Henry Reeve

Royal and Republican France

A series of essays reprinted from the 'Edinburgh', 'Quarterly' and 'British and foreign' reviews. Vol. 2

Henry Reeve

Royal and Republican France
A series of essays reprinted from the 'Edinburgh', 'Quarterly' and 'British and foreign' reviews.
Vol. 2

ISBN/EAN: 9783337071103

Printed in Europe, USA, Canada, Australia, Japan

Cover: Foto ©ninafisch / pixelio.de

More available books at **www.hansebooks.com**

ROYAL AND REPUBLICAN

FRANCE.

*A SERIES OF ESSAYS REPRINTED FROM THE 'EDINBURGH,'
'QUARTERLY,' AND 'BRITISH AND FOREIGN' REVIEWS*

BY

HENRY REEVE,

CORRESPONDING MEMBER OF THE FRENCH INSTITUTE.

IN TWO VOLUMES.
VOL. II.

LONDON:
LONGMANS, GREEN, AND CO.
1872.

The right of translation is reserved.

CONTENTS

OF

THE SECOND VOLUME.

	PAGE
CHATEAUBRIAND	1
LOUIS PHILIPPE	41
ALEXIS DE TOCQUEVILLE	77
AGRICULTURAL FRANCE	191
FRANCE IN 1870.	237
COMMUNAL FRANCE	311
EPILOGUE	393

CHATEAUBRIAND.

CHATEAUBRIAND.[1]

MONSIEUR de Chateaubriand has somewhere observed that the Government of Louis XVIII. was the best resting-place of France on the declivity of revolutions. The force of this remark is increased by the impartiality of advancing time, and the experience of more deplorable vicissitudes. Whether under the yoke of the Second Empire or amidst the convulsions which have followed it, when the condition of that great nation is such that we are more disposed to avert our eyes from its sufferings than to commemorate and applaud its sacrifices for freedom, the fifteen years of the Restoration deserve to be remembered as an era of extraordinary promise; and we the more lament the bigotry and the follies which hurried it to a grievous and early termination. The Government of the French Restoration combined the varied and abundant talents of more than one age. Amongst its elder

[1] This paper was first published in the *Edinburgh Review*, No. 198, for April 1853, as a review of a book entitled—
Politique de la Restauration en 1822 *et* 1823. Par M. le Comte de Marcellus, Ancien Ministre Plénipotentiaire. Paris : 1853.

servants and advisers, the lofty traditions, the great names, and the refined manners of the old French Court were not yet extinct, for the Duc de Richelieu and the Duc Mathieu de Montmorency sate in its councils ; to these were added the statesmanlike prudence of M. de Villèle, the judgment of M. de Serre, the brilliancy and eloquence of M. de Chateaubriand. The Chamber of Peers, hereditary in rank and independent by position, included all that was most eminent in the military and civil service of the Empire, as well as of the Royalist party. The Chamber of Deputies was alternately swayed by the austere gravity of M. Royer-Collard, and the vehement eloquence of Manuel or General Foy. The schools teemed with the instruction and the eloquence of the first thinkers of the age. Guizot had evoked the genius of philosophical history and constitutional government; Victor Cousin rekindled among the countrymen of Descartes the august but almost extinct traditions of a school of ideal philosophy ; Villemain gave new life to literary criticism ; whilst Thierry, Thiers, and Mignet opened their career by the narrative of revolutions whose influence was heightened by the force and fidelity of the language in which they clothed these events. Even poetry revived once more on the prosaic soil of France; for Lamartine opened a vein of sentiment in meditative verse which none of his countrymen had attempted; Casimir Delavigne and Victor Hugo gave a romantic colour to the lyrics of a new age; and Béranger, the most national of French writers since La Fontaine, found, in the slight melody of his songs, touches to stir the hearts of a people. Why pursue the contrast which these recollections suggest to the mind? We cannot recall a more mysterious reverse in human affairs than that this short and splendid period should have 'left no traces on the French nation, except in the imperishable pages of her literature; and that by far the greater part of the men we have named—illustrious in every department of philosophy and government—should have survived the constitution they founded, the monarchy they served, the liberty they loved, and even the epoch they adorned.

This reflection may suffice to account for the peculiar interest with which we turn to the political annals of the Restoration, even in the diffuse and inaccurate pages of M. de Lamartine's last historical production. But Louis XVIII. deserves a more trustworthy historian, and we have no doubt that the memoirs and the correspondence of his reign will gradually disclose to the world the existence of far greater ability and liberality than was supposed to exist at the Bourbon Court; especially, for example, the extensive collection of historical and personal reminiscences, still in manuscript, to which the venerable Chancellor Duke Pasquier put the finishing touch but a short time before his death. The volume before us is one of the earliest contributions to the history of this period; and although we can place neither M. de Chateaubriand nor M. de Marcellus in the first rank of the political servants of the Crown of France, their private and authentic correspondence is extremely characteristic, and it deserves the more notice in this country as it concerns transactions in which the British Cabinet of 1823 played a very prominent part.

It was upon the 16th of September, 1822, that Mr. Canning relinquished the Governor-Generalship of India to which he had been appointed, and received, for the second time, the seals of the Foreign Office, then vacant by the death of Lord 'Londonderry, which had taken place about a month before. M. de Chateaubriand had been up to that time the ambassador of France in London; and M. de Marcellus, then a young diplomatist of twenty-four, had just joined the embassy as its secretary. The moment was one pregnant with interest, for the

Congress of Verona was about to assemble. The question of the intervention of the Holy Alliance in the internal affairs of Spain loured on the political horizon. The Eastern question was to be considered; the ascendancy of Austria over Italy consolidated; and the questions of the Slave Trade and of piracy in the American seas discussed. But, more than all the rest, a change of vital moment had taken place, for the first time since 1815, in the spirit of the Foreign Minister of England. Lord Castlereagh had framed and followed a system of policy more conformable to the views of Prince Metternich than to the public opinion and interests of the English people, for he had sacrificed the popularity and, in some degree, the influence of the British Cabinet to an habitual compliance with the views of the Continental confederacy. Upon the occurrence of the melancholy event which terminated his career, Prince Metternich spoke of it as 'an irreparable loss,' and the expression was never forgotten or forgiven by Lord Londonderry's successor. Mr. Canning was often wrong in his judgment, often misled by his own vivid imaginative powers; but he aspired to restore England to the independence and the spirit of her own proud and free policy in the councils of Europe; and whilst the House of

Commons rang with his eloquence, and the world with his fame, he found himself opposed by the diplomatic maxims, the manœuvres, the artifices, and the resentment of every other Court, not excepting that of France. This change might have given an immediate and peculiar interest to the duties which M. de Chateaubriand still discharged at the Court of St. James. But the ambition of that singular personage was already directed to higher objects. London afforded no sufficient field to his insatiable vanity. At the very moment when Mr. Canning took office, Chateaubriand aspired to figure amongst the plenipotentiaries of France at Verona, to defeat his rivals and to supplant his colleagues on the most active scene of European politics, and eventually to assume, on the fall of M. de Montmorency, the direction of the foreign policy of the House of Bourbon. Never were the emulous and often conflicting tendencies of French and English diplomacy swayed by two men in whom an enthusiastic temperament and inordinate personal ambition were more conspicuous than in M. de Chateaubriand and in Mr. Canning; never did these dangerous gifts acquire a greater ascendancy over the traditions of official routine and the rules of public law. The contest, which began in a familiar correspondence between the two Ministers, ended in a duel of orations, from the tribune of the Chamber of Deputies to the Treasury bench in the House of Commons; and the world was as much interested and excited by the knightly bearing of the two antagonists as by the questions which called them into the lists and agitated the world.

When M. de Chateaubriand extorted, not without difficulty, from M. de Villèle, his nomination as plenipotentiary to the Congress of Verona, he retained his titular appointment as French ambassador in London; and M. de Marcellus, who had joined the embassy only a few days before, was left in the responsible position of *chargé d'affaires*. The position of the young diplomatist was a singular one. He had not completed his twenty-fifth year, but his rise had been rapid, and his talents were remarkable. The property of his family was considerable, and its royalism enthusiastic. Young Marcellus entered the diplomatic service early, by an appointment to the Turkish Embassy, in which capacity he learned modern Greek, and performed at least one service which deserves to perpetuate his name. He had the good fortune to purchase the Venus of Milo for the French Government, and to place in the noble statue gallery of the Louvre its most beautiful and precious ornament. Chateaubriand and Marcellus had met in the East, and were afterwards wont to console themselves for the fogs of London and the turmoil of diplomacy by wafting a sigh to the Ægean for the glory and freedom of Greece. They were thus designated to act together in Portland Place, but, owing to the departure of M. de Chateaubriand the correspondence now before us is the chief record of their intimacy. Marcellus was directed to supply his chief at Verona with ample private information as to the state of affairs in England, whilst his official despatches were addressed to the Department of Foreign Affairs in Paris; and he acquitted himself so agreeably of this task that the secret correspondence was kept up in this form after M. de Chateaubriand became Minister of Foreign Affairs, to the great amusement not only of the Minister himself, but of the King, who combined a royal appetite for gossip with a taste for the art of diplomacy and the refined pastimes of social life.

M. de Chateaubriand has himself informed the world in that portion of his reminiscences which he called the 'Congress of Verona,' that the intervention of France in the internal affairs of Spain had been an object of his constant and passionate solicitude during the whole period of his embassy to this country. He regarded a diplomatic triumph by the Ministers of Louis XVIII. as a necessary compensation for the Treaties of 1815, and a military expedition under the Duke of Angoulême as no less essential to the stability of the monarchy and the honour of the King's arms ; but he had to brave the opposition of England and to surmount the manifest repugnance of the ablest counsellor of the Crown, M. de Villèle, and possibly of Louis XVIII. himself. Two years earlier Lord Castlereagh had expressed, in a confidential minute on the affairs of Spain, communicated to the Four Great Courts in May 1820, the dissent of this country from a precautionary interference in the internal affairs of the Peninsula, especially as there was no ground for asserting that the Spanish revolution endangered the tranquillity of Europe. Mr. Canning went further, and his first instruction to the Duke of Wellington, who was then at Paris on his way to Verona, was couched in the following terms :—

> If there be any determined project to interfere by force or by menace in the present struggle in Spain, so convinced are His Majesty's Government of the uselessness and danger of such interference—so objectionable does it appear to them in principle as well as utterly impracticable in execution, that, when the necessity arises, or (I would rather say) when the opportunity offers, I am to instruct Your Grace at once frankly and peremptorily to declare,

that to any such interference, come what may, His Majesty will not be a party. (Sept. 27, 1822.)

The conflict between these opposite opinions was carried on at Verona, and the policy of this country was defended with great firmness and ability by the Duke of Wellington against the demands of France and the instigation of the Northern Courts. It was not till the termination of the Congress in December that the march of events became more rapid and the rival policy of the war party in France and the peace party in England openly opposed. M. de Chateaubriand reached Paris from Verona on the 18th of December, 1822. The train which he had already laid was ready to explode. The moderation of M. de Villèle was overcome. M. de Montmorency resigned, and on the 29th of December the diplomatist, who had already in a subordinate position been the most active promoter of the Spanish war, was gazetted in the 'Moniteur' as Minister of Foreign Affairs. Mr. Canning appears, however, not to have at once penetrated the real effect of this change, and to have attributed to M. de Montmorency the warlike language which was really inspired at Verona by M. de Chateaubriand. 'What!' said he to M. de Marcellus, 'M. de Villèle, whom the Duke has just found to be entirely opposed to the system of hostilities, wins the day, and M. de Montmorency, who, at Paris as well as Verona, was for an immediate march, quits the Cabinet. If his resignation is a pledge of peace, he will not be regretted here. *But I do not understand the attitude M. de Chateaubriand* will assume in all this.' 'He will explain it himself,' replied Marcellus; 'but be well assured beforehand that France will relax none of her measures, and that she will adopt the most effectual arrangements to put down anarchy and the revolution in Spain.' The private correspondence between the two Ministers, already published in the 'Congress of Verona,' demonstrates how entirely Mr. Canning had misconceived the real views and intentions of his opponent. The instructions contained in M. de Chateaubriand's private note to Marcellus of the 27th of January distinctly show what was passing at the Tuileries :—

Say that we wish for peace, but that we are preparing for war: that we do not refuse the good offices of England to bring about this peace; but that the first condition must be that the King (of Spain) shall be at liberty to modify the monstrous constitution of the Cortes. Go on to talk of peace; we wish for it, but with security and honour, and we prefer war to the state of uncertainty and revolutionary peril in which we find ourselves. To-morrow I will send you the King's speech. *It is very warlike*, though not entirely shutting the door against peace.

On the morrow the speech arrived, and M. de

Marcellus was instructed to communicate it to the British Minister.

He read it eagerly, but when he came to the paragraph, which he read aloud, 'That Ferdinand should *be free to give to his subjects* the institutions they can only receive from him, and which, by securing their tranquillity, will dissipate the natural apprehensions of France, and that from that moment hostilities will cease,'— 'What a principle!' said Mr. Canning, 'and what an abuse! Is that your deliberate opinion? You are going beyond the rigour of absolute monarchy, as it has so long existed in Spain, for even there the Cortes had by their remonstrances the right of extorting concessions from the Crown; but you require that Ferdinand should model or replace institutions by his own will and pleasure. Are you making a crusade for a political theory? Do you want to propagate your Charter as Mahomet did the Koran? I know what is meant by war for conquest, which does not last—war for a change of succession, which has cost us so dear—war for commercial interests, which is the most rational of all But war to modify the power of two Chambers, or to extend the prerogative of the Crown, passes my comprehension. The doctrine of constitutions emanating from the throne is odious to us. The British Constitution is the result of a long series of victories gained by the people over their sovereigns. Have you forgotten that kings ought not to give institutions, but institutions alone to make kings?'

This argument was certainly a strange one to address to the Minister of Louis XVIII., who had recovered his throne, seven years before, with the assistance of England, and upon the principle of legitimacy, and who had solemnized his restoration by granting the Charter. Accordingly, M. de Marcellus retorted,—

'Perfectly true of England since her *terrible* revolution—but in Spain, governed by an ancient and traditional dynasty, will you not allow that things may pass as in France? Let me remind you, on my side, that we owe our Charter to Louis XVIII.' 'Dreadful maxim,' continued the Minister, without listening to me : 'a king *free!* Is there any king who deserves to be a free king, in the precise sense of the term? No sovereign is free but a despot or a usurper, the curses of the world—terrific comets which glare and set in blood. Our Constitution leaves the Crown an apparent right of choosing its Ministers—but can it exercise this privilege? Look at our history. Do you think the first Georges were free to reject the Cabinets imposed on them, especially the Walpole Administration? Could George III., with his limited and almost always extinguished faculties, make a choice? No, happily for England, he could not. And George IV.—do you think (here his voice became emphatic, and he pressed my arm)—do you think I should be His Minister, if he were *free* to choose? Can he forget that I have constantly declined to share in the excesses of his youth, and that I have constantly opposed his favourites and his tastes? He hates me for my resistance, for my political attitude, and, above all, for my knowledge of his married life. Yet he was *not free* to exclude me from the Cabinet.

'Well, then,' added Mr. Canning, calming himself, as if exhausted by his own energy, 'you are going to march into Spain?' Then, tapping me on the shoulder, 'You think, young man, that this war will be short. I think otherwise—I, who am on the brink of old age. In 1793—I am old enough to go back to that time—Mr. Pitt, with 'The patriot's heart, the prophet's mind' (and he recited with emphasis this verse of his earlier days)—Mr. Pitt told me that a certain war, declared against a great nation then in a revolution, would be short also—yet this war outlived Mr. Pitt.'

We have no reason to doubt the sincerity of M. de Marcellus' intentions, but we cannot persuade ourselves that these reminiscences are not overcoloured. Nor can we attach the same degree of credit to that part of this volume which consists of recollections written thirty years after the events and conversations to which they relate, as we do to the correspondence bearing the date of the period. This distinction must be borne in mind if this book be ever regarded as materials for history. The conversations appear to consist of fragments of Canning's public speeches dressed up with more or less verisimilitude —the letters may be considered as more accurate pictures of the events of the day. In the instance we have just quoted, the absurdity of a confidential conversation of this kind between a Minister and a French *chargé d'affaires* of twenty-four upon the repugnance then subsisting between that Minister and the King,—the historical inaccuracy of the statement that George II. and George III. did not in great measure choose their own Ministers,—and the total want of penetration into the real question at issue between France and Spain, are almost incredible in a man occupying the position then filled by Mr.Canning. But, at the same time, we find in the contemporary private letters annexed to these reminiscences, abundant evidence of a strange absence of judgment, temper, and moderation. Mr. Canning continued to argue the Spanish question upon the principles which Lord Somers might have applied to the House of Stuart, or Lord Chatham to the Family Compact: such arguments produced their effect in the House of Commons, but they could only strengthen the opposite conviction in the mind of a French Minister. On one occasion Mr. Canning said,—

'Since Ferdinand, like James II., resists the will of the nation, let us apply the English method to Spain. What will be the consequence? Ferdinand's expulsion.' And then he added, as if carried away by a passion he could not master—'Hearken to me well. This example may extend to yourselves.' And, speaking loud, his glittering eyes fixed on mine,—' You are not ignorant that a departure from the principle of legitimacy, almost similar to our own, *is meditated and plotted in France at this moment.* You know the progress it has made in the party of the Opposition calling itself Moderate. *The head to be crowned is there.*'

These terrible words, spoken in 1823, struck me to the heart like an insult. I cannot express the indignation I felt at them. Meanwhile the Minister, embarrassed and dejected, paced up and down while I vented my indignation.

And well he might; for, however curious and prophetic this speech has in the sequel turned out to be, it was as offensive a diplomatic communication as could be made to the envoy of a reigning and allied Sovereign, without even the apology of a rational object in making it. On the contrary, the very

VOL. II. C

argument used by the French Court in favour of the Spanish intervention was the peril of revolutionary contagion, and Mr. Canning is here represented to have strengthened the case he was combating by this extraordinary allusion to the Duke of Orleans. M. de Marcellus informs his readers that he textually reported this conversation in his regular despatch. His despatch was even circulated to the principal embassies ; but he was told not to report any more such observations in future. We are curious to learn whether any trace of such a statement is to be found in the records of his regular official correspondence.

As a contrast to this scene we are tempted to extract another in which Mr. Canning's versatile and theatrical character is exhibited in another shape; and, in spite of some suspicion of a heightened tint of sentimentality, we are inclined to think the sketch is in the main true.

I found the Minister, one day, alone and pensive in the grounds of his little park at Gloucester Lodge. Walking over the smooth English grass, with a book in his hand, under the budding trees—' A truce,' said he, ' to politics to-day ! I am weary of them. Let us read some Virgil. In my little domain, like the old man of Galesus, *cui pauca relicti jugera ruris erant*, I was looking over the Georgics. I was here—can anything be more touching than these verses—

'Hi motus animorum, atque hæc certamina tanta
Pulveris exigui jactu compressa quiescent.'

Having spoken these verses, the Minister dropped his arm, as if overcome by thought.

'It must all end, then, in this "little dust!" What have I gained by so many battles? Many enemies, a thousand calumnies. Sometimes restrained by the timidity or the simplicity of my colleagues—sometimes thwarted by the want of sense among my partisans—always embarrassed by the displeasure of the King, I can execute nothing—I can attempt nothing of that which an inward and solemn voice seems to dictate. I said the other day, in my sorrow—I am like a bird which, instead of soaring to the cliffs and precipices, flies over the fens and skims the ground. I am wasted by internal controversies, and I shall die in a fit of dejection like my predecessor and unfortunate adversary, Lord Castlereagh. How often have I not been tempted to fly, from society and from power, to the literature which was the food of my boyhood, the only refuge which is impenetrable to the delusions of fate. Literature is more than a consolation to me—it is my hope and my refuge—it is, moreover, the freemasonry of liberal minds. Would it not have been better for M. de Chateaubriand and for me if we had never raised to our lips this poisoned cup of power which overpowers us with giddiness? Literature would have brought us together, without reserve and without bitterness. . . .' Then Mr. Canning, raising his eyes and his bald forehead to Heaven, repeated, with that harmonious voice which was one of his great charms, the lines of Hamlet—

'Oh, God! oh, God!
How weary, stale, flat, and unprofitable
Seem to me all the uses of this world!'

'Yet,' he added, 'still that desire of fame, which cannot at my age be called ambition, drives me back to public affairs and influences me. Human fame—mockery! The ancients made her a goddess—a woman to be more seductive—and she is dressed in all the attractions of patriotism. At this moment, when I should so much like to dream with Virgil, I must go to encounter Brougham at the House of Commons. Come with me; I know he is going to attack me directly, but I will not yield an inch. I will take you to Westminster.'[1]

We started, and, as we crossed the crowd at the door of the House, Mr. Canning smiled, and said to me, 'In the critical state of our relations with France and Spain, what will all these spectators and even my own colleagues think of our long conference and of our open intimacy? They will send off couriers—the funds will rise—and yet we have discussed nothing to-day but a few literary subjects and quoted a few melancholy verses.'

The termination of this Brompton eclogue was indeed a strange and abrupt one. The debate began with more than ordinary warmth. It was the night when Mr. Brougham accused Mr. Canning of tergiversation on the Catholic Question. The Minister, whose overwrought nerves had sought relief in the 'Georgics' that morning, exclaimed in a voice of thunder, 'It is false;' and Mr. Bankes

[1] By a singular coincidence, on the same evening, a few hours later, Mr. Brougham described the position of the Minister in a passage which may be remembered as a masterpiece of invective, yet not dissimilar from the terms he had himself employed. He described the Secretary for Foreign Affairs at the moment 'when he had to decide whether he should go to India to honourable exile, or take office in England and not submit to his sentence of transportation, but be condemned to hard labour in his own country, *doomed to the disquiet of a divided council—sitting with his enemies and pitied by his friends—with his hands chained and tied down on all those lines of operation which his own sentiments and wishes would have led him to adopt.'* The fierce chief of the Opposition little knew how deeply the lines he was tracing were already graven on the Minister's heart.

moved that both the orators should be taken into custody by the serjeant-at-arms. Louis XVIII., who was amused with the incident, directed M. de Chateaubriand to inquire whether 'Mr. Bankes' was a son of Sir Joseph Banks, 'le grand navigateur,' whom he had known in London. Marcellus replied, with infinite self-possession, ' M. Bankes is not the son of the great naturalist, Captain Cook's companion, whom the King knew in London, *but he is his near relation, and perhaps even his nephew.*' Nor does the ex-*chargé d'affaires* appear even now to have discovered the absurdity of his blunder.

We have been led, however, somewhat to anticipate the course of events. Parliament opened on the 4th of February, five days after the French Chambers; but the King's Speech only repeated the declaration that the Government would not be a party to proceedings which might be deemed an interference in the internal affairs of Spain, without holding out much hope of averting the calamity of war between France and that country. In the debate on the Address, Mr. Brougham delivered one of the most splendid and intemperate orations of his whole parliamentary career, against the policy of ' The Three Gentlemen of Verona,' as he called the Holy Alliance. But it was not till the 14th April that the official correspondence was laid upon the table, with full explanations of the course pursued in these transactions by the British Government. In the course of the powerful and comprehensive speech of Mr. Canning, he expressed exactly the same opinion on 'the extraordinary speech with which the French Ministers opened the Chambers,' that M. de Marcellus records; and he even went so far as to declare that there was 'not a man in the House who thought with more *disgust and abhorrence* than he did of the construction to which the words of that speech were liable.' It is satisfactory to find, in looking back to the terms applied fifty years ago to the policy of Foreign States, and to our relations with them, that, although we may want the fervid eloquence of a Canning or a Brougham, our discussions have gained very considerably in temper, discretion, and forbearance.

M. de Chateaubriand, who had dictated the French King's Speech, was intoxicated with the stimulus he had applied to the military passions of France. 'We cannot,' said he to Marcellus, 'keep our army of observation on the frontier without exposing it to corruption. We cannot withdraw it without dishonouring the white cockade and disgusting our troops.' The Duke of Wellington smiled gravely on the arrival of the French King's Speech, and said to Marcellus, 'You must confess some of your people in Paris are very unreasonable.' 'No doubt,' retorted the *chargé d'affaires*; 'but they are in a minority, which is more than can be said at Madrid or in London.' The effect of the speech in England was violent. The English funds fell, whilst those of France rose; the Press thundered, and the 'Times' repeated the arguments of Mr. Canning. The Foreign Minister seemed to hesitate as to the length to which public opinion would drive him, for the time was already past when Mr. Canning could or would resist it. M. de Marcellus remained, however, unshaken by these demonstrations; and, with considerable firmness and penetration, he continued to assure his Government that the worst they had to fear from England was an angry neutrality. About this time he described Mr. Canning's position in the following severe but not inaccurate terms :—

Let us not be mistaken as to Mr. Canning. He still vibrates between those monarchical opinions which have been the basis of his fame, and that popular favour which is now his surest road to power; but, as he lends his ear more willingly to the popular voice, and spreads his sail to the breeze, it may be seen beforehand to which side he will lean. A disciple of Pitt, and hitherto a Tory, he will become a half-Whig, and adopt democratic principles if those principles prevail. He is instinctively out of humour with the aristocracy and even the high Opposition : he is feared rather than beloved by the King ; but the people are with him. The people, struck by his talents, have placed him where he is; and the people will keep him there, if he obeys the people.

Some months later, when M. de Chateaubriand had taken up an absurd notion that the Marquis of Hastings, who had just returned from India, was likely to supersede Mr. Canning as Foreign Minister, or, at least, to be sent as ambassador to Paris, Marcellus announced with the same good sense,—

> Do not imagine that Mr. Canning is approaching the close of his ministerial career. I have seen how he reached power, what obstacles he has thrown aside, what antipathies he has overcome, and I have not to reproach myself with having for one instant deceived my Court by the illusion or the hope of his approaching fall. George IV. boasted a little when he said that he would drive out his Ministers if they said he was mad. He would wish to forget for the moment that English kings have no will of their own, and Mr. Canning in office is a proof of it.

The impression produced on the French Government by Mr. Canning's intemperate speech of the 14th April, and by the open avowal of his hopes for the triumph of the Spanish Cortes, was one of extreme irritation at the expressions used, mingled with the assurance that, in spite of this torrent of invective, France had nothing else to fear from the displeasure of England. M. de Chateaubriand still preserved in public a decorous attitude, and spoke with more temper than Mr. Canning had shown ; but his private notes display the coarsest and most vulgar resentment; thus, for instance, on the 26th April, he writes,—

The neutrality of England is established beyond a doubt, as I expected. But don't trust the wiles of Mr. Canning. He is stirring the coals there, and trying to stir them here, underhand. As for myself, I shall never recriminate with the English. Even on Thursday, I shall answer them politely. But their cowardly insults have given me the measure of the capacity and honour of these men, and I have done with them.

To this tirade Marcellus replies with excellent taste to his irritated chief :—

I see well enough here that temper and passion are bad counsellors. It is time to end these recriminations. They ought not to alter our system in Paris ; they will not upset Mr. Canning in London. These altercations of the tribune and the cabinet will not certainly prevail over the noble characters of two superior men ; but they may leave some clouds on the most elevated and well-constituted minds.

The position of the French *chargé d'affaires* in London at this time was curious and perplexing. He had received orders from Paris to suspend the intimacy of his communications with Mr. Canning, in consequence of the violent language of the British Government ; but he continued to dance with Miss Canning, and even to give balls, at which that accomplished young lady, who is still, under another name, one of the most distinguished ornaments of London society, was evidently the most welcome guest. Indeed, M. de Marcellus would have us believe that there was something beyond diplomacy in his early predilection for Mr. Canning's family, and that on one occasion the English Secretary of State himself said to him, '*Allez danser, mon gendre*,' whilst the rival Minister in France promised his faithful agent a good embassy for his wedding present. We do not wish to dispute the accuracy of M. de Marcellus' juvenile recollections; and he appears unconscious of the fatuity with which he dwelt at the time on these sentimental episodes in his official career. But we must be permitted to question exceedingly whether Mr. Canning would or could have permitted himself, in the relative position of the two parties, a joke of so questionable a point upon his own daughter. In spite of his success at Almacks, and of the playful style in which Mr. Canning himself treated the *bouderie* of his young antagonist, M. de Marcellus had to hold his ground against the all but unanimous expression of English popular feeling. When the Duke of St. Lorenzo arrived in London, having been compelled by the rupture of the two Courts to withdraw from his post

of Spanish Ambassador in Paris, he was received
with popular acclamation, whilst the mob threw dirt
and broke windows at the French Embassy in
Portland Place. The parish of Marylebone offered
to pay the damage; but this parochial indemnity
was declined by the aggrieved diplomatist, who
seems perfectly unconscious that it was offered him
as the legal compensation for a breach of the peace.

But, in the higher spheres of political and social
life, the course of these events was regarded with
very different sentiments. The Tory aristocracy
were favourable to the policy of the Holy Alliance.
The Duke of Wellington, though he had steadily
opposed the projects contemplated at Verona, always
foresaw and predicted the success of the French expedition in Spain, and more than once encouraged
the *chargé d'affaires* to disregard the clamour around
him, and to urge his Court to advance resolutely to
the great object of its policy. '*J'ai vu M. Crocker*,'
writes the *chargé d'affaires*, 'il est excellent.' Lord
Westmoreland spoke out, and exhorted the French
Ministers to smother this time the Jacobin party.
' Let them not mind the clatter of the Opposition,
which is only the old Imperial furniture that Louis
XVIII. has repaired and regilt, but which will crack
if he leans on it. Every one of these bawlers, who

want now to prevent you from entering Spain, were as quiet as mutes fifteen years ago, when a traitorous aggression set fire to the Peninsula. Write what I say to M. de Chateaubriand.'

The 'bawlers' here alluded to by the Lord Privy Seal in Lord Liverpool's Cabinet, were probably no other than Manuel and General Foy; for this remark was made at the very time of the scandalous expulsion of the former of these orators from the Chamber of Deputies. M. de Chateaubriand, whose constitutional ardour was ere long to be displayed in a different manner, when it had to revenge his own fall from power, talked of that outrage on the privileges of the Chamber as ' a scene that every one here (in Paris) has laughed at.' And, a day or two later, ' You see the humbug of our Liberals! They are ashamed of themselves, for on this motion of Manuel they could not raise four street-sweepers to rebellion.' He suppressed the fact that *sixty-two* of the most distinguished members of the Chamber of Deputies had signed an indignant protest against it. Even in the high Tory circles of London, not a voice was raised to palliate that outrage, which so forcibly recalled one of the most ominous passages in British history—the seizure of the four members by Charles I. The presentiment that a Government supported by so violent a majority would perish by violence became general ; and M. de Marcellus was again driven to his last expedient of giving a ball. It was honoured, he informs his Government, by the presence of all the Ministers, and even of the Lord Mayor. The rank and beauty of the Court of George IV. came to dance at the bachelor diplomatist's, and Count d'Orsay shone conspicuous amongst a constellation of dandies. Louis XVIII. was amused by the happy audacity of his young envoy, and Chateaubriand laughed his fill at the '*insulaires*,' who were set hopping to stop their mouths. These pleasant passages occurred, however, before the speech of Mr. Canning had opened a wider breach between the two Governments.

But although the parliamentary debate of the 14th of April had inflamed the wound, there was one man in the kingdom who took the earliest opportunity to mark the difference of opinion he entertained—and that was George IV. At the levee on the 21st of April, the King expressed to M. de Marcellus, in terms which we do not find quoted in this volume, his favourable sentiments on the Spanish campaign. The 'Times' newspaper some days afterwards commented on this incident with great violence, hinting that, if the King had really expressed his cordial wishes for the success of the French army, he must be in a state which neither the gout nor any physical malady could account for ;—in short, that he was insane. M. de Marcellus seized the opportunity with promptitude and dexterity to write an energetic letter to Mr. Canning, and to repudiate in the strongest terms the offensive insinuation of the 'Times.' This protest was laid before the King, who was pleased by it, and said (though *not* to Mr. Canning)—

'I never addressed to M. de Marcellus the language imputed to me : but such good wishes for the cause of France are certainly at the bottom of my heart, and I owed nothing less to the French *chargé d'affaires*. Whilst he is struggling against the malice and the conspirators of all countries, pardoned but not cured, and the Duke of St. Lorenzo is carried in triumph by the populace, I certainly am the last to forsake him ! My Ministers have expressed in Parliament their wishes against France, with which we are at peace. This is not an honest neutrality ; and as I have suffered by this conduct, which Europe may consider inconsistent with my political principles, I have endeavoured to restore the balance, by paying to M. de Marcellus those attentions which others have confined to the agents of the Cortes of Spain.' Such were the King's words—repeated to me (says our author) by the '*cœur discret*' which received them. You may rely upon it.

The '*cœur discret*' was no doubt one of the clandestine ornaments of the Court of that beloved sovereign,—but before such an authority we suspend our investigations. Nor can we determine whether reports of this nature are not be classed with those exercises of the imagination which were found to amuse Louis XVIII. Another passage in M. de Marcellus' reminiscences on this subject is, however, still more extraordinary :—

The King (George IV.) gave a ball, at which I was disposed to dance the more gaily as my friends and brothers were fighting gallantly in Spain,—that is the rule of diplomacy. At this ball Mr. Canning came up to me. Politicians who have been talking in the morning have always something to add in the evening. I was led aside by the Minister into the recess of a window far from the drawing-room (I confess to my great regret), when George IV. perceived us and, approaching us, said—

'Well, my dear Marcellus, things have changed their aspect since we met. You are triumphant in Spain, and I am enchanted at it. But they say King Ferdinand has taken back as his Ministers at Cadiz the very men who deposed him at Seville,— that is a weakness I shall never imitate, though they have tried to make me out to be mad, as you know better than anyone. But as I said just now to Lord Liverpool, ' If my Ministers declared me to be mad, I might recover my senses, but they would not recover their places.'

Mr. Canning already looked out of countenance, when the King turned to him and said, 'What were you saying there, Canning, to the young representative of France?' 'Sire,' said the Minister, ' I was boasting to him of the excellence of representative government, and explaining to him, at the same time, the "forced labour" of the House of Commons, which is its result. M. de Marcellus is a listener here, not being old enough to become an orator at home.'

' I know it,' rejoined the King ; ' and you have had very painful things to listen to. I sincerely pitied you for all you have had to hear and to endure. If your lips had not been closed, you would have had plenty to say in reply.' 'Sire,' said I, 'the sailor forgets the storm when calm returns.' 'So much the better,' said the King; 'but don't be dazzled with our system of government which they boast so much of. It has its advantages, but it has its evils. I have never forgotten what a King, who was also a man of wit, said to me of it. "Your English Government," he declared, "is only fit to protect adventurers, and intimidate honest men." What do you say to that, Canning?' And as the Minister faltered and hesitated to reply, the King continued, 'At any rate, for the welfare of mankind, we ought not to wish any other people to have our institutions. What does pretty well for us would be worthless elsewhere. Every soil does not produce the same fruits and the same minerals; and it is the same with nations. Remember this, Marcellus: it is my unalterable conviction.' Upon this George IV. turned on his heel, with a look and a searching smile at me. Mr. Canning had some difficulty to keep his temper. At last he said, ' Representative government has one other advantage which His Majesty has forgotten: it enables Ministers to listen in silence to the taunts of a sovereign who has no other means to vent his resentment.'

If this story had been related by an ordinary traveller at a foreign Court, we should have set it down for a clumsy and impudent invention. This picture of George IV., stalking away from the ballroom at Carlton House at a time when he could not walk without difficulty, and following about his guests in order to insult his principal Secretary of State, to repudiate the policy of his Government, and to traduce the institutions of his country,—is too burlesque to be credited. But when we remember the position which M. de Marcellus filled in this country, the favours he received from the King, the regard shown him by Mr. Canning, and the toleration of English society for his vanity and presumption, the publication of such 'reminiscences' becomes an offence of greater magnitude, and we are compelled to place the good breeding and good sense of M. de Marcellus on the same level as his veracity. As we find in another passage of this correspondence that he thought it incumbent on him to report, for the information of His Most Christian Majesty's Government, the fact that a sudden rise had just taken place in the price of wives at Smithfield market, from ten to twenty-two shillings a-piece, we are tempted to class his recollections of Carlton House and of Smithfield under the same head.

Even at this distance of time it is surprising that one of the survivors in these transactions should volunteer to disclose the impertinent levity and bad faith with which they were conducted; for M. de Chateaubriand, under whose orders he served, fares no better in these papers than M. de Marcellus himself. The two following examples of his political morality require no comment. The Spanish war had gone on successfully, for the Cortes could oppose no effectual resistance. But the object of the campaign was almost as remote as ever, because the King of Spain was still in the hands of the Liberal party, and some apprehensions were expressed that he might be shipped off to the Canary Islands. At this stage of the war, M. de Chateaubriand wrote the following despatch to his *chargé d'affaires* in London :—

It cannot be dissembled that nothing is ended as long as we have not got the King. How to get him? That is the difficulty; and England might have great influence upon it. My opinion is that the King can only be got by a *coup monté* at Seville or Cadiz. *Could not you find in London some of those enterprising fellows, so common in that country, who would carry him off for one or two millions?* Think about it. C.

So much for the chivalrous defender of the sacred persons of Bourbon kings, supported by constitutional government.

Again, in May 1823, a Conference of the Great Powers took place in London, on the subject of the Slave Trade, which had been brought before the Congress of Verona by the Duke of Wellington, and on which M. de Chateaubriand had written one of his most celebrated state papers. M. de Marcellus supplies us with the secret instructions he received on this subject.

Paris : May 12, 1823.

This is what you will have to do with reference to this conference on the Slave Trade. You will be present at it, once : you will talk very philanthropically; but you will show that in the present state of things, and of politics in Europe and America, it is difficult to arrive at any general measure. You will avoid as much as possible any further conferences, and the matter will drop.

C.

In the same spirit Marcellus replies, that Mr. Canning wanted this '*semblant de conférence*' for a motion announced by Mr. Buxton in the House of Commons.

So much for the philanthropist and the compassionate author of 'Atala' and 'The Martyrs;' whose tears were ever ready to flow for imaginary sorrows, or for his own personal wrongs.

We have already quoted more than enough to show in how odious a spirit these transactions were conducted by the French Government, and to what a degree they bore the stamp of the vanity and presumption of their principal authors. But it is impossible, on the other hand, to award to Mr. Canning the praise of foresight or judgment; we seek in vain for traces of these qualities either in this volume, or in the authentic despatches of the British Secretary of State at this period. In condemning the principle of the French intervéntion in Spain, he undoubtedly had with him the immense majority of this nation and of Parliament. But his vehement antipathy to the measure deceived him as to the facility with which it might be executed, and the results it might produce to the Bourbon Monarchy He buoyed himself up with hopes of an heroic resistance on the part of the Spanish constitutionalists to a well-appointed French army; and even calculated on the disaffection of the Duc d'Angoulême's forces when arrayed against the liberal cause. The Duke of Wellington, who knew the Spaniards and the French army infinitely better than Mr. Canning, scouted these objections, though he too had condemned the principle of the intervention. The result was, the unresisted advance of the French troops from the Bidassoa to Seville, and a success equal to M. de Chateaubriand's fondest expectations, purchased with scarcely the loss of a company of infantry. Mr. Canning had entirely failed to estimate the fact, that, in the southern countries of Europe, the lower orders of the people and the masses of the rural population are sometimes as well disposed to support absolute government as liberal institutions; and that the love of freedom has possessed itself of a class, but not of the nation.

The French intervention of 1823 in Spain produced several results which might be considered favourable to the principles then contended for in

France by the Government of the Restoration. It flattered the army, which displayed consummate discipline, and took the field, for the first time since the Revolution, under the white cockade. It satisfied the Royalist majority in the Chamber of Deputies, which seldom found King Louis XVIII. as royalist as itself; and it established close and confidential relations between France and the three great Continental Powers, leaving this country entirely isolated in Europe. 'I knew how it would end,' said the Duke of Wellington to M. de Marcellus. 'They have followed their notions of resentment; and what is the result? Everything is done without us, or in spite of us. We are separated from the Continent. *Penitus toto divisos orbe;*' for even the old Duke quoted Latin on the occasion. 'Well, we deserved to be left out; for our part in all this has not been what it ought to have been.' The Duke spoke truly, not because Mr. Canning had professed a different principle to France, but because he had asserted it with pique, and carried it to the length of resentment.

'They say,' said Mr. Canning, the other day, 'that I have been mistaken on this affair of Spain. It is better to be mistaken once than twice, and better to be mistaken twice than to confess oneself mistaken at all.'

In these enigmatical subtleties the great interests of nations are lost. Mr. Canning persists in considering the triumph of France as his defeat, and everything which may lessen our success is a relief to his bitterness.

Yet, in writing these lines just before he had quitted London, on the arrival of Prince Polignac as ambassador, M. de Marcellus pointed out the possibility of healing even these wounds, by skilful concessions to the vanity of the great English Minister. To this overture Chateaubriand replied, in a tone implying that he was not the man to undertake that task, and that all confidential relations between himself and Mr. Canning were at an end for ever :—

I do not believe in the fall of Mr. Canning, and I think, with you, that he must be flattered to be brought over: but wounded *amour propre* never repents, never returns, never forgives, when it is not controlled in the mind by lofty sentiments, and a generous inclination to make sacrifices. Mr. Canning has nothing of this. He is a man of talent, of learning, and of wit, but he has nothing about him great or sincere, and his ambition will always prevail over his principles.

These are harsh words, and they convey the judgment of an embittered antagonist, though a successful one. They were pronounced by a Minister intoxicated with the triumph of his policy and convinced of the stability of his power. Who would have said, when they were written, that in a few weeks from that time this brilliant statesman would be overthrown by his colleague M. de Villèle, and suddenly abandoned by the Court to the ignominy of a peremptory dismissal ? M. de Chateaubriand himself was to give the world a memorable example of that 'wounded *amour propre* which never repents and never forgives,' and the discarded Minister of the Restoration became its most formidable assailant. More fortunate than his rival, Mr. Canning retained power long enough to efface, by the increasing lustre of his career, the recollections of his failure on the Spanish question, until he, too, perished under the fierce and systematic hostility of his former colleagues, who, even in Lord Liverpool's Cabinet, had not concealed their dissent from many of his opinions. We can place no implicit reliance on the fidelity of M. de Marcellus' narrative, for he has evidently embellished his youthful reminiscences, and exaggerated the importance of the part he played. It is unfortunate that, with so strong a desire to show off M. de Chateaubriand, Mr. Canning, and himself, he should leave on our minds so low an impression of the wisdom, the dignity, and the good faith of the personages who figure most conspicuously in these curious pages.

LOUIS PHILIPPE.

LOUIS PHILIPPE.[1]

OF the millions, in this country and elsewhere, who hailed the French Revolution of 1830 with a sudden enthusiasm or a liberal sympathy, few have as yet paused to contemplate that event and its consequences as matters of history, apart from questions of temporary interest, and with rather more deliberation than usually belongs to the correspondents of the daily papers. The focus of historical truth cannot be brought to the burning-point till we have arrived at a certain distance from the lights and flashes of the hour. It is not given to any man to have his life tolerably well written until he has completed it: even the events of the earlier part of the

---

[1] This paper was first published in the *British and Foreign Review*, No. 33, for June 1844, as a review of the work entitled—*Révolution française. Histoire de Dix Ans,* 1830-1840. Par M. Louis Blanc. Paris : Pagnerre. 4 vols. 8vo. 1843. Louis Philippe was on the throne, and nothing foretold the ignominious termination of his reign; but it is not without interest to remark how the terror and uncertainty of the future were already felt through the security of the present.

present century are still in the questionable light of half-remembered, ill-recorded things; and the difficulty of arriving at a complete survey of the reign of Louis Philippe is as great as that of measuring with the eye an eminence on which the observer may chance to be standing. No one qualification of accuracy, political principle, or good sense has fitted M. Louis Blanc for the arduous and thankless office of a contemporary historian. The eagerness and curiosity with which more than one edition of this work has been devoured by the public, may be taken as a sufficient proof that the demand for information as to what passed between the years 1830 and 1840, in the upper as well as in the lower regions of French politics, is at least as keen as the demand which is supplied by graver historians. But it is indeed equally clear that the fruit has been plucked before it is ripe; and that what is here passed off as a history of a great nation for a space of ten years of its existence, is in fact little more than the framework of the 'Annual Register,' stuffed out with personal reminiscences, or anecdotes of more questionable authenticity, and seasoned with the venom of an ill-natured pamphleteer. The time is, we hope, not very far distant when the judgment of men upon the events of the King's reign will be formed upon more trustworthy evidence and in a more candid spirit.

M. Louis Blanc does not for one instant perplex his readers by an affectation of candour or impartiality. He writes with the avowed purpose of extolling all the genuine characteristics and agents of the revolutionary principle in France, and of decrying all those men and things by whose influence the revolutionary principle has been reduced into subjection. In his eyes the temporary triumph of the real leaders of the people—the nameless heroes of July—was at once converted into a miserable and shameful defeat, by the intervention of those representatives of the middle classes who then established and maintained a constitution of their own creation and a sovereign of their own choice. Thirteen years of the government of the *bourgeoisie* are, in the opinion of M. Louis Blanc and his friends, an excessive and over-grievous expiation of the thirty-six hours of supreme power which they enjoyed in 1830 at the Hotel de Ville. The conflict was hardly over before the prize was carried off by other hands; and the victory was hardly proclaimed before the period of defeat and constraint began. In other words, M. Louis Blanc is one of those persons whose views of society and of government are founded upon those of the Comité de Salut public, somewhat tinged and inflated by the subsequent flourishes of the Imperial *régime*; and who look upon the whole body of French citizens as recreants and cravens, as long as they are not carrying the torch of liberty and equality round the world. It is impossible for those who have observed with close attention the social and political state of France, to conceal from themselves that the elements of discord, which have been raging and struggling for half a century in the various and appalling shapes of the Revolution, are still in existence—checked but not eradicated, lulled but not annihilated. In the mouths of too many of the political personages of the day, liberty and patriotism and the dignity of France are terms not altogether distinct from those fatal aberrations which led to the blasphemies, the frenzies, and the bloodshed of the Reign of Terror: that is to say, such politicians are willing to purchase the use of power by any sacrifices of duty, justice, or prudence; and, provided the revolutionary element is at work, they care not at what risk even to themselves. There are in reality two parties in France, and only two: the one consisting of such men as these; the other still professing to find, in the institutions of a constitutional monarchy and in the despotic forms of administrative power, a safeguard for the destinies of the country. In the ordinary course of affairs, and even in the midst of political debates, this real distinction is not always acknowledged or observed. Oftentimes it has been obscured by minor differences, or concealed by less important divisions; but in the first hour of real passion the mask falls aside, and every man discovers in his neighbour a legitimate descendant either of the authors of the great French Revolution or of its victims. If indeed, even amongst those who are more indulgent than we can be ourselves to the scenes of the first Revolution, there existed a steadfast adherence to the principles of rational liberty and a resolute demand for those institutions upon which in the hour of trial the existence of freedom depends, we should be tempted to excuse their failings in consideration of their object. But it must be confessed that that object is not freedom, but power. They may be eager to circumscribe the prerogative and the influence of the party they oppose, but they are not less ready to use all that prerogative and that influence whenever the vicissitudes of political fortune have thrown them into place. Thus the central administration of France, and all the machinery of an absolute government with which it is surrounded, is popular with all parties, or at least with all party-leaders, because they all intend to use it for their own purposes when the opportunity occurs. The tolerance which encourages the growth of independent powers in the State,—the civil courage which relies on the alliance of such powers rather than on their subordination,—that mutual confidence in the principles and practice of freedom which extends from the throne of a constitutional king to the broad basis of municipal administration, have no place in France; and it is certain that nothing would more effectually tend to crush whatever seeds of real freedom may have crept into the French political system, than the presence at the head of affairs of those arbitrary patriots, those imperious friends of the people, those despotic demagogues, whom M. Louis Blanc describes as the victims and martyrs of our time.[1]

In the narrative of the events of July 1830, which

[1] This prediction was realised to the letter in 1848, four years after the publication of this article, when M. Louis Blanc made his appearance as a member of the Provisional Government at the Hotel de Ville, and continued to play a part in the drama of that most absurd revolution, until he was compelled to escape from France for his participation in the revolt of June against the Assembly. And I may be permitted to add that the preceding remarks on the character of French politicians and statesmen are as applicable to the existing Government and Assembly at Versailles as they were nearly thirty years ago to the persons to whom they were originally applied. [1872.]

forms one of the principal and the least objectionable parts of these volumes, the mind is confounded by the spectacle of the men who were suddenly raised to the position of supreme authority in France. The first brawler who had the courage to draw on a proscribed uniform—the first prate-apace who caught the ear of the mob—the first accident that hit the fancy of the crowd by a bit of ribbon or a snatch of song—was straightway enthroned at the Hotel de Ville, and lorded it in the capital. In spite of the author's manifest intention to blacken all the agents of the House of Orleans, and in particular to throw the deepest shades of insult and slander over the King, he has not attempted to assert the existence of any serious conspiracy against the government of Charles X. On the 26th and 27th of July, the only effect of the ordinances on the leaders of the Opposition was that of consternation. Sebastiani talked of writing a letter to the King; Dupin maintained that the Chamber was really dissolved; the boldest proposed a stoppage of the supplies; Casimir Perier recommended moderation, and acknowledged the defeat of the Opposition. Assuredly, if at that moment the people had not taken fire at the sight of the tricolor flag—if the fatal nomination of Marmont, the most unpopular name in France, had not added fuel to the flame, and if the principal organs of the press had not adopted the determination to act for themselves,— neither the Liberal deputies nor the Liberal electors would on that day have saved the liberties of France. The Government had prepared itself for a struggle with the parliamentary Opposition, and in that it would have, at least for a time, succeeded; it had not prepared itself for a collision with the people, and in the streets of Paris it perished.

We have before us the note-book of an English gentleman, whose observations on the position of affairs some months before this event are exceedingly curious, for they show that the accession of the Duke of Orleans was already far more discussed than M. Louis Blanc is disposed to admit. The following passage was noted down in Paris on the 8th of March, 1830.

After all, nobody has an idea how things will turn out, or what are Polignac's intentions or his resources. Lord Stuart told me that he knew nothing, but that when he saw all the ministers perfectly calm and satisfied, and heard them constantly say all would be well, although France seemed to be against them, and a clear majority in both Chambers, he could not help thinking they must have some reason for such confidence, and something in reserve of which people were not aware. Lady K——, with whom I had a long talk, told me that she did not believe it possible they could stand; that there was no revolutionary spirit abroad, but a strong determination to provide for the stability of their institutions, a disgust at the obstinacy and pretensions of the King, *and a desire to substitute the Orleans for the reigning branch,* which was becoming very general; that Polignac is wholly ignorant of France, and will not listen to the opinions of those who could enlighten him. It is supposed that the King is determined to push matters to extremity, to try the Chambers, and, if his ministry are beaten, to dissolve them, and govern *par ordonnance du Roi;* then to try and influence the elections, and obtain a Chamber more favourable than the present. Somebody told her the other day of a conversation which Polignac had recently had with the King, in which His Majesty said to him, ' Jules, est-ce que vous m'êtes très-dévoué ? ' —' Mais oui, Sire, pouvez vous en douter?'—' Jusqu'à aller à l'échafaud ?'—' Mais oui, Sire, s'il le faut.'—'Alors tout ira bien.' It is supposed there will be an address against the Government by about 250 to 130 [it was 220 to 180]. All the names presented to the King (yesterday) for the presidency are obnoxious to him ; but he named Royer-Collard, who had twice as many votes as any of the others. It was remarked at the Séance royale that the King dropped his hat, and that the Duke of Orleans picked it up, and they always make a great deal of these trifles. The Duke of Orleans is, however, very well with the Court, and will not stir, let what will happen, though he probably feels like Macbeth before the murder of Duncan,—

' If chance will have me king, why let chance crown me,
Without my stir.'[1]

We know few instances of political prediction more striking than this record, which was confirmed to the letter nearly five months afterwards. Nothing can more accurately describe the position of the future King of the French.

[1] This quotation is from the manuscript journal of Mr. Charles Greville, who visited Paris in March 1830. He communicated it to the writer of this paper, and allowed him to use the passage, in 1844.

The efforts of the people were no sooner crowned with success, than the eagerness of a new race of aspirants became manifest. Men like M. Guizot, Audry de Puyraveau, Dupin, and Casimir Perier, had contented themselves with a protest, which indicated a reluctant submission. But names before unknown, or known only by the accomplishments most remote from the duties of government, were put forward as the daring founders of a new dynasty. Béranger, the song-writer, became, according to our author, 'the soul of the Orleanist party.' Laffitte and his friends had only recovered from their dread of the absolutism of the Court, to fall into equally lively apprehensions of the absolutism of the people. A Government, or at least a round table with four people sitting at it, was organised at the Hotel de Ville under the auspices of Lafayette ; but every one felt that a more substantial form was required to consolidate the revolution, and MM. Thiers, Mignet, Larréguy, and Laffitte got up a proclamation in the name of the Duke of Orleans. The crown was disposed of by a hand-bill, and the dynasty enthroned by a placard.

Thiers and M. Ary Scheffer, the painter (the latter of whom was intimate with the Orleans family), were deputed to proceed to Neuilly upon this business. The scene deserves to be extracted :—

At the chateau of Neuilly the two negotiators were received by the Duchess of Orleans. Her husband was absent. Whilst M. Thiers explained the object of the message, the austere countenance of the Duchess displayed the greatest emotion; and when she learnt that it was proposed to transfer to her house a crown snatched from an aged Sovereign who had always shown himself so faithful a kinsman and so generous a friend, she exclaimed to M. Scheffer, 'How could you, sir, undertake such a mission? As for this other gentleman, I can conceive it; he knows us but little; but you, sir, who have had so many opportunities of knowing us—we shall never forgive you!' The two envoys were not a little embarrassed by so noble a repugnance, when Madame Adelaide came in, followed by Madame de Montjouy.

Madame Adelaide had too virile a mind and too little of pious affection in her heart to yield to family considerations. Nevertheless, struck as she was by the dangers which encompassed her brother, she exclaimed, ' Make what you please of my brother, —a president, a national guard—anything but proscription!' These words were the plain expression of the feelings of the Prince himself at that moment. But what M. Thiers came to offer was the crown, and Madame Adelaide had no mind to reject so seductive an offer. Wholly devoted to the Duke her brother, whose views she shared, and over whom she exercised some influence, she had dreamed for him of that greatness of which she thought him worthy. One thought only appeared to embarrass her: what would Europe think of them? To mount that throne from which Louis XVI. descended to go to the scaffold, was it not to raise an alarm in all the royal houses, and to put in jeopardy the peace of the world?

M. Thiers replied that these apprehensions were unfounded; that England, still mindful of the fall of the Stuarts, would applaud a result so conformable to the example of her own history; that the more absolute sovereigns would acknowledge their obligations to the Duke of Orleans, if he made his elevation repress the passions then let loose; that there was a greatness in saving France; that if it was too late for the principle of legitimacy, that of monarchy might still be preserved; that, after all, the Duke of Orleans had only the choice of perils, and that in the present state of things to fly from the possible dangers of royalty, was to confront the inevitable storms of the Republic.

Such reasons as these were not calculated to touch the humble and pious soul of the Duchess of Orleans, but they were readily adopted by Madame Adelaide. 'A child of Paris,' as she called herself, she offered to go amongst the Parisians; and M. de Montesquiou was sent to apprise the Duke.

He had taken refuge at Raincy. Upon learning what was taking place, he started in his carriage; M. de Montesquiou preceded him on horseback. Suddenly the noise of the wheels appears to recede. M. de Montesquiou looks round; the carriage of the Prince was returning to Raincy at full speed. Such was the natural effect of the uncertainty which tormented the Duke of Orleans.

This hesitation arose from no want of what is commonly called courage, for of that virtue the King of the French has on all occasions given the most undeniable proofs, and it may be regarded as the noblest quality of his character. But the courage which is founded on moral dignity—the courage which dares at all risks to undertake and to perfect what is right, to reject and repel what is wrong—the courage which rises to be a living principle of justice, energy, and power—must be placed far above the gift of equanimity in scenes of danger; and to this height the temper of Louis Philippe's mind has never risen. He is one of the greatest kings who ever reigned by little means. When we review the dangers which he has surmounted, the influence which he has acquired, the prosperity to which he has raised his people, the splendour of his edifices, the personal ascendancy he has exercised over all those who have served him, and the importance of the space his reign must fill in the annals of Europe, we are tempted to place him as high as he stands in the public opinion of England. But when we examine his character in its minor details—his constant sacrifice of the future to the present, and of the great to the convenient—his practice of governing men by their vices, rather than by their virtues —his cynical disbelief in the grand principles of political integrity, which is attested by his most intimate counsellors and servants—the instability of all his purposes, except those which centre in his own family interests,—we are compelled to admit that impartial history, whilst it applauds the services he has rendered to his country, will assign a lower rank to the moral greatness of his character. ' C'est un homme,' said one of his best and noblest ministers, when he withdrew from the Cabinet, ' qu'on peut conseiller, mais qu'on ne peut pas servir.'

We disbelieve many, if not all, of the sinister

accusations and imputations which are collected in the slanderous pages of the volumes before us. If Louis Philippe's government has been devoid of that generous and heroic spirit which prompts the greatest actions of a prince—too often at no small cost to his own people and to the rest of the world—it deserves at least to be for ever remembered as a government free from all sanguinary crimes. Springing from a fierce revolution, and surrounded by the armed and menacing factions of the Republic, the Empire, and the ancient Monarchy, it has never departed from a measure of clemency and humanity worthy of the highest praise; and, for the first time in the history of the world, a vast revolution has been consolidated without the shedding of one drop of blood for political opinions, and even by the extension of an unprecedented mercy to the assassins of the king. In a country in which the first object was to quench political passions, the Government wisely began by extinguishing its own. The objects which Louis Philippe has pursued have been uniformly attained, not by violence or menace, or fear, or open-handed force, but by patience, perseverance, caution, address, sometimes by corruption and deceit. If fear has ever been used as a means of government, it has been instilled into the nation not as fear of the

Government, but fear of the enemies of the Government. Whatever may be the faults of the Court, they rise into virtues when they are contrasted with the crimes and follies of its opponents.

Nothing gives us a meaner opinion of the political attainments and capacity of the party in France to which M. Louis Blanc belongs, than their stupid prejudices and gross ignorance on all those economical questions which constitute the science, in contradistinction to the art, of government. It must be acknowledged that this retrograde move in political economy is not confined to the popular party; but amongst them we are the more forcibly struck by it, inasmuch as it tends directly to injure the very interests they most profess to defend. Throughout these volumes the plain truths of political economy are never alluded to without a sort of angry hostility: they are denounced as the pestilential exhalations of this country: they are inveighed against as the heartless inventions of perfidious intriguers: and the propagation of false maxims of English political economy is made the bugbear in peace, just as the gold of Pitt and Cobourg was the bugbear in the war.

The frightful disturbances which broke out at Lyons in October 1831, were preceded by a resolution on the part of the Trades to the following effect :—

Considering that it is notorious that many of the manufacturers do actually pay too low wages for weaving, it is expedient that a minimum tariff of wages be fixed for the price of weaving.

M. Bouvier Dumolard, the prefect, yielded at first to this fatal demand, and it was settled that a minimum rate of wages should be fixed by a committee consisting of twenty-two weavers and twenty-two manufacturers. M. Louis Blanc does not seem to suspect the very obvious truth, that to fix such a tariff by a combination was to condemn the master-weavers to cease work altogether, if the market value of labour and freedom of contract were to be controlled by the authority either of the populace or of the Government.

Nothing (says our author) assuredly is more conformable to the laws of justice and humanity. Even supposing that the measure was illegal—even if it had not been authorised in 1789 by the Constituent Assembly, in 1793 by the Convention, and in 1811 by the Empire, was it not imperiously demanded by the state of affairs? Was that the time to abstain, between the violated laws of humanity and the imminence of civil war? A power, which, under such circumstances, cannot be arbitrary, ought to abdicate. M. Bouvier Dumolard might and ought himself to have fixed the tariff: he wanted the courage to do it, and contented himself with bringing the two parties together. But such was then the strange falsehood of the notions current amongst the public on the rights of trade and the liberty of business, that the conduct of the prefect, timid as it was, was loudly blamed by the manufacturers, and considered as an excess of power.

As might have been anticipated, such measures as these did not prevent a very frightful conflict. Some days later, Marshal Soult entered Lyons with the Prince Royal and an army of 20,000 men, but not before the city had been deluged with blood; for the victory of the workmen, at first, was as complete as that of the people of Paris had been on the 28th of July. M. Louis Blanc mourns over their defeat, and adds :—

> In the violent debates to which this insurrection gave rise in Parliament, nothing was said of the establishment of a minimum of wages, or of the necessity of making the State intervene in the affairs of industry, or of the modifications required by the oppressive discipline of competition, or of the scientific modes to be adopted to prevent the recurrence of such a disaster. No, a great quarrel occurred in the Chamber, and that was all.

It is to the credit of the Chamber of Deputies of 1831 that nothing *was* said of such 'scientific modes' as these; but we are not a little amused at the complacency with which our author associates his *science* with the madness of an ignorant and desperate populace.

The insurrection at Lyons was, however, a far less formidable danger than the great disturbances in Paris on the 5th and 6th of June 1832. Even the revolution which had overturned the throne two years before, commenced with less of popular excitement and republican desperation. At one moment the battle was almost won by the insurgents. The presence and encouragement of a few great names might have turned the scale; but they remained either faithful to the Court or distrustful of the anarchists, and the Government triumphed. Our limits forbid us to borrow the picture of this conflict, which M. Louis Blanc has drawn with the spirit of an enthusiastic partisan, but we must make room for the following account of the King's conduct at this emergency. The battle of the 6th of June was hardly terminated, and the city was still crowded with troops and stained with gore, when—

At noon the King left the Tuileries, accompanied by the Ministers of War, of the Interior, and of Commerce, and he reviewed the troops on the Place Louis XV. and the Champs Elysées. Thence he went by the Boulevards to the Bastille, crossed the Faubourg St. Antoine, and came back along the quays to his palace by the Louvre. Although the revolt was by this time almost entirely conquered [the attack on the Cloitre St. Méry had not begun] the King's long ride was an act of courage; and the National Guard which saluted him with acclamations as he passed, knew not how near death was to him in several quarters of the town. On the quay, not far from the Place de Grève, a young woman had levelled a musket at him, from a high window, and only failed to fire it because the weight of the piece made her hand shake. Certainly the King on this occasion did not hesitate to risk his person, smiling calmly to all about him, comforting the wounded, approaching the hostile or sullen groups of the people, and restraining those of his escort who sought to cover him with their own bodies.

At three o'clock an open barouche, in which were Arago, Laffitte, and Odilon Barrot drove into the Tuileries. A man unknown to them rushed forward to their horses' heads and exclaimed, 'Take care, gentlemen! M. Guizot has just left the King's apartments: your lives are not in safety.' Surprised rather than alarmed by this incident, the three commissioners were announced. M. Laffitte had studied the King's character in the course of a long intimacy; and on the threshold of the royal closet he said to his colleagues, 'Let us be firm: he will try to make us laugh.'

The object of these deputies was to state the grievances of the Liberal Opposition, to which the King with his usual address opposed the enormous difficulties of his position.

Some curious incidents marked this interview. They had scarcely begun to speak when a sinister sound was heard. 'It is the cannon,' said the King, 'which has been brought up to force the Cloitre St. Méry, without losing too many troops.' Something was said of the extreme forbearance of his policy to the Legitimists. 'I have always remembered,' said he, 'the remark of Kersaint: Charles I. had his head cut off, and England saw his son re-ascend the throne: James II. was only banished, and his family died out on the Continent.'

The chief characteristic, however, of the King's conversation was his fear that the honour of the political system which had been followed should be attributed to Casimir Perier. This honour he altogether assumed for himself; he insisted upon it, he reverted to it, evidently for the purpose of representing his late

Minister as the docile instrument of a superior mind. He dwelt a good deal on the imperturbable firmness of his will—a will which had only once given way, and that was in abandoning the *fleurs de lis*, which belong as much to the younger as to the elder branch of the Bourbons. Amongst other things which fell from him in the torrent of conversation, the deputies were struck by an observation, hazardous enough in the mouth of a diplomatic king: 'The element of revolutions exists in all the nations of Europe, but they have not all got the stuff of a Duke of Orleans to put it down.'

We now turn to the view which our author and his party take of the foreign relations of the new Government. At the very moment of his accession, the position which the new sovereign assumed is stated by himself with characteristic ingenuity, in the following very curious letter to the Emperor Nicholas :—

Monsieur mon Frère,

J'annonce mon avénement à la couronne à Votre Majesté par la lettre que le général Athalin lui présentera en mon nom ; mais j'ai besoin de lui parler avec une entière confiance sur les suites de la catastrophe que j'aurais tant voulu prévenir.

Il y avait longtemps que je regrettais que le roi Charles et son gouvernement ne suivissent pas une marche mieux calculée pour répondre à l'attente et au vœu de la nation. J'étais bien loin, pourtant, de prévoir les prodigieux événements qui viennent de se passer, et je croyais même qu'à défaut de cette allure franche et loyale dans l'esprit de la Charte et de nos institutions, qu'il était impossible d'obtenir, il aurait suffi d'un peu de prudence et de modération, pour que ce gouvernement pût aller longtemps comme il allait. Mais, depuis le 8 août 1829, la nouvelle composition du nouveau ministère m'avait fort alarmé. Je voyais à quel point cette composition était odieuse et suspecte à la nation, et je partageais l'inquiétude générale sur les mesures que nous devions en attendre. Néanmoins, l'attachement aux lois, l'amour de l'ordre, ont fait de tels progrès en France, que la résistance à ce ministère ne serait certainement pas sortie des voies parlementaires, si, dans son délire, ce ministère lui-même n'eût donné le fatal signal par la plus audacieuse violation de la Charte et par l'abolition de toutes les garanties de notre liberté nationale, pour lesquelles il n'est guère de Français qui ne soit prêt à verser son sang. Aucun excès n'a suivi cette lutte terrible.

Mais il était difficile qu'il n'en résultât pas quelque ébranlement dans notre état social ; et cette même exaltation des esprits, qui les avait détournés de tant de désordres, les portait en même temps vers des essais de théorie politique qui auraient précipité la France et peut-être l'Europe dans de terribles calamités. C'est dans cette situation, Sire, que tous les yeux se sont tournés vers moi. Les vaincus eux-mêmes m'ont cru nécessaire à leur salut. Je l'étais encore plus, peut-être, pour que les vainqueurs ne laissassent pas dégénérer la victoire. J'ai donc accepté cette tâche noble et pénible, et j'ai écarté toutes les considérations personnelles qui se réunissaient pour me faire désirer d'en être dispensé, parce que j'ai senti que la moindre hésitation de ma part pourrait compromettre l'avenir de la France et le repos de tous nos voisins. Le titre de lieutenant-général, qui laissait tout en question, excitait une confiance dangereuse, et il fallait se hâter de sortir de l'état provisoire, tant pour inspirer la confiance nécessaire, que pour sauver cette Charte si essentielle à conserver, dont feu l'empereur, votre auguste frère, connaissait si bien l'importance, et qui aurait été très-compromise, si on n'eût promptement satisfait et rassuré les esprits.

Il n'échappera ni à la perspicacité de Votre Majesté, ni à sa haute sagesse que, pour atteindre ce but salutaire, il est bien désirable que les affaires de Paris soient envisagées sous leur véritable aspect, et que l'Europe, rendant justice aux motifs qui m'ont dirigé, entoure mon gouvernement de la confiance qu'il a droit d'inspirer. Que Votre Majesté veuille bien ne pas perdre de vue que tant que le roi Charles X a régné sur la France, j'ai été le plus soumis et le plus fidèle de ses sujets, et que ce n'est qu'au moment que j'ai vu l'action des lois paralysée et l'exercice de l'autorité royale totalement anéantie, que j'ai cru de mon devoir de déférer au vœu national, en acceptant la couronne à laquelle j'ai été appelé. C'est sur vous, Sire, que la France a surtout les yeux fixés. Elle aime à voir dans la Russie son allié le plus naturel et le plus puissant. J'en ai pour garantie le noble caractère et toutes les qualités qui distinguent Votre Majesté Impériale.

Je la prie d'agréer les assurances de la haute estime et de l'inaliénable amitié avec laquelle je suis,

Monsieur mon frère, de Votre Majesté Impériale, le bon frère,

LOUIS-PHILIPPE.

The haughty and contemptuous reply of Nicholas to this effusion quenched at once all hopes of restoring that alliance between Russia and France which had been the work of the Restoration; and this letter was the first of a series of affronts which the two monarchs continued to aim at each other from the opposite extremities of Europe :—

J'ai reçu des mains du général Athalin la lettre dont il a été porteur. Des événements à jamais déplorables ont placé Votre Majesté dans une cruelle alternative. Elle a pris une détermination qui lui a paru la seule propre à sauver la France des plus grandes calamités, et je ne me prononcerai pas sur les considérations qui ont guidé Votre Majesté, mais je forme des vœux pour que la Providence divine veuille bénir ses intentions et les efforts qu'elle va faire pour le bonheur du peuple français. De concert avec mes alliés, je me plais à accueillir le désir que Votre Majesté a exprimé d'entretenir des relations de paix et d'amitié avec tous

Etats d'Europe. Tant qu'elles seront basées sur les traités existants et sur la ferme volonté de respecter les droits et obligations, ainsi que l'état de possession territoriale, qu'ils ont consacrés, l'Europe y trouvera une garantie de la paix, si nécessaire au repos de la France elle-même. Appelé conjointement avec mes alliés, à cultiver avec la France, sous son gouvernement, ces relations conservatrices, j'y apporterai, pour ma part, toute la sollicitude qu'elles réclament, et les dispositions dont j'aime à offrir à Votre Majesté l'assurance, en retour des sentiments qu'elle m'a exprimés. Je la prie d'agréer en même temps, etc. etc.

NICOLAS.

To hold such language in justification of his own royalty, and to receive such a reply—stripped of the ordinary form of 'Monsieur mon Frère,' which Louis Philippe himself had studiously adopted— was what had never before befallen a prince of the house of Bourbon or a king of France. But whilst M. Louis Blanc records with manifest satisfaction every incident of the reign which may be construed into a humiliation or a blunder, he either omits from ignorance or distorts from passion those facts and those principles which have justly entitled the government of Louis Philippe to the respect of the world.

One of the first and severest trials of the power which had been so recently constituted, was the impeachment of the ministers of Charles X. The generous passions which had inspired the people in the day of battle, had indeed degenerated in

December into the more brutal and vindictive fury of a revolution. The King had shown, from the moment of his accession, a determination that no blood should be shed. Even the ordinary executions of condemned criminals were stopped, lest the sight of the guillotine should act upon the popular imagination. If M. de Polignac and his colleagues had been tried by an ordinary tribunal, or by a popular assembly, their doom would have been inevitable. The Chamber of Peers almost sunk under the terror of the trial, when the gates of the Luxembourg were surrounded by the mob—the fidelity of the troops was doubtful—the ascendancy of Lafayette over the National Guard was all that was interposed between the deliberations of the senate and a massacre by the people. In that terrible crisis, the firmness of Louis Philippe saved the prisoners, and prevented the imminent danger of bloodshed on the scaffold. Will it be credited that a writer who now dares to show his name in print has recorded these details only to sneer at the precautions of the Court, and has deliberately advocated a sentence of death which even the excitement of the moment could not have justified? By the diabolical spirit in which such passages of this work are conceived, the absence of crimes is imputed to the Government as a disgrace; and whenever an outbreak of popular violence takes place, the desperadoes who perished in their vain and sanguinary attempts are exalted to the rank of heroes and martyrs.

It would be unjust to M. Louis Blanc to pass an irrevocable condemnation on his account of matters collected from sources of original information, or to argue against his whole work from the unparalleled absurdities which he has published about our own country. In spite of the interest which he professes to feel for the cause of Poland, no opportunity is neglected of inculcating the importance of a good understanding between France and Russia. But to England the author never expresses anything but the most malignant hatred, in terms which indicate a gross and grotesque ignorance of the people and policy of Great Britain. Take, for instance, the following paragraph :—

In England the excitement caused by the revolution was profound. The newspapers lauded the heroism of the Parisians, and subscriptions were everywhere opened for the wounded. These demonstrations *were sincere and disinterested on the part of the Radicals alone.* The Whigs burst forth into transports of joy, because in their hopes they had always connected the movement which was to raise them to power with the triumph of French liberalism. But the Tories—strange to say—the Tories themselves showed their insensibility to the misfortune of a royal family, and the Wellington Administration seemed to smile upon a crisis which, however, was the forerunner of its own downfall. The fact is that there was here, for the Tories, a question far higher than party questions—that, namely, of the supremacy of England in Europe. The English aristocracy, like all aristocracies, forwards and accomplishes its designs with much foresight and consistency. It was known that, under Charles X., a proposal had been made for ceding to the French the left bank of the Rhine, and to the Russians, Constantinople. It was also known that the Duke of Orleans is an Englishman by taste and inclination, to use his own words in a letter written to the Bishop of Llandaff in 1804. Hence all the parties in England combined, if not to celebrate the victory which had been gained in France over the monarchy, at least to insult the conquered monarch.

On this side of the Channel these lines require no answer; but it is impossible to repress a feeling of indignation at the propagation of such knavish falsehood amongst the very people whose prejudices and passions predispose them to receive it. When therefore we find M. Louis Blanc eager to blast every patriotic effort, to tarnish every lofty reputation, to sneer at every deep and prudent mark of sympathy with the people, and to misrepresent every measure of the Government, we only beg the reader to compute his general veracity and fairness by the standard here applied to ourselves.[1]

[1] In spite of his virulent abuse of England, and his abhorrence of its tyrannical government, it was to England that M. Louis Blanc betook himself when he was driven out of France; and here he remained for upwards of twenty years, a harmless insignificant

Like Louis Philippe, in the letter we have cited, M. Louis Blanc considers Russia the most natural and powerful ally of France. The King found out his mistake ; the historian persists in it. Our author settles the Eastern Question by an alliance between Russia, France, and Prussia, against England and Austria, which would have the following 'desired and foreseen consequences'—

The definitive establishment of the Russians at Constantinople and the consecration of their preponderance in Asia ; the establishment of France in Syria and in Egypt, and the consecration [again] of her preponderance in the Mediterranean as a French lake ; the re-constitution of the kingdom of Poland, with the addition of Gallicia; the aggrandisement of Prussia at the expense of Austria, as the price of the frontier of the Rhine ceded to France ; and, as a necessary consequence of the ruin of Austria, the independence of Italy.

We have extracted this pleasing proposal chiefly for the sake of the note which follows it : it characterises the ignorance and want of principle of the party by whom the King and the statesmen of France have been assailed.

person, employed in writing a most mendacious history of the French Revolution from the papers in the British Museum. In the autumn of 1870 he returned to France, and was elected a member of the Assembly which met at Bordeaux; he still occupies a seat there, but has subsided for the present into total obscurity, being generally supposed in France to have more violence in his opinions than courage in defence of them. [1872.]

It may perhaps be objected to this system, that it would have been strange to prefer, after the Revolution of July, the alliance of a despot to that of a constitutional monarchy, by which this revolution had been ardently applauded. No one, assuredly, has more esteem and admiration for the great people of England than we have, provided it be separated from its Government. But, to speak frankly, we do not see why we should sympathise with the English constitutional system, which consecrates the most execrable tyranny which ever existed. What political bond is there between a nation which, like our own, in order to extirpate aristocratic power, has consented to pass through all the convulsions of the most formidable anarchy, to be exhausted by a war without a precedent or a parallel, and to be half drowned in the blood of Europe and in her own—and a nation, like that of England, which only exists by the excesses and permanent usurpations of aristocracy? Have we so soon forgotten that it was against the principles of our immortal Revolution that England drove the whole Continent, whose wrath was in her pay alone?

As for the reception which England gave to the Revolution of July, how long have such manifestations been relied on by statesmen? When the Belgian question arose, did the sympathy of the English for our revolution prevent them from opposing our most legitimate pretensions?

To imagine that Russia would have rejected an alliance of interests eminently favourable to her, through monarchical zeal, especially as she has so little to fear from the propagation of our ideas, is really puerile.

We are not much addicted to celebrate the good qualities of the Emperor of Russia; but we do not hesitate to express our conviction that, rather than stoop to an alliance with the worst principles and the puny descendants of the French Convention, the Emperor Nicholas would renounce the greatest projects of aggrandisement which could be offered to him.

The Revolution of 1830 was hailed in this country with as hearty and spontaneous a burst of sympathy as ever rose from the heart of a free people. The French have now, for the most part, forgotten the service rendered them by England at that crisis, when, unprepared as they were for war, the whole of Continental Europe was against them. It is, however, not the less true that the active co-operation of England not only prevented war, but actually brought to a successful issue all the negotiations in which the two countries jointly engaged. M. Louis Blanc has not recorded these events in the spirit of the men who accomplished such important changes in the structure of Europe without any of the horrors in which he chiefly delights, but rather in the factious temper of those who incessantly labour to thwart the Government in all its foreign relations. The hostility to this country often expressed by the public organs of France is not, we are disposed to think, universally spread amongst the people; but we cannot doubt that it is identified with the doctrines of the revolutionary party, and that it is one of the most convenient forms for keeping up the passions of the adherents to that cause. We have not so mean an opinion of French statesmen as to think that they would deliberately sacrifice the peace of the world and the order of society to the mere acquisition of personal power. But there were, and are, in France men who have the instinct of the Revolution with all its indiscriminating intensity; and they are capable of letting loose, in a moment of difficulty, a force which it would require more than another Louis Philippe to bring into subordination again.

The principal resource of the King, as a means of internal government, has been to engross men by the promotion of their material interests. He has made no appeals to their loyalty, he has never trusted himself within reach of those more expansive sympathies by which sovereigns like Louis XIV. and Napoleon converted the French people into the most servile, all-enduring subjects of Europe—enthusiastic in their bondage. He knew that these passions and sympathies were cold towards himself, or, if roused, that they might be turned against him; but the interests of the community were within his reach, and upon them he founded his throne. He founded a throne, but has he founded a dynasty? For our own part, the only expression we can use at the present time is, that it is not impossible that the dynasty may subsist, but that its fate depends on the characters of two princes, one of whom is still a babe, and the other has grown to manhood with few of the better qualities of his family. Politically speaking, however, we cannot deplore the melancholy and premature death of the Duke of Orleans. His varied acquirements, his affable manners, and his quick parts gave a charm to his character, and had earned for him the reputation of being one of the most amiable men in Europe; but his acknowledged taste for war, and the want of straightforwardness in his political relations, would probably have made him one of the most dangerous kings that ever mounted the throne.[1]

It is impossible to 'contemplate without anxiety the prospects of a nation, where the past has exhausted every imaginable combination of government, and the present contains so few solid pledges for the future. France endured the bad kings of her ancient monarchy for the sake of that monarchy; she exulted in the still more oppressive institutions of the imperial *régime* for the sake of the Emperor; but under the dynasty of Orleans she neither upholds

---

[1] I must remind the reader that these remarks were written in 1844. They are curious from what follows. [1872].

the monarchy for the sake of the prince nor the prince for the sake of the monarchy. The feelings of unwavering allegiance and of ardent loyalty are both extinct; the throne is supported by the bare but general conviction of its necessity. It remains to be seen whether any of those great institutions which tower over the stream of ages, can be based upon no sounder principle than the convenience or the mutual fears of a community. King Louis Philippe has remained the master in every popular commotion and in almost every parliamentary struggle; he has reigned with undoubted power and with signal success; but that success has failed to restore the prestige of monarchy to his house, or to concentrate upon himself or his descendants the affections of the people. He deserves those affections; he deserves far more—the respectful gratitude of a nation which he has raised to the highest pitch of internal prosperity that it has yet enjoyed; but he will be more highly estimated in future ages than in his own, as he is already more revered in foreign countries than in France.

This paper has been retained in this collection because it describes, not inaccurately, the weakness inherent in the King's Government, even at the height of its power in 1844, and the increasing hostility of the principles and agents of the revolution, even to the most liberal and enlightened Government which had or has existed in France. The reign of Louis Philippe was not perfect. Nothing in this world is perfect. But when we remember the paltry motives which led to the Revolution of 1848, and the fatal consequences which have followed that overthrow of the constitutional monarchy, it may be regarded as the most disastrous event in French history. [1872.]

ALEXIS DE TOCQUEVILLE.

ALEXIS DE TOCQUEVILLE.[1]

I.

A DOMINICAN monk, whose eloquence has for the first time raised a brother of his order to a seat in

[1] These papers were first published in the *Edinburgh Review*, No. 230, for April 1861, and in the same Review, No. 250, for October 1865, as reviews of the following works :—1. *Œuvres et Correspondance inédites d'Alexis de Tocqueville.* Publiées et précédées d'une Notice, par Gustave de Beaumont, Membre de l'Institut. 2 tomes. Paris : 1860. 2. *Discours de réception à l'Académie française.* Par le R. P. H. D. Lacordaire—des Frères Prêcheurs, le 24 janvier 1861. Paris. 3. *Discours de M. Guizot, Directeur de l'Académie française, en réponse au Discours prononcé par M. Lacordaire pour sa réception à l'Académie française.* Paris : 1861. And also of the posthumous works published by M. de Beaumont at a later period.—The first of these papers has already been in part republished in the form of an introductory notice prefixed to the last edition of the English translation of the 'Democracy in America,' and perhaps I owe some apology to the reader for reproducing it in this place. But I am conscious that if there be any truth or merit in the opinions I have formed on the state of France and the history of her revolutions, their value is due in great part to the author of that memorable book. I had the good fortune to translate it into English when I was about one and twenty, and from that time till the date of his death in 1859 I lived in the intimacy of unbroken friendship with Alexis de Tocqueville. I was well acquainted with his opinions on many subjects which he never imparted to the world ; my own opinions were no doubt affected by the influence of that pure and subtle intellect ; and the highest merit I would venture to claim for them is their conformity with his principles. This collection of papers relating to France, and to the state of society in that country, would therefore have been incomplete if it did not contain these notices of M. de Tocqueville and of his writings.

the Academy of France,—an historian and statesman to whom in politics Alexis de Tocqueville had been habitually opposed,—a friend who had shared for thirty years his affections, his thoughts, and almost every incident of his life, have within the last few weeks pronounced and recorded their homage to this illustrious and virtuous man, whose premature death is an irreparable loss to letters, to his country, to those who loved him, and to the age.

Nothing is more diverse than the points from which these eminent persons approached their common subject—nothing more unlike than the distinctive features most attractive to each of them in M. de Tocqueville's character; yet such was the simplicity, the truth, the native beauty of his mind, that voices of different tones blend in perfect harmony over his tomb, and the monument which adorns it, though raised by many hands, is of one conception and design. Perhaps of the three writers whose names we have cited, Father Lacordaire has best succeeded in tracing and expressing, by the light of his own genius, the extraordinary elevation and moral dignity of M. de Tocqueville's life. The part M. Guizot had to perform in his official capacity as the Director of the French Academy, was of a more modest kind, and, with his usual good taste, he confined himself to it, dwelling less on the circumstances which had separated him from M. de Tocqueville in public life than on the principles which united them in a common love of literature, philosophy, and freedom. But M. de Beaumont's biographical notice of his friend, accompanied as it is by a selection from his private letters, and by some unpublished fragments of his works, is by far the most valuable memorial we as yet possess of him. M. de Beaumont has executed this task with a conscientious desire to present to the world a fair and accurate portrait of the man he loved. He has abstained from needless and intrusive panegyric. He has contented himself with a guarded selection from the papers placed in his hands. He has carefully avoided all that could wound personal sensitiveness, and he has performed a very difficult part with skill and good taste. The book has excited a degree of attention in France not commonly bestowed in these days upon publications of so serious a character, an edition of 4,000 copies having been rapidly sold; and we have no doubt that it will retain its place as one of the most valuable contributions to modern biography.

But whilst we share the gratification which this publication has excited, and rejoice to mark so strong a disposition in France to do honour to the exalted qualities of a man who lived above his age, it must in candour be admitted that M. de Beaumont has not escaped all the inconveniences of contemporary biography. When the life of a distinguished man is written within a few months of his death by those who have enjoyed his intimacy, there is a risk that the private incidents of his domestic circle will assume an excessive degree of importance, whilst the principles which regulated his public conduct, and even the public events in which he took part, cannot be fully and completely explained. No one will read without affectionate interest the expressions, which abound in these volumes, of Alexis de Tocqueville's devotion to his wife, his father, and his friends. In these relations he was a model of tenderness and fidelity; and, happily for himself, the ties of domestic life and of friendship filled a larger space in his existence than the pursuit of literary fame or the efforts of political ambition. But posterity, regarding him as one of the most profound thinkers and accomplished writers of this century, will naturally look rather to his public life than to his private virtues. And in this respect the volumes before us leave the tale of his life untold.

He exclaimed in early youth to his intimate friend, who is now his biographer: ' Il n'y a pas à dire, c'est *l'homme politique* qu'il faut faire en nous.' His studies, his journeys, his pursuits were already directed to a life of political action. He engaged in politics with matchless ardour, and with an ambition the more intense that it was absolutely free from the slightest taint of personal interest. He pursued this noble enterprise for fifteen years, in the contests of parliamentary debate, in the paroxysms of revolution, in the ranks of a constituent assembly, in the service of the President of the Republic, and in the direction of the department of foreign affairs. He witnessed the catastrophe which extinguished the liberties of his country, and realised the darkest of his own marvellous predictions; but subjection to despotic power wasted him like an incurable disease, and amongst the causes which doubtless contributed to exhaust his delicate and sensitive frame, was the ever-recurring thought that he who survives the freedom and the dignity of his country has already lived too long. Some traces of these feelings may be found in M. de Beaumont's volumes; indeed, they pervade every letter in the latter portion of this collection: but of the political events and opinions connected with these passionate sentiments we find scarcely any record. Since the revolution of February 1848 a thick darkness has settled over the history of the French nation. Men have learned to whisper their opinions. The former divisions of party appear ludicrous and mischievous when they are measured by that great chasm which yawns between Imperial despotism and constitutional freedom. Those who, like M. de Tocqueville himself, have actually written a record of the political events in which they took part, bury their manuscripts or deposit them in foreign countries, till better times shall vindicate the rights of history. Thus, although we cannot admit that the life of such a man as Tocqueville has been adequately written, so long as the strongest of his opinions and the most notable of his actions are passed over in silence, we must be content for the present with what M. de Beaumont has given us, and with the promise that at some future period Tocqueville's political correspondence will also be made known to the world.

On the other hand, it is perfectly true that the private details of M. de Tocqueville's birth, parentage, and connections which are to be found in these volumes powerfully contribute to explain the true bearing of his political opinions; and this is the chief result which the public can draw from so uneventful a biography. It is not, however, an unimportant result, if it removes a misconception

which has very generally prevailed as to the spirit
and design of his principal writings. Because M.
de Tocqueville based his literary and political
reputation on the study of democracy and democratic
institutions, it was hastily inferred that these institutions were the object of his own predilections.
Because he described with perfect impartiality the
means by which the American people appeared to
have succeeded in combining a highly democratic
state of society with a free and regular government,
it was supposed that M. de Tocqueville carried a
love of democracy to the length of republicanism.
Even among some of his intimate friends an opinion
existed that his political principles had in them
something extreme and revolutionary, and his own
family, ardently attached to the royalist party in
France, were half alarmed at the audacity and the
fame of the most illustrious member of their house.
The truth is, that his celebrated book on American
democracy had, as M. Guizot remarks in his address,
the singular good fortune to find equal favour in the
eyes of opposite parties. It was hailed with equal
satisfaction by the ardent friends of democracy and
by those who dread the exclusive predominance of
democratic power. The former were gratified by
M. de Tocqueville's admission of the preponderance

of this great element in modern societies, and by his prediction of its future dominion over the world ; the latter were no less struck by the acuteness with which he pointed out its tendency to favour absolute government, and to degrade the noblest faculties of man. His doctrine of the universal extension of social equality was applauded by Mr. Mill and Mr. Grote; his doctrine of the tyranny of democratic majorities was quoted with extraordinary effect by Sir Robert Peel, when he was laying the foundations of the great party of conservative resistance, after the popular movement of 1832. But no party objects whatever entered into the mind of M. de Tocqueville himself. Even in this controversy, which may be said to have formed the business of his life, because he saw more clearly than any other man that the fate and freedom of the world depend on it, he maintained an inviolable impartiality, the more difficult and meritorious that his personal sympathies inclined to the cause of aristocracy, although the result of his profound political observations led him to believe that the cause of aristocratic government was irreparably lost, and that democracy must hereafter be mistress of the world. This apparent contradiction was perfectly well explained by himself in a letter to his friend Stoffels, which deserves to be cited. Stoffels had imagined that the tendency of his theories was radical and almost revolutionary; he replied that his love of liberty was tempered by so great a respect for justice and so genuine a love of law and order, that he might fairly pass for a Liberal of a new sort, not to be confounded with most of the democrats of the time.

The political object of the work is this : I have sought to show what a democratic people is in our days, and by this delineation, executed with rigorous accuracy, my design has been to produce a twofold effect on my cotemporaries. To those who make to themselves an ideal democracy, a brilliant vision which they think it easy to realise, I undertake to show that they have arrayed their picture in false colours ; that the democratic government they advocate, if it be of real advantage to those who can support it, has not the lofty features they ascribe to it ; and, moreover, that this government can only be maintained on certain conditions of intelligence, private morality, and religious faith, which we do not possess; and that its political results are not to be obtained without labour. To those for whom the word 'democracy' is synonymous with disturbance, anarchy, spoliation, and murder, I have attempted to show that the government of democracy may be reconciled with respect for property, with deference for rights, with safety to freedom, with reverence for religion ; that if democratic government is less favourable than another to some of the finer parts of human nature, it has also great and noble elements ; and that perhaps, after all, it is the will of God to shed an inferior grade of happiness over the totality of mankind, not to confer a greater share of it on a smaller number, or to raise the few to the verge of perfection. I have undertaken to demonstrate to them that whatever their opinion on this point may be, it is too late to deliberate, that society is advancing and dragging them along with itself towards equality of conditions; that the sole remaining alternative lies between evils henceforth inevitable ; that the question is not whether aristocracy or democracy can be maintained, but whether we are to live under a democratic society devoid indeed of poetry and greatness, but at least orderly and moral, or under a democratic society lawless and depraved, abandoned to the frenzy of revolution, or subjected to a yoke heavier than any of those which have crushed mankind since the fall of the Roman Empire. I have sought to calm the ardour of the former class of persons, and, without discouragement, to point out the only path before them. I have sought to allay the terrors of the latter, and to bend their minds to the idea of an inevitable future, so that with less impetuosity on the one hand, and less resistance on the other, the world may advance more peaceably to the necessary fulfilment of its destiny. This is the fundamental idea of the book—an idea which connects all its other ideas in a single web, and which you ought to have discerned more clearly than you have done. There are, however, as yet very few persons who understand it. Many people of opposite opinions are pleased with it, not because they understand me, but because they find in my book, considered on one side only, certain arguments favourable to their own passion of the moment. But I have confidence in the future, and I hope the day will come when everybody will see clearly what a few only perceive at present.

Perhaps even now that day predicted by the author has not yet entirely arrived. The book itself, far from having suffered from the lapse of time, has gained in authority and interest from the inexhaustible depth, the unflinching truth, and the extraordinary foresight which are its characteristics. It is, and it will remain, by far the greatest work of political philosophy of this age; for it embraces futurity itself, and that with no uncertain range. But the world has not yet entirely taken the full measure of it, and the deeper insight which these biographical details may give into the purpose of the author are of great assistance to a more thorough comprehension of his design.

In a letter to one of his English friends, he expresses with greater precision his own personal relations to the undertaking :—

People want to make me a party man, which I am not. They ascribe to me passions when I have only opinions,—or rather but one passion, the love of freedom and of human dignity. All forms of government are in my eyes but means to satisfy this sacred and lawful passion of man. Democratic and aristocratic prejudices are alternately ascribed to me. I should perhaps have had these or those had I been born in another century or in another country; but the accident of my birth has easily enabled me to defend myself against either tendency. I came into the world at the end of a long revolution, which after having destroyed the former state of things had created nothing lasting in its place. Aristocracy was already dead when I began to live, and democracy was not yet in existence. No instinct, therefore, impelled me blindly towards one or the other. I was an inhabitant of a country which had been for forty years trying everything and stopping definitively at nothing. I was not, therefore, easily addicted to political illusions. Belonging myself to the old aristocracy of my country, I had no natural hatred or jealousy of aristocracy : nor had I any natural love of it, for people only attach themselves to what is in existence. I was near enough to judge it with knowledge, far enough to judge it without passion. The same may be said of the democratic element. No interest gave me a natural or necessary propensity to democracy; nor had democracy inflicted on me any personal injury. I had no particular motive to love it or to hate it, independently of my own reason. In a word, I was so well balanced between the past and the future that I did not feel myself naturally and instinctively drawn towards one or the other, and it was no great effort to me to take a tranquil survey of both sides.

The maintenance of this state of philosophical impartiality, widely remote from indifference, was one of the great objects of M. de Tocqueville through life, and it is one of the finest qualities of his writings. He was, as an ingenious writer expresses it, essentially ' binocular ;' he saw correctly because he saw the object in two positions at once, the angle of one point of vision correcting the obliquity of the other. But we are rather inclined to attribute this singular rectitude of judgment to the skill with which he preserved the balance between his sympathies and his understanding than to the absence of those passions to which other men are more apt to yield. A few details of his earlier life will explain our meaning.

The family of Clerel, or, as it was anciently spelt, Clarel, has been established for many centuries in the peninsula of the Cotentin, on the Norman coast,

and the village and lands of Tocqueville give them
their territorial designation. The Clerels figure in
the roll of Battle Abbey, among the companions of
the Conqueror, for an extraordinary number of the
gallant Norman adventurers who overran Britain,
and filled the world with their exploits, drew their
first breath in some manor-house of this district.
Tradition indeed relates that the village of Tocqueville owed its name to a Norman chief, or sea rover,
called Toki, whose tumulus may still be seen on the
high ground above the château; and certainly this
point commands a vast range of sea and land of no
common historic interest—hard by, Barfleur, now a
neglected port, but once famous in the annals of
English royalty and English wars; to the east, the
Hogue; to the west, Cherbourg. On this spot the
seigneurs of Tocqueville have dwelt for many generations, leading the life of the country gentlemen of
France before the Revolution, always ready to pay
their debt to their country with their blood, for their
descendant relates in one of these letters that his
grandfather and his great-uncle perished on the
field of battle or died of their wounds; seeking their
amusements in field sports or in the neighbouring
county town of Valognes; proud of their gentle
descent, though not entitled to be ranked among the

highest order of the French nobility. Their actual residence at Tocqueville dates from about 250 years ago. Before that time the Clerels lived on an estate at Rampan near St. Ló, and the family was known as Clerel de Rampan. Several of the Seigneurs de Rampan figure in the annals of the Parliament of Rouen in the seventeenth century ; and as the spirit and learning of the French provincial magistracy— the old parliamentary spirit—was the very salt of the nation, before the Revolution of 1789, it may be said that Alexis de Tocqueville inherited the qualities for which this order of men was justly conspicuous. But when he himself went to the bar, an old country neighbour, well versed in Norman pedigrees, the Countess de Blangy, who had inherited the domain of the Abbé St.-Pierre in the same district, said to the young *stagiaire*, ' Souvenez-vous, Monsieur, que votre famille a toujours été de la noblesse d'épée.' She was right in point of fact. The Clerels had always been soldiers, and long before 1789 the family bore the title of Count. That title, subsequently conferred by Louis XVIII. on the father of Alexis, was no more than the recognition of an ancient distinction. It is still borne by the elder brother and representative of the house ; but Alexis himself always refused to adopt it, and he mentions in one of his letters to Madame Swéchine, that titles had long ago lost, in his estimation and in France, all meaning and all value.

The Château de Tocqueville consisted originally of what might be termed, north of the Tweed, a peel, flanked by a huge tower of enormous solidity, and this part of the edifice is probably as old as the battle of Agincourt. Such was the type of the Norman manor-house of the fifteenth century. But when the gentry of the Cotentin had ceased to dread the incursions of English marauders, their houses expanded, and in the reign of Louis XIII. the château was considerably enlarged. A quadrangle was built, which served partly for the residence of the family, and partly for farm buildings, the windows looking out on the farm-yard in the middle. A large dovecote, though now guiltless of pigeons, still marks the ancient seignorial right of the lord to keep his pigeons at the expense of his peasantry; and a stain over the door indicates the spot from which the Revolution of '93 tore the escutcheon of the family. The quadrangle has made way for the convenience of a modern approach, and the old château has assumed the elegance of a mansion of the nineteenth century : but every stone of it tells of the past. Alexis de Tocqueville came into possession of this residence by a family arrangement in 1837. He speaks of it in one of his letters at that time as 'mon pauvre vieux Tocqueville,' a sort of big farm-house, which had not been inhabited for half a century. Indeed at that time the floors were gone, and the roof was in danger, though happily the old 'girouette féodale' still turned on the big tower. But its aspect was speedily changed; it became for the next twenty years the scene of uninterrupted domestic happiness, and of never-failing rural interests, a repose after the contests of political life, a retreat in the dark hour of national adversity, and the scene of literary labour, of liberal hospitality, of counsel and consolation to all who needed or asked for them. But we are anticipating the course of events.

At an early age the father of Alexis entered into possession of this inheritance, then surrounded with all its seignorial rights, and contracted a marriage with Mdlle. Lapeletier de Rosambo, a granddaughter of M. de Malesherbes. The marriage was celebrated at Malesherbes in 1793; and, extraordinary as it may seem, we derive this information from the lively recollections of an eminent man, who was present at the nuptials, and danced on that occasion for the last time in his life. We need hardly add that there was but one person living at the time this paper was first published to whom this description could apply, and that we refer to the Lyndhurst of France, Chancellor Pasquier, then in his ninety-fourth year, and in the full possession of his memory and his wit. This connection with a house so distinguished as that of the Lamoignons proves the consideration at that time enjoyed by the Clerels of Tocqueville.[1] The life of M. de Malesherbes was patriarchal. Disgraced by the Court, though adored by the nation and venerated by Europe, he too had retired to his country residence, and devoted his leisure to the improvement of agriculture and the introduction of rare trees, until the horrors of the Revolution recalled him to the side of that master whom he had sought in vain to counsel. The defence of Louis XVI. by M. de Malesherbes at the bar of the Convention, and his sublime attachment to the King in that tremendous hour, is the most glorious event of his life, but the whole course of it had been equally great and pure. It was he who asserted in 1771, in the language of a

[1] M. de Tocqueville's connexion with the old Marquise d'Aguesseau was also by his mother's side, Madame d'Aguesseau being one of the three daughters in whom the Lamoignon family expired. One of her sisters married Count Molé's father, and the other M. Feydeau de Brou. The paternal grandfather of Alexis de Tocqueville married Mdlle. de Damas Crux, whence the Duc de Damas was his great-uncle.

remonstrance which his great-grandson would not have disavowed, 'that the right of self-government belongs to everybody and every community, as a right of nature and a right of reason ; that since powerful ministers had made it a matter of political principle not to allow a National Assembly to be convoked, they had come at last to quash the deliberations of every village, and that a government had been introduced in France more fatal than despotism, and worthy of Oriental barbarism.'

After the execution of the King M. de Malesherbes returned to his country-seat. And it was at this very time and under these distressing and alarming circumstances, that the Count de Tocqueville married his granddaughter. Barely six months had passed after the marriage, Malesherbes still living on his estate with the several branches of his descendants, when his eldest daughter and her husband, M. de Rosambo, were torn from him by the revolutionary emissaries. A few days later Malesherbes himself and all the other members of his family were also seized; and on the 22nd April 1794 he was sent to the scaffold with his daughter, his granddaughter, recently married to M. de Chateaubriand, and her husband, the elder brother of the well-known statesman and writer. They were executed before his eyes, and his own death instantly followed that of those he loved. M. and Madame de Tocqueville, she being a sister of Madame de Chateaubriand, were arrested at the same time, and remained for several months in the Conciergerie, until they were liberated by the fall of Robespierre. We remember to have heard that the first thing they did after their liberation was to drive about Paris for a whole day in a hackney coach, partly for the enjoyment of the sense of freedom, and partly from the confusion of mind produced by the scenes they had witnessed and the perils they had escaped. They returned, however, to their family mansion : the plate had been buried, and was saved ; a service of Dresden china had also been buried in another part of the grounds, but the clue to the hiding-place was lost, and it has never been recovered. The Tocquevilles never emigrated ; they therefore retained their landed property, and continued to live peaceably upon it. In 1805 Alexis, their third son, was born in Paris ; but soon afterwards, being still an infant, he was brought to Tocqueville in a panier slung across a horse, with his nurse on a pillion. In those primitive times, not seventy years ago, there was no such thing as a road for wheeled carriages from the mansion of a country gentleman to the village, or even from the village to the chief town of the department.

We have related these details because, independently of the interest they may possess, they serve to show the influence of the Revolution on the last and present generations of the French. In the higher ranks of society, more especially, there is hardly a family in which events of the deepest tragic interest have not occurred within living memory; and if the actual witnesses of those dreadful scenes have now almost disappeared, their children received from them in early life impressions which no time can efface. When Alexis de Tocqueville was born, less than eleven years had elapsed since the most illustrious members of his mother's family had perished on the scaffold. The age of martyrs was still near. Is it yet over? Tocqueville himself was wont to say that he lived in a country where no man could foretell with certainty whether he should die in his bed or on the block. These traditions doubtless contributed to produce on a mind naturally so sensitive and so reflective, impressions of which he was himself scarcely conscious. His family was ardently royalist, and might be compared to a high Tory family on this side the water; with some change of conditions, their prejudices and disposition of the mind were the same. His education was scanty, being conducted apparently by an Abbé Lesueur, whose death, during his absence in America, he affectionately deplores. But that which was not scanty and not deficient was the high principle, the lofty conception of truth and duty, the unselfish dignity with which his father, like himself, was completely imbued. On the Count's death, in 1856, Alexis wrote to M. de Corcelle, one of his most intimate and highly-valued friends : 'You are right. If I am worth anything, I owe it above all to my education, to those examples of uprightness, simplicity, and honour which I found about me in coming into the world and as I advanced in life. I owe my parents much more than existence.'

The following anecdote, related by himself in a charming letter to Lady Theresa Lewis, recalls these impressions of his early life. Speaking of Lady Theresa's 'Friends and Contemporaries of Lord Clarendon,' then lately published, he says—

One feeling above all lives in your pages, though it be dead in the hearts of our generation—I mean that sort of idolatry of royalty which ennobled obedience, and made men capable of acts of self-sacrifice, not only to the principle of government, but to the person of the sovereign. It may be 'said that this feeling is gradually disappearing entirely from the world. In some countries, as in France, not a trace of it remains. I met with it again in your narrative, and the more kindly as the scenes to which it belongs carry me back to the earliest days of my childhood. I remember even now, as if it were still before me, one evening in a château where my father was then living, and where some family rejoicings had brought together a large number of our near relations. The servants had retired. We were all sitting round the hearth. My mother, who had a sweet and touching voice, began to sing an air well known in our civil disturbances, to words relating to Louis XVI. and his death. When she ceased every one was in tears, not for the personal sufferings they had undergone, not even for the loss of so many of our own blood on the field of civil war and on the scaffold, but for the fate of a man who had died fifteen years before, and whom most of those present had never seen. But that man had been the King.

Alexis de Tocqueville was ten years old at the Restoration in 1815, and his father became successively prefect at Metz, at Amiens, and at Versailles. He was also raised, very deservedly, to the rank of a peer of France. These mutations had some effect on the earlier career of his son. In 1822 he gained the prize of rhetoric at the Academy of Metz; and in 1827 he entered the profession of the magistracy, as Juge Auditeur at Versailles. In the interval he had made a tour in Italy, of which some record has been preserved. Probably Alexis de Tocqueville had then never heard of the celebrated passage in Gibbon's Memoirs, where that great historian relates that the idea of his 'Decline and Fall' came into his mind as he sate amidst the ruins of the Capitol and heard the voices of the barefooted friars singing vespers in the Temple of Jupiter. But a similar vision seems to have passed before the mind of another youthful traveller on the same spot: as Tocqueville describes in his journal, a procession of barefooted friars mounting the steps of the Ara Cœli, whilst a shepherd calls his goats browsing in the Forum, the past history of Rome rises before him, and he traces the extinction of her greatness to the day when her liberties fell beneath the sceptre of imperial power.

The following years were eagerly devoted to extend the range of his education, as well as to qualify himself for his legal functions; but it is easy to perceive that his ambition would never have contented itself with the honours of the bench, and, in those days more especially, the whole youth of France had embarked with inconceivable energy in historical researches, in literary controversies, in philosophical theories, which called forth the full powers of a mind earnest in the pursuit of all knowledge. In political affairs he took as yet no part, but his sympathies were entirely on the side of the liberal party, whilst his remarkable foresight enabled him to discern the perils of the monarchy. In

August 1829, on the formation of the Polignac ministry, a year before the celebrated ordinances, he wrote—

These ministers can neither summon a new chamber with the present law of election, nor pass a new law of election in the existing chambers. They are launched then on the plan of *coups d'état*, of laws by ordinance ; that is, the question lies between the royal power and the popular power—a conflict in closed lists, a conflict in which, in my opinion, the popular power only stakes its present, but the royal authority will stake both present and future. If this ministry falls, the Crown will suffer much from its fall ; for it is the creation of the Crown, and it will cause securities to be taken hereafter which will still further restrict a power already too limited. God grant that the House of Bourbon may not one day repent what has just been done !'

The revolution which in 1830 realised these sinister predictions, was a severe, if not a fatal blow to the hopes of a man of five-and-twenty entering with M. de Tocqueville's prospects and opinions on public life. It was not only that his personal chances of advancement in the world were at an end, and that his family, deeply imbued with the passions of the Royalist party, viewed with horror a new form of popular government. These considerations had small weight with a mind alike disinterested and independent. But it became manifest in 1830 that the passions of the French Revolution had slumbered but were not extinct. Another experiment had failed—another form of government had been overthrown. To use an expression of his own, 'The Revolution has not stopped. It no longer, indeed, brings to light any great novelties, but it still keeps everything afloat. The mighty wheel turns and brings nothing up, but it seems that it will turn for ever.' What then was this blind but irresistible force which swept before it in ever-recurring paroxysms the institutions, the orders, the government of the country ? Not merely the love of freedom, for freedom has existed in England for nearly two hundred years, without any grave perturbation of social order, and it has existed for eighty years in the United States, combined with a purely democratic state of society. Nor indeed had the love of freedom acquired any permanent hold over the French people. They adored it in 1789, they were indifferent to it in 1800; and the same phenomenon has since been repeated.

Accustomed though we be to the fleeting inconsistency of men, there is something astonishing in so vast a change in the moral inclinations of a people ; so much selfishness succeeding to so much patriotism, so much indifference to so much passion, so much fear to so much heroism, so great a scorn for that which had been so vehemently desired and so dearly purchased. A change so complete and so abrupt cannot be explained by the customary laws of the moral world. The temperament of our nation is so peculiar that the general study of mankind fails to embrace it. France is for ever taking by surprise even those who have made her the special object of their researches ; a nation more apt than any other to comprehend a great design and to embrace it, capable of all that can be achieved by a single effort of whatever magnitude, but unable to abide long at this high level, because she is ever swayed by sensations and not by principles, and her instincts are better than her morality ; a people civilised among all civilised nations of the earth, yet, in some respects, still more akin to the savage state than any of them, for the characteristic of savages is to decide on the sudden impulse of the moment, unconscious of the past and careless of the future.

This inconstancy in the pursuit of political objects, this inability to estimate the true value of such objects or to retain them, and lastly the malignant passions which the Revolution had arrayed against all social, intellectual, and moral superiority, were the evil powers which M. de Tocqueville was resolved to combat and to resist. The shock of the Revolution of 1830 was scarcely needed to teach him that a deep gulf lay fixed between the principles to which he was immutably attached and the dreams which his countrymen were determined madly and vainly to pursue. He was led, or rather compelled, to the study of democratic institutions, not by any natural sympathy with popular agitation or any illusion as to the results of it, but by consternation at the ravages it had already made, and by a deep-seated dread of its furthest consequences. Throughout his writings, throughout his parliamentary career, throughout his correspondence, the conviction may be traced that modern democracy tends to the establishment of absolute power, unless it be counteracted by a genuine love and practice of freedom. The modern theory of democracy is not so much a love of freedom as the love of a particular kind of power. Democratic power differs in its origin, but not at all in its nature, from other forms of absolutism. It is as impatient of control, as liable to overleap the restraint of law, as much addicted to flatterers and abuses, as the most arbitrary monarchy or the corruptest oligarchy. He perceived that freedom itself could with difficulty be practised or maintained in countries where high principles were giving way to low interests; where the spirit of personal dignity and independence was crushed by the Government and hated by the masses; where, to use his own illustration, the impulses of savage life prevailed over the laws of civilisation, and revolution triumphed over tradition. He perceived, too, that as the ruling principle of democracies is the principle of interest, so the principle of aristocracies, if they are to last, must be that of duty. It is apparent from what we have already said of his descent and education, that he belonged by nature to a chosen order of men. Indeed, the extreme delicacy of his physical organisation, the fastidious refinement of his tastes, the exquisite charm of his manners, made him the very type of a high-bred gentleman; and if these were in him the outward signs of distinction, not less was he ennobled by the very soul of chivalry, by that purity and simplicity of character which are the truest nobility, and by a combination of manly virtues with an almost feminine grace,—qualities which Englishmen are wont to trace to an ideal perfection in the person of Sir Philip Sidney.

Conceive such a man placed by fate on the brink of the French Revolution, stripped of the traditions of the past by one blast of that great convulsion, robbed by another blast of the hopes of the future, hating with an equal hatred the abominations of the Ancien Régime, the crimes of the Revolution, and the iron yoke of the French Empire, whether imposed by the military genius of one Napoleon, or by the civil craft of another; and all this time viewing with almost superhuman penetration and with patriotic despondency the gradual decline of the French people from that standard of moral dignity and public spirit which could alone enable them to fulfil the generous aspirations of their forefathers! Well aware of the difficulty, perhaps the impracticability, of so great an enterprise, he never ceased to contend for those genuine principles of liberty which could alone, as he thought, preserve society and civilisation from the greatest calamities. He held 'that the first duty which is at this time imposed upon those who direct public affairs is to educate the democracy; to warm its faith, if that be possible; to purify its morals; to direct its energies; to substitute a knowledge of business for its inexperience, and an acquaintance with its true interests for its blind propensities. A new science of politics is indispensable to a new world.'[1]

Such were the views, still probably indistinct, which led the young 'Juge Auditeur' to throw up his office at Versailles, and in the company of M. Gustave de Beaumont to proceed in 1831 to the United States. A mission was given them by Count Montalivet to examine the Penitentiary System, then recently introduced in America: they performed this part of their duty conscientiously; but the real motive of their journey was to examine the political institutions of the American people, and

[1] Introduction to *Democracy in America*, vol. i. p. xxii.

the imperishable result of it is the book entitled
'Democracy in America.'

M. de Tocqueville was not thirty years old when
his great work appeared. He woke one morning,
like Byron, and found himself famous. 'I feel,'
said he, in a letter to his friend Stoffels, written in
February 1835, 'like a lady of the Court of
Napoleon, whom the Emperor took it into his head
to make a Duchess. That evening, as she heard
herself announced by her new title when she came
to Court, she forgot to whom it belonged, and
ranged herself on one side to let the lady pass whose
name had just been called. I assure you this is
just my case. I ask myself if it be *I* that they are
talking about? and when the fact is established, I
infer that the world must consist of a poor set of
people, since a book of my making, the range of
which I know so well, has had the effect this appears
to produce.' His first interview with Gosselin, the
publisher, was by no means flattering. That great
man consented with some hesitation to strike off an
edition of 500 copies, and Tocqueville remarked
that it was rather a humiliating condition of the
profession of authors to have to treat one's bookseller
as if he were a superior being. Nine months afterwards the tables were turned. ' I went yesterday

to see Gosselin, who received me with the most expansive countenance in the world, exclaiming, "Ah ça! mais il paraît que vous avez fait un chef-d'œuvre!"' The success of the book was indeed prodigious. It was instantly translated into all languages. It has become a text-book of constitutional law in the United States, where the English translation has run through numberless editions. It shortly afterwards opened to Tocqueville the doors of the French Institute, and eventually of the Academy. M. Royer-Collard affirmed that, since Montesquieu, nothing like it had appeared. Even the compositors and readers in the printing office testified their interest in the production of it.

Soon after the publication of his first two volumes in 1835, M. de Tocqueville paid a visit (though not his first visit) to England. He was received by many Englishmen with attention and hospitality, which soon ripened into cordial friendship and the deepest mutual regard. Indeed, no inconsiderable portion of the collection of letters now given to the public mark the strong attachment and the sedulous interest with which he kept up his connexions with English society. Perhaps, indeed, there was no society now in existence to which he may be said so naturally to have belonged as that which he met with in this country. In the polished circles of Lansdowne House and Holland House, his manners and his powers of conversation ensured him a cordial reception ; he found there not only the easy citizenship of good-breeding, but the same deep interest in the progress of mankind, and the same ardent attachment to every great and free object which had become the ruling passion of his life. His own ideal of social excellence and political greatness lay precisely in the combination of aristocratic tastes with popular interests, and in that independence of position and character which is never more complete than when it is united to a high sense of the duties and obligations of property and station. That is what he found in the Whig society of this country. Twenty years elapsed before he revisited England, and was again received with all the honours that could be paid by society to one of the most eminent and interesting men of the time. But during the whole of that interval his intimacy with his English friends had been strengthened and increased, partly by correspondence, and partly by their visits to his own country-house in Normandy. It is no light praise to say that, of all the men we have known, he had the loftiest and most entire conception of friendship. His confidence and his affection were not easily given; they were given to few; but when given, his friends became a portion of himself; none of them was ever in the faintest degree slighted, or neglected, or forgotten ; between them and him, each in his respective manner, there was entire communion ; not one of them ever broke from that charmed circle, nor did the vicissitudes of life at all affect the unalterable tenderness of his regard. It is not less interesting to us to know that the first and only object of his affections, who became his wife, and who in that name comprised the strongest and purest ties of human existence—his constant companion, counsellor, and friend; with whom no place was solitary to him, and without whom no society was attractive—was an Englishwoman, who brought him for her portion that best of gifts, the comfort and the trust of English domestic life. Although it be somewhat out of its chronological place, we are here tempted to quote a short letter in which he conveyed to M. de Corcelle his impression of England on his last visit in 1857.

Tocqueville, July 29, 1857.—I should have so much to say about England, which I saw again after the lapse of twenty years, and with a larger experience of men, that several letters would be requisite to convey to you the impressions I received and the ideas suggested to my mind by the spectacle before my eyes.

It is the greatest spectacle in the world, though not everything in it is great. Especially things are to be seen there which are wholly unknown in the rest of Europe, and which singularly gratified me.

Doubtless there exists in the lower classes a certain amount of feeling hostile to the other classes of society; but this feeling is not perceptible, and that which is perceptible is the union and accord which exist between all men belonging to the educated classes, from the lower tradesmen to the highest aristocracy, to defend society and direct it in common. I did not envy England her wealth and her power, but I envied her this; and I breathed when I found myself for the first time for so many years out of the reach of those class hatreds and jealousies which, after having been the source of all our misfortunes, have ended in the destruction of our freedom.

England has given me a second joy which I had long been deprived of. I found there a complete harmony between the world of religion and the world of politics, between private virtues and public virtues, between Christianity and freedom. I heard Christians of all denominations advocating free institutions as necessary, not only to the welfare, but to the moral being of society; and I nowhere met that sort of moral monster now so common all over the Continent, where men of religion are the advocates of despotism, leaving to those who are without religion the honour of raising their voice for freedom.

Our limits forbid us to enter as fully as we could wish on M. de Tocqueville's Correspondence with his English friends, though these letters will be read with extreme interest in this country, because they touch on topics more familiar to ourselves, and, we must add, more agreeable, than the gloomy aspect of modern French society. But one or two of his observations may find a place here.

In common with all the French Liberals, Tocqueville had been bitterly wounded by the disposition of a certain class of English politicians to make light of the overthrow of liberty in France, and even to express a servile admiration for Louis Napoleon, because it suited the interests of this country to conciliate that personage, and even to contract an alliance with him. Some trace of this feeling may be perceived in the following passage of a letter to Mrs. Grote, written in 1857 :—

> What you say of the simple nature of the English mind has always struck me. It consists in a downright perception, somewhat narrow, but distinct, which enables you to see thoroughly what you are looking at, and to do thoroughly what you have in hand, but not to see several things at once. This is probably the cause of a peculiarity of the English mind in politics, which has always surprised me. In the eyes of the English, that cause which is most useful to England is always the cause of justice. The man or the Government which serves the interests of England has all sorts of good qualities ; he who hurts those interests, all sorts of defects. So that it would seem that the *criterion* of what is right, or noble, or just is to be found in the degree of favour or opposition to English interests. The same thing occurs to some extent in the judgment of all nations ; but it is manifested in England to a degree which astonishes a foreigner. England is often accused on this account of a political Machiavellism, which, in my opinion, not only does not exist among you more, but rather less than elsewhere. The principal reason of this phenomenon consists,

I think, in the inability to see two things at once ; and, on the other hand, in the laudable desire to connect the actions of one's country with something loftier and more stable than interest, even than national interest. You want to make a thing answer, and with that intent you accept this or that man, this or that Government ; that is all you see. You overlook or scarcely perceive his faults, because the whole attention is absorbed by a single object. In France, things have often been done in politics which were convenient though unjust, but their convenience did not conceal their injustice. We have even sometimes made use of great scoundrels, but without imputing to them the smallest virtue.

As for the sort of indifference the English seem now-a-days to show for the freedom of several nations on the Continent, which appear themselves to have forgotten that they once were, and might again be, free, I think it very natural. On this point strangers cannot be expected to feel for us more than we feel ourselves. I grant then that you may very fairly not seek to destroy bad Governments, which are endured by the countries living under them ; but don't tell us they are good Governments. The times, I confess, are not favourable to the exercise of the great and ancient influence of England as a liberal power in the world. But let her, at least for a time, lay that influence on one side. She cannot in one country claim the advantages of despotism, and in another, as in Italy, the honour of liberalism. Let her choose.

One of the subjects connected with the politics of this country which had long excited M. de Tocqueville's curiosity and spirit of reflection was the government of our Indian dependencies. He was possessed with the idea that the civilisation of Europe was more and more destined in this and in

future ages to subdue the barbarism of the East.
With this impression he plunged at one time into
the study of the affairs of Algeria; he visited the
country, and nearly lost his life, between Philippe-
ville and Constantine, from exposure to the climate,
which was all but fatal to his sensitive frame. On
the outbreak of hostilities between Great Britain and
China, in 1840, he observed :—

> If I were an Englishman I should not see without anxiety the expeditions now in preparation against China. Here then is the mobility of Europe pitted against the immobility of the Chinese! 'Tis a great event, especially if one remembers that this is only the sequence, the last link in a multitude of events of the same kind which gradually push the European race abroad, and subject successively to its empire, or to its influence, all other races. There is happening in our days, without our perceiving it, a thing more vast and more extraordinary than the establishment of the Roman Empire. I mean the subjection of four portions of the globe by the fifth. Let us not think too ill of our age and of ourselves. Men are small but events are great.

Under the same impression he had collected and
read a vast quantity of materials for the history of
British power in India, and at one time meditated a
book on the subject; but he gave it up from the
conviction that he ought first to visit the country.
These circumstances inspired him with the most
intense interest and excitement when the great
revolt of 1857 broke out in Bengal, and the letters

written to several of his English friends during this period are eminently instructive. Nothing can be finer or more profound than the words in which one of the letters concludes : 'Je crois que les horribles évènements de l'Inde ne sont en aucune façon un soulèvement contre l'oppression ; *c'est une révolte de la barbarie contre l'orgueil :*' and in his opinion one of the chief difficulties for the future Government of India would arise from the dangerous necessity of bringing a larger number of dominant Englishmen into contact and collision with the Hindoo population. The following letter to Lady Theresa Lewis contains a more ample view of the subject :—

India is almost as great a subject of anxiety to us at Tocqueville as it is to you in London. My wife speaks and thinks of it incessantly, and more than one mail has kept her awake at night. For myself, there is nothing now in the world which interests me more than the destiny of your great nation. You may therefore conceive with what interest we have read all you say of the present state of affairs in the East. I agree with you that there was probably more of *accident* in the outbreak than was at first supposed; but I think with you again, that the accident led up to the action of certain general causes and set them in motion. To these general causes I would add this one. The people of England, who are the only civilised people who still govern themselves aristocratically, are led by a strange caprice of fortune to strike down or crush aristocracy wherever else it exists. That is the inscrutable task of every *master*, be he foreign or native. You have been carrying it on for a century in India with prudence, but with perseverance. You have respected the native princes and the native aristocracy as much as was compatible with your dominion. But day by day you have compressed, enfeebled, or destroyed some of those foreign if not hostile powers, which were in your dominions though not within your grasp. The time is come when each of these princes and classes clearly perceives (with the aid of the light you have yourselves diffused) that they are all destined to pass under this roller. It is a question of time. This one to-day, that one to-morrow. They have already enough experience and intelligence to see this ; they have still enough strength to hope to resist the destiny that awaits them. This is therefore the most critical instant of a dominion such as yours. But it is a matter of astonishment and of joy that this common sentiment has not found a man to represent it better than the miscreants who have as yet risen against you. I think that if that had occurred, you would have seen almost all the little princes who still people Northern India, and all the principal races which inhabit it, march at once against you instead of remaining spectators.

I am less inclined to concur in your opinion when you say that the loss of India would not weaken England, and that it is chiefly from a sort of heroical vanity that the people of England care for maintaining their hold on that country. I have often heard this opinion expressed by very enlightened Englishmen, but have never shared it.

It is true that, materially speaking, the Government of India costs more than it brings in ; that it requires efforts at a distance which may, at certain moments, paralyse the action of England under circumstances more directly affecting her ;—I admit it. Perhaps it would have been better to hang Clive than to make him a lord. But I am not the less persuaded that at this time of day the loss of India would be a great diminution in the rank of England among the nations of the earth. Among many reasons for this opinion, I confine myself to the following :—

There has never been anything so extraordinary under the sun as the conquest, and still more the government, of India by the

English; nothing which, from all points of the globe, more attracts the eyes of mankind to that little island whose very name was to the Greeks unknown. Do you conceive, Madam, that a nation which has once filled this amazing space in the imagination of our race, can withdraw from it with impunity? For my part I do not think so. I think the English are obeying an instinct, which is not only heroical but true, and a real motive of conservation, in their resolution to keep India at any cost since it belongs to them. I add that I am perfectly certain they will keep it, though perhaps under less favourable circumstances.

I am certain that you agree with me in desiring from the bottom of my heart that their victory may be as little tinged as possible by the vindictive passions which are naturally excited in their hearts. The civilised world is now on their side. It pities their sufferings; it admires their endurance. Nothing would be more easy than to turn against them this sympathetic opinion of Europe by exceeding the proper bounds of repression. Symptoms of this change are already perceptible. You have undoubtedly had to do with savages whose barbarity surpasses all known limits, and you have seen in India horrors at which the imagination recoils. But you have no right to be the masters of those pitiless savages except inasmuch as you are worthier than they. It is your business to punish, not to imitate them; and it would be to imitate them if, for example, as many people propose, the population of Delhi were massacred. Forgive me the warmth with which I express myself. I love the glory of England too passionately—for it is in my eyes that of freedom herself—not to desire fervently that the English may be as great in their victory as they have hitherto been in the struggle; and it seems to me that all who are in power, or who act upon the public mind in England, must work together for this end.

This noble passage is so characteristic of M. de Tocqueville's enlightened regard for this country, that we have stepped out of our course to cite it. It was his wont to discuss with his correspondents all the great topics of the day and the books he read with the same eloquence and earnestness ; and even from this limited collection of his letters, a multitude of other examples of not inferior interest might be culled. But we must now return to the business of his life.

In 1837, when Alexis de Tocqueville had not been long settled in the old family château of his house, he came forward as a candidate for the representation of the arrondissement of Valognes in his own department. His reception was not very flattering. A trace of the old revolutionary prejudices lingered in the neighbourhood ; a cry of *Pas de nobles !* was got up : his opponent, a retired cotton-spinner who had built a big house, said : ' Prenez garde ! il va vous ramener les pigeons,' pointing to the mighty dovecote of Tocqueville Manor ; and, in short, the aristocratic though liberal candidate was defeated. He was himself surprised at the intensity of the democratic passions which sent up the large Norman farmers to vote against him. ' My opponents admit,' said he, ' that I have none of the prejudices they ascribe to the nobility ; but there is something in the head of these fellows against us which resembles the instinctive aversion of the Americans to men of colour.' So that, by a curious coincidence, at the very moment when the 'Democracy in America' was in everybody's hands, and generally regarded as a vindication of democratic institutions, the democracy of his own county rejected the author for his aristocratic descent.

It is true that his opponent also had the support of the Government, and that by M. de Tocqueville's own act and choice. When Tocqueville's name was first announced as a candidate, Count Molé, then Prime Minister of France, gave orders that he should have all the support the Government could afford him, and this without the slightest pre-engagement or even inquiry as to the line he intended to follow in politics. M. Molé was his kinsman, and no slight admirer of his works. But this proceeding on the part of the Minister ruffled the sensitive pride of Tocqueville. He instantly wrote to M. Molé to decline the support of the Government, and to insist on standing in a position of absolute independence if he were to be elected at all. M. Molé's answer, which is published in this correspondence, though not written without warmth, is a masterpiece of dignity, good sense, and good breeding. He protested against the supposition that because he had proffered the support of the Government without conditions to a man whom he esteemed, this support was to be considered as an intolerable burden or a humiliating bargain; he observed with truth that isolation is not independence, and that a deputy is more or less engaged to whatever party may return him; lastly, he urged that the ministerial party was not a mere band of dependants, but a body of men acting together from convictions in defence of the parliamentary institutions of the country, a task at no time easy, and certainly rendered more difficult by the opposition and hostility of M. de Tocqueville's own character. This correspondence left no unfriendly feeling between these two eminent men; they were both of them consummate gentlemen, and each knew that the other was contending, not for an interest, but for a principle. Men of that stamp are more eager to sacrifice a personal interest than to trade upon it.

Two years later, at the general election of 1839, when M. de Tocqueville had made his way in the department, and had become an object of real attachment to his immediate neighbours, and of respect to all the country round, he was elected to the Chamber of Deputies by a great majority, and he retained his seat under all circumstances as long as there was a free Parliament in France.

Nevertheless we have adverted to this occurrence because it marks the first important step of M. de Tocqueville in public life by a fixed predetermination to join the Opposition, and to owe nothing at any time to the King's Government. We take the liberty to say that this step on his part, and on the part of several of the able men with whom he acted, was a most unfortunate one for his own public utility, and for the welfare of parliamentary government in France. That form of government was not so firmly established that it could resist the attacks of those who were in the main sincerely attached to the constitution, though they disapproved the policy of the Ministry and the Court; and no one repeated more emphatically than M. de Tocqueville his prophetic warnings, that it was not this or that Minister, this or that system, but representative government itself which was at stake and in danger. The fixed idea of his life was that the constitution would be undermined by the democratic passions of the nation and encroached upon by the insincerity of the Court, until nothing stable would remain, and the overthrow of the parliamentary system would be followed at no distant time by the despotism of a single ruler. But with a foreknowledge of this danger, which no one else possessed to the same degree, and which as expressed in his earlier writings and speeches looks like a gleam of superhuman intelligence, what political conduct ought he to have pursued? He thought it his duty to throw the weight of his lofty intellect and unblemished character on the side of the Opposition. But what was that Opposition? He himself admits in one of his letters that there never had been a real constituted Opposition in France capable of fighting its way to a majority, and then assuming the direction of affairs. M. Thiers, if he was to be considered its head, was certainly quite as far removed from Tocqueville's standard of political morality as M. Guizot. To thwart the schemes of the Court, and once or twice a year to deliver a few set speeches against the policy of a Cabinet, was, after all, a wretched substitute for true political life. He acknowledged himself that he had no party spirit, yet he acted with those to whom party spirit was the sole guide, on the principle, as he himself expressed it, ' On n'a quelque chance de maîtriser les mauvaises passions du peuple, qu'en partageant celles qui sont bonnes.' Under this influence his votes on some of the party divisions of the day were votes which we disapproved at the time, and to which we look back with regret. They failed to promote any good object; they assisted to strengthen the very evil they were designed to oppose.

M. de Beaumont observes with great candour that Tocqueville was not fitted by nature for opposition; he had none of the passions which belong to it; his speeches were earnest, but not impetuous; his caution and conscientiousness restrained him from extreme steps; and in the tribune of the Chamber he fell far short of the greatest orators of his time. The most useful acts of his parliamentary life were his reports on the question of negro emancipation in the French colonies, on prison discipline, and on the administration of Algeria, which are masterpieces of their kind, and have since been republished with his principal speeches.

In our judgment the result of his political career would have been still more honourable to himself, and far more useful to his country, if, instead of wasting long years in the sterile warfare of opposition, he had joined the Cabinet. He would there have acquired a practical knowledge of affairs, which, in fact, he never fully obtained, and he would have thrown his clear discernment and disinterested patriotism on the side of a more liberal and dignified policy. To those of his friends who sometimes ventured to urge this course upon him, he was wont to reply, 'It may be so. But I hold it to be impossible to serve the King. When he is gone we shall see.' There was a radical incompatibility between Tocqueville's chivalrous conception of high political principles, not one of which he would have sacrificed for the wealth of empires, and the system of expedients in which the King was no mean proficient, and which he regarded as the art of government. Perhaps, too, there was a latent trace of resentment, almost unconsciously entertained, on the part of the royalist gentleman against the son of the Duke of Orleans and the King of the Barricades. But in this M. de Tocqueville was wrong. Had the King been a thousand times less worthy of respect than Louis Philippe actually was, he was not the less the head of the State, and it was not consistent with practical political wisdom to stand aloof from the Court. The parliamentary government of England continued to strike root under the two first Georges, who, both as sovereigns and men, were immeasurably below the King of the French. Had Sir Robert Walpole thrown his talents on the side of opposition, the House of Hanover might have been overthrown, but we know not who would have been the gainer by it. Doubtless the Government of Louis Philippe and M. Guizot committed errors which led to its political destruction; but what is equally certain is that for a long period of years the Opposition were the unconscious tools of those factions which eventually upset the dynasty and the constitution itself.

At length the storm came. By no man had it been so clearly foreseen as by M. de Tocqueville, and for several months before the catastrophe he had carefully abstained from all participation in that mad system of agitation which produced the popular banquets and republican demonstrations of 1847. On the 27th January 1848, soon after the opening of the last session of the Constitutional Parliament, he rose in the Chamber of Deputies, and said—

> They tell me that there is no danger because there are no disturbances; they say that, as there is no visible perturbation on the surface of society, there are no revolutions beneath it. Gentlemen, allow me to say that I think you wrong. Disturbance is not abroad, but it has laid hold of men's minds. The working classes are quiet, and are not agitated as they have sometimes been by political passions; but can you not perceive that these passions, which were political, are now social? Can you not see that opinions and ideas are spreading amongst them which tend not only to overthrow this or that law, this or that minister, or even this or that Government, but society itself, and to shake the foundations on which it rests? Can you not hear what is daily repeated, that everything which is above their own condition is incapable

and unworthy to govern them ; that the present division of wealth in the world is unjust; that property rests upon no equitable basis? And are you not aware that when such opinions as these take root, when they are widely diffused, when they penetrate the masses, they will bring about, sooner or later—I know not when, I know not how—the most tremendous revolutions. Such, Sir, is my conviction ; we are slumbering on a volcano. I am certain of it.

Within four weeks the explosion took place. The King fled. The Republic was proclaimed ; and not only the Republic, but all the demoniac passions of a socialist revolution were let loose on France.

Then, indeed, neither Tocqueville nor any one of his political friends hesitated as to the part they were called upon to pursue. In the first Revolution the sanguinary violence of a small faction had prevailed over the great majority of the nation. Under the second Republic, the nation itself, appealed to by universal suffrage, gave an unequivocal answer to the call, and elected an Assembly firmly resolved to defend property and public order. An attempt was made by the Revolutionists to annihilate the Assembly itself : it escaped by a miracle : a few days later the fate of the nation hung on the issue of a battle in the streets of Paris. Thanks to the courage and union of the Assembly, the law triumphed, and the country was saved. In all these events M. de Tocqueville took an active part ; and we are informed by his biographer that the volume in which he has recorded them, for the information of posterity, is complete, and will one day see the light. Tocqueville had naturally been selected by the constituent body as one of the members of the Committee to frame the new Republican constitution ; and it is a curious example of the difficulty of governing human affairs that a constitution, now universally acknowledged to be a masterpiece of absurdity, was the work of several men of undoubted intellectual power and political foresight. An attempt was made by Tocqueville to induce his colleagues to adopt the principle of a second Chamber ; but this and every other attempt to construct the machinery of a true republican Government utterly failed. The Republic was destined to a short-lived existence, between the frenzy of democratic socialism on the one hand, and the violence of that popular reaction which speedily adopted as its chief Louis Napoleon Bonaparte. The newly-elected President of the Republic had long appreciated the philosophical insight of M. de Tocqueville into the nature of democratic institutions, and may have inferred that the predictions of a single dominion, with which his books abound, were naturally to be fulfilled by a restoration of the

Empire. Soon after his election to the Presidency he invited M. de Tocqueville to dinner, placed him by his side, and paid him marked attentions. On leaving the Elysée, Tocqueville said, 'I have been dining with a man who believes in his own hereditary right to the crown as firmly as Charles X. himself.'

One chance remained to avert the final catastrophe. It was possible that the President might still be content to accept a constitutional position; to govern by responsible Ministers who hoped to effect a revision of the constitution by legal means. At any rate, to abandon or to oppose him was to compel him to resort to an immediate *coup d'état*. On this principle M. Odilon Barrot and the leading Liberals formed an Administration on the 2nd June, 1849, in which M. de Tocqueville took the important office of Minister of Foreign Affairs. We shall not enter at length into the transactions in which he was engaged. As he said, on quitting his office four months later, 'I have contributed to maintain order on the 13th June, to preserve the general peace, to improve the relations of France and England. These are recollections which give some value to my passage through affairs. I need hardly say anything to you of the cause which led to the fall of the

Cabinet. The President chooses to govern alone, and to have mere agents and creatures in his Ministers. Perhaps he is right. I don't examine that question, but we were not the men to serve him on these terms.'

On one point, however, we think it proper to enter into some further details, although M. de Beaumont has passed it over in silence. We allude to the expedition against Rome. That celebrated expedition, even more embarrassing in its consequences than it was supposed to be at the time, occurred while M. de Tocqueville held the Foreign Department in France. He conducted the first negotiations with the Pope; and it is therefore of importance to show precisely what were then his own views and those of the French Government. For this purpose we shall translate two letters, not included in M. de Beaumont's collection, which were addressed by M. de Tocqueville to an English friend at that time :—

Paris, 9th July, 1849.—I attach so much importance to the opinion of enlightened men in England, that I sit down to write you a few lines, though I have but little time for this sort of correspondence; but I want to furnish you with the latest information on this affair of Rome. I am better placed than any one to speak of it, for, as you have remarked, I am an entire stranger to all the decisive measures which have hitherto marked the course of this proceeding. When I took office the order to attack Rome was already given; it might even be supposed that Rome was already taken; at any rate, it was certain that our army was *committed;* and things having got to this point, it was impossible to recede. Not a public man in France, whoever he might be, either could or would have receded. I have therefore only assumed the responsibility of the acts which have followed or will follow the aggression, not of the aggression itself. My mind is therefore able to judge it freely.

The actual state of the case is judged with severity; but you lose sight of what the case might have become. Allow me to remind you of it. Is it true—yes or no—that the Catholic Powers were resolved to restore the Pope? Is it true—yes or no—that Austria had announced that she was going to enter the States of the Church and to march on Rome, in order to overthrow the Roman Republic? Do you doubt that they would have done as they said? Let us then take these first points for certain. Now here are others which are not less so. If the Austrians, Neapolitans, and Spaniards had arrived before Rome, do you doubt, in the first place, that they would have caused far greater ravages than we have done, and that they would have bombarded Rome in earnest, instead of the imaginary bombardment of which your consul has calumniously accused us? and, secondly, do you doubt that their triumph would have been not only the overthrow of the Republic, but the extinction of all liberty and the mere return of the old priestly government? You cannot question it, I hope.. I take these points therefore also for certain.

How then, I ask the public men of England, do they think that it was for the interest of your country to allow Austria to acquire so great a preponderance over the whole Italian peninsula? And to the philanthropists, to the liberals, to the archæologists of England, I say, What! does the ancient animosity against France blind you to that degree that you prefer to see the Roman

Republic destroyed by main force by the soldiers and the principles of Austria rather than by ours?

I know well enough, between ourselves, where the weak point of our expedition lies,—it is on the side of republican France. Yes; the French may fairly say to their own Government that there is in this expedition something repugnant perhaps to the principle of the sovereignty of the people, which is the basis of our whole political edifice. But why should not foreign countries, and especially enlightened England, prefer that we took this task upon ourselves instead of leaving it to others? For you surely can't suppose we have any desire to establish ourselves in the Papal dominions. We go there evidently for a purpose which is extremely clear and intelligible, especially to England—to prevent the omnipotent influence which Austria exercises over the north of Italy from extending over the whole peninsula, and the total destruction of all equipoise there; and to save the Roman States and the whole of Italy from the inevitable return of the Old Court, and from the restoration, not of the lawful sovereign, but of the abuses of that ancient and bad government. We have never had any other objects, nor shall we ever have any others. The reestablishment of the Pope, made upon these conditions, is all we desire, and I cannot conceive that there is anything in this to wound, in any respect, the instincts and the just susceptibility of England. The odd thing is, that the Austrian Government, which might fairly have some reason to take umbrage at our enterprise, has never made the least objection to it, and that our friendly relations with Austria are not the least impaired. It is strange that it should be Englishmen, and principally English Tories, who attack us.

In a subsequent letter, written ten days later, he said :—

I should not be without uneasiness as to the result of the debate to-morrow in the House of Lords, if the principal organ of the

Government in that House were not the Marquis of Lansdowne, whose tact and moderation I know. As to the intentions of the French Government in the conduct of the affair of Rome, the English Cabinet must be sufficiently informed. I have taken effectual measures to satisfy them that we have no secret end in this enterprise, and that we have never ceased to desire, on the one hand the restoration of the temporal authority of the Pope, which we consider as a necessary condition of liberty and peace of conscience in the Catholic world; and, on the other hand, a guarantee of liberal institutions to the Roman States. I protest to you that we desire nothing so much as to get out of this affair of Rome, and to evacuate the Roman territory, as soon as we can do so with honour. But these conditions must be attained, or we will stay in Italy, whatever be the risks and political embarrassments which may result from it, at least as long as I am minister, I answer for it.

We have quoted these letters inasmuch as they contain a statement from his own pen of the grounds on which M. de Tocqueville accepted the responsibility of the Roman expedition, and they have also a very curious bearing on the subsequent course of events. It is scarcely necessary to point out that it was from the fatal blunder of France in consenting to play the part of Austria that this long series of embarrassments arose; for the honour of France became in a manner pledged to the maintenance of a government which she could not control, which did come back without any liberal conditions at all, and long remained, what Lord Derby called it, the plague spot on the Italian soil. These dangers, which escaped M. de Tocqueville's great discernment, were nevertheless apparent in this country and elsewhere to men of inferior powers but of greater practical experience in political affairs.

By a sort of Nemesis the Roman expedition was made the pretext of the downfall of the Cabinet, The President had always disapproved the enterprise, but, weary with long negotiations, he chose to take the matter into his own hands; his celebrated letter to Edgar Ney was a death-blow to ministerial responsibility in France, and from that moment the violent dissolution of the Assembly and the change of government were only a question of means and of time. Tocqueville retired for some months from the scene, for indeed his frail body, exhausted by the fatigues of office, needed repose. He spent the winter at Sorrento, and there laid the basis of the last of his works, which might be termed the Genesis of the French Revolution, traced by him back to its true source, in the vicious institutions of the 'ancien régime.' He already perceived that in the impending contest between the President of the Republic and the Assembly all the chances were in favour of Louis Napoleon. In January 1851 he writes:—

The general aspect of the time seems to me to be a movement

of the nations away from liberty and towards concentration and permanence of power. The circumstance that the most eminent parliamentary chiefs and the best known military commanders are almost all opposed to this movement, does not reassure me ; for we live in a democratic age, and a society in which individual men, even the greatest of them, count for very little. To form my opinion, I listen neither to those who exalt nor to those who depreciate the talents of the pretender. At such times it is not the man we must look at, but that which raises the man and brings him into power. A dwarf on the crest of a huge wave may be washed to the top of a cliff, which a giant could not scale from the sands below.

Nevertheless, soon afterwards, upon his return to France, M. de Tocqueville drew up the celebrated Report of the Committee on the Revision of the Constitution, which was presented to the National Assembly on the 8th July, 1851. This document is of the highest excellence, and has since been included in the general edition of his works. He traced in it with masterly precision the fatal situation in which the Constitution had flung the French nation, between two contending powers incapable of union, yet destined both of them to come to an end almost simultaneously, leaving the country without an Assembly and without a Government: and he demonstrated that the only possible mode of diverting the impending catastrophe was to alter and amend the organic law of the State. This memorable Report may be regarded as the last public act of his life.

As the crisis approached, in the autumn of 1851, he writes in increasing perplexity :—

> How little we feel ourselves masters of events at such times! There is but one determination that I am always certain to follow, and that is, to bring our liberties triumphant through this crisis, or to fall with them. All the rest is secondary; but this is a question of life and death.

And, in common with all that was illustrious in the last free Parliament of France, he did fall. M. de Tocqueville was included in that wholesale act of proscription of the 2nd December, 1851, which, with a sort of insolent derision more odious than the tyranny that prompted it, sent the orators, statesmen, generals, and patriots of France in a felon's cart to the common gaol. Their detention lasted not long, but long enough to place their country under the feet of a master, to annihilate the law, to silence the voice of many of them for ever, and to accomplish that revolution which had haunted M. de Tocqueville through life, when a democratic people, weary of anarchy and incapable of self-government, precipitates itself at the feet of despotic authority. The scene itself was described by M. de Tocqueville himself with indignant animation, for it need be now no more a secret that the narrative of the *coup d'état* published immediately afterwards by the 'Times' newspaper of the 11th December, 1851, was from his pen.

We renounce the painful, the impracticable task of describing the effects of this blow on M. de Tocqueville's mind. It was not the loss of the objects of common ambition, it was not the closing to himself of that career of public utility to which he was passionately attached and devoted ; it was the sense of the moral wreck of his country, and of the extinction of the very source of all true public virtue by her own act.

In May 1852 he wrote to M. de Beaumont :—

Work is at present impossible to me. I attribute this painful incapacity to the disturbing conversations one is always having in Paris. If I were in the country I should attribute it to solitude. The truth is it proceeds from a sickness of the soul, and will not cease till that is better, which can only come with time, the great healer of sorrow, as everybody knows : we must wait as patiently as we can till its effects are felt. Yet this sorrow, like all true and lawful sorrows, is dear to me as well as poignant. The sight of all that is done, and still more the opinion formed of it, galls every fibre of pride, of rectitude, and of dignity in my frame. I should be grieved to be less sorrowful. On this score, indeed, I have no reason to complain; for, in truth, I am sorrowful to the death. I have reached my present age through many different circumstances, but with one cause, that of regular liberty. Is this cause lost beyond recovery? I feared it was so in 1848; I fear it still more now, though I am not convinced that this country is not destined again to see constitutional institutions. But will it see them last—these or any others? 'Tis sand. It is in vain to ask whether it will abide, but what are the winds that will displace it?

I enclose a copy of the letter addressed to the electors of my department, in which I resign my seat in the *Conseil général*. I could not take the oath now exacted. This consequence of the 2nd December is perhaps that portion of the event which is personally most painful to myself. I enjoyed in my department a position of unalloyed gratification. It gave me the moral direction of all the chief local affairs, a sort of government of men's minds founded on personal regard, independently of political opinions. This part of my public duties cast a sort of light on my private life, which was very agreeable. But these are very petty miseries.'

We shall imitate the reserve of M. de Beaumont in abstaining from entering more fully into the causes of this revolution as they appeared to Tocqueville's mind, nor is the time yet come when the burning language in which he denounced the authors of it can with propriety be made public. But the following observations on the probable duration and character of the Imperial power are so just that we permit ourselves to cite them from an unpublished letter. When read by the light of subsequent events it is one of the most striking of his political predictions, for it was written about eighteen years before the German War and the fall of the Empire.

Although this Government has established itself by one of the greatest crimes recorded in history, nevertheless *it will last for some length of time*, unless it precipitates itself to destruction. It will last till its excesses, its wars, its corruptions, have effaced in the public mind the dread of socialism—a change requiring time. God grant that in the interval it may not end in a manner almost as prejudicial to us as to itself—*in some extravagant foreign enterprise.* We know it but too well in France, Governments never escape the law of their origin. This Government, which comes by the army, which can only last by the army, which traces back its popularity and even its essence to the recollections of military glory—*this Government will be fatally impelled to seek for aggrandisement of territory* and for exclusive influence abroad ; *in other words, to war.* That at last is what I fear, and what all reasonable men dread as I do. *War would assuredly be its death, but its death would perhaps cost dear.*

Henceforth the life of Alexis de Tocqueville was spent in comparative seclusion, and in total estrangement from public affairs. Educated as a French boy, in colleges and towns, he had not acquired in early life any taste for country life or country pursuits. In one of his letters he remarks that from the age of nine to the age of twenty-four he had never spent six weeks in the country at a time ; in another letter he expresses his astonishment that people should be able to lead the life of vegetables. But one of the effects of the revolutions to which society in France has been subjected is to teach a wiser lesson. The Revolution of 1789 had forcibly broken the relations formerly existing between the landed proprietors and the peasantry. The revolutions of 1830 and of 1851, by detaching considerable portions of the upper classes, enjoying the largest amount of landed property and of intellectual cultivation, from the government of the day, have thrown these classes back to their natural position on their own estates. The consequence is that of late years the improvement of agriculture, the restoration of country houses, and a more active participation in rural interests and pursuits, have become engrossing objects of life to the best portion of the French aristocracy. Alexis de Tocqueville applied himself early, and with increasing success, to this laudable and dignified task. He sought in the first place to heal the breach made by the Revolution of 1789 between the cottage and the château, some traces of which were perceptible at his first election in 1837. The simplicity of his manners, the entire absence of any tinge of pride or pretension in his intercourse with persons of all ranks, the genuine interest he felt in their concerns, the patience with which he was ever ready to listen to them, and the readiness with which he placed the stores of his own wisdom and judgment within their reach, inspired the peasantry before long with unfeigned confidence and affection. He practised to the letter, as Father Lacordaire has observed, the divine command 'Whosoever will be chief among you, let him be your servant.' Speaking of him to a stranger, one of the Norman farmers said, 'The people are very fond of M. de Tocqueville, but it must be confessed he is very grateful for it.' In 1848, on the proclamation of universal suffrage, the whole population of the district voted by acclamation in his favour. While the election was going on, as he leaned exhausted with fatigue against a doorpost, one of the peasants, not personally known to him, came up with Norman frankness and said, 'I am surprised, Monsieur de Tocqueville, that you are tired, for did not every one of us bring you here in his pocket?' He was wont to say that in the hearts of these honest fellows the honour and virtue of the French character had taken refuge, that 'Maître Jean' and 'Maître Pierre,' the worthies and notables of the village, were the only titles of dignity which no revolutions could obliterate; and that his peasant neighbours were the only people with whom he cared to converse beyond the circle of his intimate friends. This relish for the homely fare of a rural district was greatly augmented by his inexhaustible sense of the humorous. His biographers appear to have thought it inconsistent with the dignity of a philosophic Academician to admit his love of fun.

When a thing presented itself, as it not uncommonly did, to his mind in a droll aspect, his merriment was unquenchable. He was, what is every day becoming more rare, especially in France, a hearty laugher; indeed his laugh, musical and cheerful as his voice, sometimes got the better of him and could not be stopped. It partook of the intensity of all the emotions which alternately swayed his sensitive and delicate nervous organisation.

Thus it was that in his own home, without the smallest attempt to humour the democratic passions of his neighbours, he did practically subdue them. He became precisely what he admired in the position of the landed gentlemen of England, independent of the State, independent of the people, but ready and willing to serve the State and to serve the people in all honour. Under these circumstances he devoted himself to the literary task he had marked out, of tracing the Revolution to its true sources; and the originality of his mind can hardly be more demonstrated than by the fact that, after all the innumerable commentaries and histories of the French Revolution which have appeared, Alexis de Tocqueville presented to the world an entirely new view of it.

The publication of this book in 1856 was followed,

in 1857, by his journey to England, to which we have already alluded. The reception he met with here was in fact the last triumph of his life. He was received on all sides with demonstrations of respect and affection; and when the time came for his return to Normandy, the Lords of the Admiralty, hearing that there was no direct steam communication from England to Cherbourg, placed a small vessel at his disposal, which landed him within a mile or two of his own park. At that time nothing appeared to indicate that his life, always precarious, was in any immediate danger. He lived by nervous power, and that seemed unexhausted; indeed, it had repeatedly carried him through dangerous and acute disorders. But in the summer of 1858 a more serious accident showed his lungs to be affected. In the autumn he was ordered to a milder climate than that of his own well-beloved domain. He repaired to Cannes, accompanied by the devoted partner of his life, and by one or two of his nearest relatives and friends. For a time he imagined that the affection of the lungs had been overcome. But, in spite of the illusions which attend the closing stages of pulmonary disease, it soon became obvious that life was ebbing away. He received with piety the last sacraments of the Church; for though faith, like every other gift of his nature, had been with him a matter of internal edification rather than of outward display, he had never ceased to entertain the most serious attachment to the Christian religion, and to that Church in which he was born. On the 16th April, 1859, he expired. By his own express desire his mortal remains were interred in the churchyard of Tocqueville, and were attended to the grave by an immense assemblage, not of those who admired him for his genius, but of those who loved him for his goodness; and a plain cross of wood, after the fashion of the country, marks the spot where whatever of him was mortal lies.

II.[1]

THE critics, who, in common with ourselves, had occasion to review four years ago the 'Memoir and the Correspondence of M. de Tocqueville' ventured to remark that, in spite of the zeal and the fidelity with which M. Gustave de Beaumont had portrayed the life and edited the papers of his illustrious friend, his task was still incomplete. Indeed, he himself informed us that much still remained in the shape of unfinished fragments and unpublished letters which might one day form part of a more extended publication. We urged him to give a larger selection of these documents to the world; for although they may not have received that exquisite finish which M. de Tocqueville himself loved to impart to all he published, yet the scattered thoughts of so powerful a mind are sometimes even more forcible and impressive than his mature compositions, and the charm of his tender and meditative letters to his family and his private friends is inexhaustible. M. de Beaumont has given ear to these observations.

[1] First published in October 1865.

Encouraged by the prodigious interest which was excited in France and throughout Europe by his former volumes, he has now enlarged the plan of them. A complete edition of the works of Tocqueville has been prepared for the press, which contains in addition to the writings already well known to all readers, a volume of the speeches and reports prepared for the Chamber of Deputies, a volume of fragments principally relating to the masterly analysis of the French Revolution on which the author was engaged at the time of his death, and an additional volume of correspondence. These publications are entirely new, and they are of great interest and value. In the selection of the volume of letters previously published, M. de Beaumont was restrained by motives of delicacy from laying before the world the confidential effusions of intimate friendship, and by motives of prudence from calling attention to the political opinions of Tocqueville, especially with reference to the Imperial Government of France. Already time, death, and the progress of events have removed some of the obstacles to publication which existed three years ago. The result is that the letters now produced have a deeper meaning and a more decided tone than those which had formerly appeared—indeed, it was for this reason that they were then withheld from the public; and many of them have a direct bearing on political affairs, to an extent which the admirers and adherents of the Imperial Government of France will probably consider indiscreet and inconvenient. We rejoice, on the contrary, that M. de Beaumont has had the courage to produce these most remarkable papers. They contain the thoughts of a man, great as a writer, but greater still by his undaunted independence and by his undying love of freedom; and we are not sure that Tocqueville, in the full enjoyment of life and intellect, ever wrote anything more likely to rouse the slumbering spirit of his country, or to guide her back from servitude to liberty, than these posthumous leaves, penned many years ago in the solitude of his Norman home and in the confidence of private friendship. There is in these volumes the same profound insight which pervades all the works of the author into the causes of the French Revolution, and those vices of democratic society which, under the First and the Second Empire, have twice thrown back the French nation from the ardent enjoyment of freedom into a submissive obedience to absolute power. And if it be true that after a vigil of seventeen years, some streaks of dawning light are again visible on the horizon—if some indications are again felt that this slumber is not to be perpetual—then it is in this language that Tocqueville, and those who like him have watched through the night in despondency, but not in despair, would address the awakened sleeper. To these passages of his correspondence we shall presently direct a more particular attention.

After long hesitation as to the choice of a subject to employ his mind on a great work, when the collapse of the Republic and the *coup d'état* of 1851 had terminated his political career, Tocqueville resolved to enter upon a philosophical investigation of the phenomena of the great Revolution, which had for sixty years swayed to and fro the destinies of his country. But with characteristic originality, he sought for the earliest indications of these phenomena in the preceding age, and he exhumed the administrative records of the old monarchy from beneath the lava of the great eruption. Probably no living Frenchman had acquired so accurate a knowledge of the state of France before the Revolution, and he said in one of his letters, 'If anybody wants to found a professorship of the old administrative law of the country, I believe I could fill it.' The result of these inquiries was the book on ' The State of France before the Revolution,' which is in every one's hands. But this was only the prelude of his task. His intention was to approach the Revolution itself; to pass lightly over the course of events, although he had mastered them with inconceivable labour and precision; and to deduce from them certain general principles which acute reflection and enlarged experience enabled him to trace throughout this protracted convulsion. For it was one of his fixed convictions that, however perplexing, unexpected, and contradictory the course of events may be, they are rigorously governed by laws of human nature as determinate as the laws of the physical world, and that these laws can be traced by a sufficient power of observation and analysis even into the regions of metaphysical abstraction, although the people and even its leaders and teachers may be totally unconscious of the influence by which their movements are directed. Above all, it was his design to arrive, through the Revolution, at the character of Napoleon Bonaparte, and at the institutions established by him in France, not only because these are subjects of extraordinary interest in themselves, but because the name of that remarkable man and the fabric of his power became the ruling forces of the Second Empire, and the key to the last form which the Revolution had then assumed.

And here we are arrested by a page or two of such eloquence and insight, that although we cannot hope to render the purity of the author's style in another tongue, and we cannot afford to dwell much longer on this portion of the volumes before us, we lay it before our readers. The fragment was written at Sorrento in 1858.

What I would seek to portray is not so much the events themselves, however surprising and however great they may be, as the spirit of those events—less the different acts of the life of Napoleon, than Napoleon himself—that singular, incomplete, but marvellous being whom it is impossible attentively to consider without contemplating one of the most strange and curious spectacles in the universe. I should desire to show what part in his prodigious enterprise was really derived from his own genius, and what was supplied to him by the state of the country and the spirit of the times—to explain how and why this indocile nation rushed at that moment of its own accord into servitude, and with what incomparable art he discovered in the working of a most democratical revolution all that was apt for despotism, and brought out of it those natural consequences.

In speaking of his internal government, I shall survey the effort of that almost divine intelligence rudely employed to compress human freedom, by a scientific and ingenious organisation of force such as none but the greatest genius of the most enlightened and the most civilised age could have conceived; and, beneath the weight of this masterly engine, society stifled to sterility—the movement of the intellect slackened, the human mind enervated, the soul contracted, till men cease to be great; and around the vast and flat horizon, whithersoever you turn, nothing stands erect but the colossal figure of the Emperor.

Turning to his foreign policy and to his conquests, I should seek to follow the furious rush of his fortune over nations and kingdoms, and to relate by what means the strange greatness of his genius was here also abetted by the strange and irregular greatness of his times. How marvellous a picture, by the hand of one who could trace it, of human power and of human weakness, would be that of this impatient and uncertain being doing and undoing his own works, tearing up and changing the boundaries of empires, and driving nations and sovereigns to despair even less by the evils he inflicted upon them than by the eternal uncertainty in which he left them as to that which they had yet to fear.

I would, lastly, explain by what a series of excesses and errors he himself drove onwards to his fall; and in spite of these excesses and errors, I would mark the gigantic trace he has left behind him in the world, not only as a recollection but as a living and durable influence: what died with him, what remains.

And to complete this long survey, I would show the purport of the Empire in the French Revolution—the place to be filled by this singular act in the strange drama, the close of which escapes us yet.

These are great objects glancing before me. But how to reach them?

These designs were not to be completed. But in every fragment of the materials formed and collected by the author for the edifice he had conceived, the reader will trace with melancholy interest the stamp of originality and genius. It is certain that if M. de Tocqueville had lived to complete his 'Essay on the Revolution,' he would have thrown new light on events which have for upwards of half a century engaged the attention of a host of writers of the highest class ; for he would have brought us nearer to its true causes, and would have demonstrated more clearly its effects on the latest generations—effects which cut short his own public life and threw a gloom over the closing years of his existence. Of these truths traces will be found in every page of the eighth volume of M. de Beaumont's collection, and we are indebted to him for the skill with which he has re-set, in a connected form, the precious, but imperfect, remains of his friend's labour. The task was one of extreme difficulty, for these fragments were traced upon unconnected scraps of paper, in a handwriting not easily deciphered, and intended only to assist the memory of the author : but the zeal and intelligence of M. de Beaumont have triumphed over these obstacles and given to the scattered thoughts of his friend as much connexion as they would admit of.

It is not, however, our intention to dwell upon the theme of the French Revolution, and we can only commend these fragments to the attentive consideration of our readers. We propose rather to turn to the additional volume of the Correspondence, and in that correspondence to follow with some detail those letters which belong to the history of M. de . Tocqueville's political life. It may be remembered that on a former occasion we expressed regret that the records of his political opinions and actions had been withheld. To a considerable extent this omission is supplied in the volume now before us, although certain significant gaps at moments of great interest remind us that more yet remains to be said, and that this volume was published under the Second Empire.

Before we proceed, however, we must linger for a moment over another class of Tocqueville's letters—we mean those addressed to his nearest relations. They present a charming picture of domestic life, and of those family relations which are nowhere more sacred than in France; for it may, perhaps, surprise some of our readers to be told that in no country upon earth are the filial relations so deferential and the fraternal relations so affectionate. In England the conjugal tie is more close and absorbing; it frequently overpowers the bonds of birth and blood. In France it seldom equals, and still more rarely weakens, the primal sanctity of the affection and respect a man pays to his parents. These virtues of the old French houses were a portion of the very nature of Alexis de Tocqueville ; and from the moment when he started on his American voyage to the close of his father's life in 1857, they pervade his correspondence. It is curious to remark, too, from the earlier letters in this collection, descriptive of his American journey, how powerfully that expedition contributed to form his character, his judgment, and even his style. His first communications to his mother are playful and affectionate, but still crude and diffuse. They have in them a certain boyishness, which long remained one of the charms of his character. For though Tocqueville came back from the United States a great philosopher, impregnated with one of the wisest works of modern thought, he was still a philosopher of seven and twenty, alive to every touch of nature and sentiment, and as ready to chase butterflies as to plant acorns. To describe a romantic evening ride to Kenilworth in a letter to the woman he loved—to relate to one of his cousins a droll return to Tocqueville, where he arrived, like Ulysses at Ithaca, driving a couple of Lord Radnor's best breed of pigs, was just as natural to him as to write the subtlest chapter of his 'Democracy;' and, contrary to the usual fate of man, in him the pleasures of sentiment and of imagination outlived the passions of political life, and remained unclouded to the last.

One other class of these letters calls for a passing

notice; they are those addressed in later years to his nephew, Baron Hubert de Tocqueville, a young man of promise whom he regarded as his heir, and to whom he addressed, upon his entry into the diplomatic service at the Courts of Vienna and Berlin, a series of kindly admonitions which are models of wisdom and good taste. They are like that epitome of the wisdom of the world delivered by Polonius to Laertes, of invaluable counsel to any young man of birth and figure about to enter the great world, and their effect will not be confined to him to whom they were addressed. Already that young gentleman had shown himself worthy of the name he bore and the estate to which he was to succeed. He left, as we have heard from members of our own embassies at the same Courts, a pleasing impression on all who knew him. But, alas! he survived his uncle but four years, and his two infant children remained the sole heirs of that old manor-house of Tocqueville, which had been rescued and repaired, after the ravages of the Revolution, to be for twenty years the seat of so much domestic happiness, so much intellectual refinement, so much genial hospitality. Since the death of Madame de Tocqueville, which occurred not very long after that of her husband, its walls are again uninhabited.

The elections of 1837 brought M. de Tocqueville into public life, and in 1839 the Department of the Manche, in whose welfare he never ceased to take an active interest, sent him to the Chamber of Deputies. The following extract from a letter to Mr. Senior, written as early as 1836, shows with what accuracy he had already measured the true state of the country:—

Here, for the present at least, we appear to have resumed our wonted course. With the exception of agriculture, which suffers a little, everything is surprisingly prosperous; for the first time for five years a sense of stability revives, and with that feeling a turn for speculation. The almost febrile activity which has ever characterised us quits the field of politics for that of material improvement. If I am not much mistaken, we are about to witness in the next few years immense progress in this direction. Nevertheless the Government would be very wrong to overrate the consequences of this happy state of affairs. The nation has been frightfully agitated; it enjoys to the full the repose at length vouchsafed to it; but the experience of all time teaches us that this repose may be fatal to those who govern France. In proportion to the cessation of the fatigue of the last few years political passions will revive; and *if the Government, whilst it is in its strength, does not redouble its caution, and study with the utmost care to respect all the susceptibility of the nation, it will be surprised to see the storm which will suddenly dash against it.* But will this be understood by our rulers? I doubt it.

The history and the fate of the Government of King Louis Philippe are written in these few lines, though they were committed to paper twelve years before the catastrophe of 1848. M. de Tocqueville never ceased to hold the same opinion, which he repeated on the eve of the Revolution of February; and in joining the Opposition his object was not so much to defeat the Government as to avert dangers which were likely, in his opinion, to lead to another overthrow of the monarchy. He received at this time the Cross of the Legion of Honour, without soliciting it, without even knowing it had been conferred upon him till he saw his name in the 'Moniteur.' 'This incident,' he said, 'has vexed me. I am annoyed to think that people will perhaps suppose I have asked for this scrap of riband, which has been so often made the price of base compliances. I would have refused it if I could : the difficulty is to find a courteous and modest mode of refusing.'

At this important moment of his life he turned for counsel to his honoured friend, M. Royer-Collard, of whom alone he was wont to say that he spoke oracles. M. Royer-Collard had then almost retired from the world; his political life was ended ; but he was the man who, in Tocqueville's eyes, had laboured under the Restoration with the greatest earnestness and elevation of purpose to reconcile the hereditary monarchy of the Bourbons with the liberty of France, and to resolve the problem of combining a powerfully centralised Administration in a democratic state of society with a Representative Chamber. Him, therefore, Tocqueville regarded with a deference he paid to no other politician, and M. Royer-Collard easily recognised in his youthful friend the same blameless and patriotic spirit which had pervaded his own life. But already his prescient eye had discovered the perishable nature of the institutions under which they were living and the dangers which still threatened the cause they loved. The letters of M. Royer-Collard himself in this volume are of uncommon interest, for they bear in every line the stamp of a wise and powerful mind. We quote from them the following passages :—

In times of instability it is not good to enter public life very young; if I had had that misfortune I should have been incapable of the conduct I pursued under the Restoration, and all I have of public life lies there. 'The great reputation' which you esteem 'the most precious thing in life,' is more easily secured at this time by such books as yours than by parliamentary activity. You have been tried as a thinker and a writer: you know not what your oratorical powers may be, and an orator needs something quite apart from talent.

He needs favourable circumstances, a certain condition of government, and a certain disposition of the public mind. His success depends on conditions which are in some sort external to himself. No, I do not hold you for an arrogant or an ambitious man. I care, indeed, less than you do for opinion—that is, the opinion of the multitude; for the opinion of the few—that is, of competent judges—is the most worthy object of ambition; it is true glory. But I speak of myself, whose visions of self-love are satisfied by what mere distinction and consideration give. There are, I know, higher missions, and yours is of the number. I acknowledge them, I honour them, I admire them, but I venture to address to them the remark that Bossuet ascribes to the great Condé, 'I think first of doing well, and leave fame to come afterwards.' . . .

The very small part I have taken in the affairs of my time has satisfied my activity, or, if you will, my ambition. It was not in me to undertake more. But to you, sir, it is given to mark far otherwise your passage on earth and to drive your furrow across it. You have begun it. You will follow it, without completing it; for no man has ever finished anything. The thoughts you have brought forth in the travail of your mind will not be understood till you are gone, and will not bear all their fruits. Yet you would be faithless to Providence if you drew back. The reward will not be the reverberation of your name (*vanitas vanitatum*); it will be altogether in the influence you will exercise over the noble of heart. . . .

Make no efforts either to come forward on the stage or to withdraw from it. You belong to Providence. Resign yourself to the coming event. You will have grounds of consolation whatever it may be. The state of our society is known to you as well as if you were an old man. Neither social order nor the government are settled. Everything would crumble at the first blow. It is true that among the characters of the day there is not a hand capable of dealing it; but the blow of a hammer is not always needed against an ill-constructed edifice; a stroke of wind may suffice.

Under the influence of these oracular counsels, rare indeed from a man of M. Royer-Collard's age and authority to one so much younger than himself,

Tocqueville entered the Chamber of Deputies. His success there as a politician and an orator was certainly far inferior to the position he had already acquired as a writer. He himself acknowledged some ten years later that 'his true value was rather in the works of the intellect; that he was worth more in thought than in action; and if he was destined to leave aught behind him, it would consist far more in what he had written than in what he had done.'

But, however unproductive these years of parliamentary life may have been in positive results to himself or to his country, they undoubtedly advanced his own education, by bringing him into closer contact with practical details, without contracting his own extended range of observation. He followed these details with scrupulous attention and a sort of enthusiastic interest, convinced that the art of government consists much less in grand displays and eloquent harangues than in a careful mastery of the details of administration. It is true, and M. de Tocqueville felt it, that these minutiæ interfere with the broader views of politics, and that the life of a man who passes the best years of his existence in a popular assembly is consumed in a conflict of petty and insignificant motives. As he wrote to his brother :—

The events and the men of our time are unquestionably small ; but does it not require the most constant and, so to speak, the most passionate attention to keep oneself free and unscathed in this labyrinth of mean and wretched passions, in this ant-heap of microscopic interests, driving in opposite directions, which cannot be classed, and which do not resolve themselves, as they ought to do, into great common opinions? The political world of our day, in its minute mobility, its perpetual and undignified confusion, absorbs the powers of my mind a thousand times more than political action of a more productive, broad, and single character. The incidents which befall us are but pin-pricks, no doubt ; but a great many pin-pricks may disturb and agitate the soul of the greatest philosopher in the world, and *à fortiori* mine, which is unhappily the least philosophical I know of.

We have already expressed our regret that at this period of his life, and at this period of French history, M. de Tocqueville and the eminent political friends with whom he acted, should have thrown their whole weight upon the side of the Opposition instead of transferring their services to the King's Government. No doubt the passions of the Opposition, in which it was unhappily the fate of M. de Tocqueville to spend his parliamentary life, were petty and contemptible ; we think the results of those passions were mischievous ; and we are persuaded that M. de Tocqueville would have rendered much greater service to his country, and would have influenced the policy of the Crown far more effectually, if he had taken office instead of jealously standing aloof from it. No man who acts with a political party and under a monarchical government can find everything to his mind. He must accept a great deal that is disagreeable and even opposed to his own views for the sake of the general result. But Tocqueville's scrupulous independence and intense sensitiveness disqualified him for the part he might otherwise have played. Whilst ten precious years were wasted in these battles of the ants, the storm was gathering below him and around him, until at length the stroke of wind predicted by M. Royer-Collard swept the fabric from the earth.

The most important event in this period of M. de Tocqueville's life was the quarrel between France and the Great Powers of Europe on the Syrian question, caused by the Treaty of the 15th July, 1840. Indeed, although he could not disguise from himself the dangers to which it exposed his country, he viewed with satisfaction any event which seemed likely to raise the politics of the day above the 'pot-au-feu démocratique et bourgeois' of the Chamber.

In these expectations he was, however, speedily disappointed; and we find him on the formation of M. Guizot's administration steadily voting against the Government, not because he approved the vociferations of a party clamorous for war, but because he held that the policy of submission the King had adopted was so irritating and degrading to a proud and high-spirited nation, that the monarchy itself ran no small risk of being overthrown. ' That,' said he, in letters to his friends in England, ' that is the real danger—the sole danger—not war for the sake of the Government, but the overthrow of the Government, and, after that, war. Never since 1830 has the peril been so great. Thrones are not upset by anarchical passions alone ; that never happens ; the bad impulse must be supported by a good instinct. The revolutionary party is reinforced for the moment by the wounded pride of the nation, which gives it a force it could not otherwise obtain. For my part I remain in the Opposition, not revolutionary, but decided, and for this among many other reasons—the only chance of controlling the bad passions of the people is by sharing with them those passions which are good.'

In a subsequent letter he deplored the estrangement of France and England as the greatest of misfortunes, not soon to be repaired. On two of these points we agree with M. de Tocqueville : we think that the Treaty of 1840, and the dispute which followed it was a heavy blow to the Monarchy of July, from which it never entirely recovered, and in spite of the *entente cordiale* between M. Guizot and Lord Aberdeen, the relations of the two countries were never, under Louis Philippe, restored to entire harmony and confidence. But we think that, in spite of these facts, M. de Tocqueville and his friends arrived at an erroneous conclusion. It is now abundantly demonstrated by the Memoirs of M. Guizot and by historical evidence, that the separation of France from the other Powers of Europe on the Eastern Question was not the result of any ill-will to France on the part of England, but of the extreme mismanagement and underhand dealing of the French Ministers of that day. Unluckily these very Ministers were the men whom the Liberal party had brought into power by the Coalition ; and when they fell, and the King called upon M. Guizot to repair the mischief they had done, he found himself confronted by this formidable array of many of the ablest men in France, who never relaxed in their hostility until they overthrew his Cabinet and the throne along with it. Whether the policy of the King were good or bad, right or wrong, this at any rate, was the worst calamity which could befall the nation. It destroyed the work of thirty years of constitutional government ; it caused a momentary but fatal alliance between the then Liberal party and the

Revolution; it placed the Liberal party itself in a hopeless situation; and the country stood thenceforward in the dire alternative of a daily struggle with anarchy or a willing submission to despotism. As early as August 1847, M. de Tocqueville perceived the approach of these dangers, and described them in the following terms :—

> You will find France tranquil and tolerably prosperous, but nevertheless uneasy. For some time past the mind of the nation has been singularly perturbed, and amidst a calm greater than we have enjoyed for a long period, the idea of the instability of the present state of things has arisen in many minds. For myself, although I view these symptoms with some alarm, I do not exaggerate their significance. I think our society is firmly established, chiefly because I see no other basis on which it can be placed, even were that desired. Yet this state of things ought to give rise to serious reflections. The system practised by the Administration for the last seventeen years has so perverted the middle class, by making constant appeals to its personal cupidity, that this class is gradually coming to be regarded by the rest of the nation as a little aristocracy so vulgar and so corrupt that it is shameful to be governed by it. If this feeling were to spread in the masses, it might one day bring about great calamities.

And on the eve of the Revolution itself, in January 1848, he delivered from the tribune of the Chamber that last memorable speech in which he adjured the Government to change its course in presence of the impending tempest, which we quoted in a former page.

M. de Beaumont has passed lightly over the actual events of 1848, which were recorded by Tocqueville in another form and may be published at some future time. He soon discovered, however, that the same subserviency to material interests which he deplored, had not been diminished by the Revolution, and that it lay not in any given institutions or ministry, but in the temper of the times. 'The Revolution of 1789 sprang (he said) from the brain and the heart of the nation; but this Revolution has partly taken its rise in the belly, and the love of material enjoyment has played an immense part in it.'

In spite of these misgivings, and with a very qualified faith in the destinies of the Republic, M. de Tocqueville thought it his duty to join the Cabinet formed by M. Barrot, under the auspices of President Bonaparte after his election, and he held in this Administration the office of Minister of Foreign Affairs. Although he was not personally responsible for the French expedition to Rome, inasmuch as the order to undertake the siege had been despatched to the army six days before he took office, yet he assumed the responsibility of that measure on grounds which have already been stated in the preceding paper, viz. the firm intention to uphold the Liberal cause in Italy, and to restore the temporal authority of the Pope, not unaccompanied by guarantees for his future good government of his dominions. It soon became apparent in this and in other matters, that the conditions on which the Ministers held office under the President were not those of constitutional responsibility and personal independence, and after a short interval of five months the Government was dissolved.

It was not disappointed ambition or wounded pride that drove M. de Tocqueville from office ; it was the conviction that universal suffrage had given an irresponsible ruler to France, who would soon find, or make, an opportunity to place himself above all law. The momentous question of the revision of the constitution, however, again found him at his post in the Assembly, to make a last attempt to repair those provisions of the constitution of 1848 which led directly and necessarily to another revolution. That constitution had limited the duration of the presidential power to four years, and had rendered the out-going President ineligible for a second term. The consequence was that from 1848 to 1851 the country was agitated by a febrile anxiety to know what would happen at the expiration of Louis Napoleon's term of office, or rather to know by what means, violent or legal, it would be prolonged. M. de Tocqueville was of opinion that the restriction placed on the elective power of the nation should be abolished—a task of great difficulty, since the constitution could only be modified by the vote of two-thirds of the Assembly. The report on the revision of the constitution was drawn up by him in this sense, and presented on the 8th of July, 1851. He describes his view of the state of affairs in the following letter :—

27th July, 1851.

I am very well satisfied with the general effect produced by my Report in France, and delighted by the opinion expressed towards myself in your country. I care almost as much for what is said of me on one side of the Channel as on the other, and I have so many feelings and ideas in common with the English, that England is become my second intellectual country.

How is it that my arguments in favour of the revision have not convinced you? The non-constitutional re-election of the President has long appeared to me extremely probable. I still think it so, although Louis Napoleon Bonaparte has effectually alienated the upper classes and almost every man of political eminence, and although, as far as I can judge, his popularity among the people is considerably diminished and daily diminishing. Nevertheless, I own to you that I persist in regarding his re-election as pretty nearly inevitable, in consequence of the absence of any possible competitor and in consequence of the general uneasiness. I think this Bonapartist current, if it be turned aside, can only be so by a revolutionary current more perilous still; and, finally, I think that if Napoleon be unconstitutionally re-elected, anything in the shape of an attack on freedom becomes possible. I was so convinced of this six months ago, that I remember to have said to you, that probably the end of all this would be to make me quit public life, in order to have no part in a Government which would attempt to destroy *de jure* or to annul *de facto* constitutional institutions, and which would perhaps succeed in the attempt for some years, from the exhaustion of the public mind. With small belief in the possibility of maintaining the Republic, which would be the government of my own choice, I should have seen without regret Louis Napoleon become our permanent chief if I had thought it possible, on the one hand, that he could rally the heads of society about him, and if, on the other hand, he would or could have been a constitutional sovereign. But I did not believe that possible, as I told you, and all I have seen since my return from Italy has convinced me more and more how much I was in the right. The President is as *impermeable* to constitutional ideas as was Charles X. himself. He has his own notion of legitimacy, and he clings to the constitutions of the Empire as the other clung to the divine right of kings. He is, moreover, more and more separated from the whole body of men who have ability or experience to conduct the government, and reduced to seek his *point d'appui* in the instincts and passions of the people strictly so called. Hence his re-election, especially if it be illegally carried, may have the worst consequences, and yet it is almost inevitable—save by a recourse to revolutionary passions, which I do not wish to rekindle in the nation. What is the deduction from all this, but to desire the revision, for the purpose either of rendering the re-election of the President impossible by changing the nature and origin of the executive power, or of rendering it less dangerous by making it legal? . . . It is possible that a crisis may occur so perilous that I myself may be of opinion that it is best that the constitution should be violated by the people ; but I shall leave that sad work to others. My hands shall never strike the flag of the law in my country. . . . In short, our situation is more complicated, more inextricable, and more obscure than it ever has been. We are still in one of those strange and terrible positions in which nothing is impossible and nothing can be foreseen. The chances are in favour of the President's re-election, and at the same time an Assembly may be returned much less presidential than is supposed; so that if Louis Napoleon does not avail himself of the first popular impulse to grasp all powers in his own hand, he may find himself again in presence of an Assembly which will not allow him to do as he pleases. In presence of this unexampled situation the nation is perfectly calm and even prosperous. People follow their avocations without plunging into great risks, but with activity and perseverance, just as if the morrow of everything was not uncertain. No doubt the dread of the term 1852 is extreme, and even, I think, exaggerated. But we have all received the education of revolutions; we know that we must live in them like soldiers in the field, who are not deterred by the chance of being killed the next day from dining and sleeping, or even from amusing themselves. That is the state we are all in ; and when I survey the attitude of the whole nation I cannot but admire it ; even with all its blunders and its foibles, it is a great people.

The project of revision failed. The consequences so clearly indicated in the preceding letter rapidly ensued. The President did 'grasp all powers into his own hands' to shake off the control of an independent Assembly, and on the 2nd December, 1851, the Republic and the freedom of France expired. It remains for us only to trace the effects of that catastrophe on his own mind, on his life, and on the French nation.

A short time after the event he wrote to M. de
Beaumont in the following terms:—

I perceive, my dear friend, that you have carried with you
into your retreat the same agitation of mind which I still find in
the bustle of the world. How should it be otherwise? Which
way are we now to look in France for objects which do not awaken
sad thoughts? And if we move out of France it would not fare
better with us; for the disease is in us as well as around us.
Lanjuinais, who is in Italy, writes that the remembrance of France
puts out the glory of the arts and of the sun.

We must, however, make up our minds to what is taking place,
and not disguise from ourselves that this will last a considerable
time. As for me, I can only recover that frame of mind which is
necessary to my studies, by satisfying myself that I am out of
public affairs for a long while, and that the thing is now to form
new habits and create new interests. This is not the way of the
world. I am continually meeting people full of the most absurd
delusions—real delusions of émigrés—who set themselves gravely
to compute how many months this Government has to live. As
for me, I stand by what I have said. *It will found nothing; but it
will last.* With far greater strength than the republican government,
it has the same advantage of being a neutral ground on which
both the monarchical parties find a temporary refuge, and which
they prefer to the camp of their former antagonists. This is especially true of the Legitimists, who are not only well received but
encouraged to come in by all sorts of petty artifices, which succeed
the more easily as many are not averse to be caught by them.
Thus, they say that the famous memorandum the President is to
leave [to designate his successor] will name the Count de Chambord. Just a case of 'Le bon billet qu'a la Châtre.' The other
day Lady Douglas told somebody that the President hated
marriage, disliked his family, and would no doubt, if not provoked,
leave the government to the lawful sovereign. All these follies,

aided by lassitude, fear, and hatred of the Orleans family, gain acceptance. Add to this the second-class ambitions of the party, the people who were hurt at not getting seats in the Chambers, or who were useless when they got there, and now declaim against what they call the reign of the lawyers, and you may fancy what a rout it is. . . .

A newspaper has published the letter in which you refuse to come forward. I have not the least doubt that we do well to stand aloof. There is nothing for us to do until liberal opinions are born again in France. I never had a more clear and certain conviction than this. My only anxiety arises from the fear that I shall not find means to occupy satisfactorily the forced and probably very long leisure this future leaves to me. I cannot as yet grasp or even clearly apprehend the subject I have chosen; this gives me some days of great dejection.

The elections are approaching without a symptom of electoral *life*. The insignificance of the thing appears to be generally felt. I think the Government will carry all its candidates; yet, if there were any combination in Paris, it might be beaten there. I have just read in the 'Moniteur' the law on the Press, or rather against the Press. Everything that can be conceived, short of the censorship, is accumulated in this decree to render all discussion illusory and all intellectual movement impossible. I especially commend to you the clause on false news, by which the mere fact is punished, without any mischievous intention. Well! in spite of all this, the day that public opinion begins to awaken they will be obliged to have recourse to the censorship, either openly or secretly. The censorship is the only known specific against the freedom of the Press.

The effect of these events on Tocqueville was to wean him altogether from society, and to throw him back upon the cherished retirement of his own home

—embellished by all the graces of domestic life and cordial friendship, enlivened by a recurrence to his literary pursuits, but embittered by the thought that he had survived the liberties of his country. In this strain he wrote to Mrs. Phillimore, the accomplished daughter of Lord Justice Knight Bruce:—

> I write to you, Madam, from the depths of the country, in which I live but little with mankind but much with my books; and as all mankind do not resemble you, I am not displeased to be separated from them. I have plunged with delight into the studies which business and revolutions had interrupted. I have commenced a great work, which I had been thinking of for the last ten years, and which I expected never to have the time or the liberty of mind to undertake; and I acknowledge to you that there are many moments in which I am selfish enough and bad Frenchman enough to be extremely happy. A sort of twinge of virtue sometimes disturbs me when I reflect that no amount of personal happiness can console a man for the ruin of the institutions which promised greatness to his country. It is hard to think, whatever may be the pleasures of private life, that this great and terrible French Revolution can finish in the thing we see before us. Believe me, Madam, this is not the end of that great drama: it is an act added to the rest, but not the close of it.

In the midst of this solitude comes one day a visitor who is thus amusingly described :—

> Last week the silence of this ancient abode was broken by the noise of carriage wheels, and we were somewhat surprised to see X. alight. He had come to spend the day with us. We received him as well as we could, and talked literature from morning to

night. He converses on that subject much better than on politics; he knows the whole eighteenth century by heart, and upon my word I thought he was going to recite to my wife the *Pucelle* of Voltaire. He would, in fact, have amused me, if it were in the power of man to amuse me for eight hours running. As I did not wish to have the air of avoiding political conversation, I said to him abruptly, 'How can you explain that the President, who has passed his life in free countries, should have destroyed freedom to this degree in our own? As for me,' I added, 'that which will always prevent me from rallying to this government is not so much even the 2nd December as what has followed it.' X. admitted, with some embarrassment, that he was surprised himself, that things had been carried too far, but that he did not despair of a return to freedom, and so fell back upon literature. I resumed the subject once more, which gave X. an opportunity to tell me that the President was surrounded with people who only blamed him for the moderation of his policy and the tardiness of his measures—people in fact who were shocked by the excess of our liberties and the small amount of power he had kept in his own hands. What irritated me the more in my guest was to see that, whilst he had sacrificed his former affections to his interests, he carefully retained his former animosities; so that after he had favoured me with a grand tirade on the crimes of the Restoration, and especially on the expedition to Spain, 'Yes,' I exclaimed, 'you are right; it is always a great crime to destroy the liberty of a people under the pretext that a bad use is made of it.' This axiom cut short the conversation, and we returned for good to Voltaire, which did not prevent us from parting very tenderly at ten in the evening.

In the autumn of 1853 he repaired to the neighbourhood of Tours, where a country-house had been hired for the winter, as the climate of Normandy was too severe for his health, always delicate. From this cottage he addressed the following letter to his friend and former chief, M. Odilon Barrot :—

As for public affairs, I imagine that you are as ignorant and as powerless as I am myself. You and I, my friend, belong to what they would have called eighty years ago 'the old Court.' Nay more, we belong to another age of the world; we are of a class of antediluvian animals who ought really to be placed in cabinets of natural history to show what the creatures were like, long ago, who were so singularly constituted as to care for freedom, legality, and sincerity—strange tastes, which presuppose organs altogether different from those of the modern inhabitants of the world. This race too will pass away, and will be followed by another, more like us than itself, I am sure; but shall we witness this fresh metamorphosis? I question it; much time must elapse in order to efface the deplorable impressions of the last few years, and to bring back the French, I do not say to a passionate love of liberty, but to a sense of their own dignity, to the habit of writing and speaking with freedom, to the desire of discussing their obedience, which is in the spirit of the age and the most ancient instinct of the race. When I think of the disasters which a handful of political adventurers have inflicted on this unhappy country—when I see that in the midst of this rich and industrious community doubts have been cast, with an air of plausibility, on the right of property itself; when I remember these things, and that the human race is composed for the most part, as in fact it is, of feeble, honest, and vulgar minds, I am disposed to forgive the prodigious moral enervation we are witnessing, and to reserve all my indignation and my scorn for the intriguers and the madmen who have thrown our poor country into these extremities.

Meanwhile the work on the 'State of France before the Revolution' proceeded. Tocqueville visited Germany in 1854, and the commencement of the Russian war in that year gave a somewhat different direction to his thoughts. Hating the Government with all his heart, he nevertheless approved its conduct in the Eastern question, upheld the English alliance, and maintained that in presence of the enemy it is the duty of every man to abstain from doing anything to increase the difficulties of a crisis in which the nation is engaged. From about this time, too, dates Tocqueville's acquaintance with Sir George Lewis, which speedily ripened into mutual admiration and cordial friendship. They were both of them men in whose eyes the work of government was the noblest exercise of the human intellect for the improvement of our race by the influence of freedom and of truth, and who may be said to have pursued politics with no other object, for they were indifferent to all the vulgar prizes of political ambition. They were both of them alike free from pretension and from prejudice, intent upon the real principles of action which may govern the world rightly, rather than upon the forms they may assume, or the accidents that may attend them. In Lewis there was a greater mass of accumulated knowledge, for his was universal; in Tocqueville a quicker vein of sentiment and perhaps a more subtle

power of discernment ; but their faculties and tastes
readily mingled in entire harmony, and few men have
more rapidly and completely known and esteemed
one another. It may be permitted to those who
shared the friendship and reverenced the character
of each of these two eminent men to record in a few
passing lines the regret which two great nations must
for ever feel that their wise and virtuous lives were,
within so short a time of one another, prematurely
closed.

The letters addressed by Tocqueville to Sir
George Lewis during the war, especially with
reference to the administration of the army, are of
extreme interest, but their length forbids us to quote
them here. We confine ourselves to one observation. He had viewed with great regret the comparative failure of the British military administration
at the outset of the war, though he attributed the
superior arrangements of the French army chiefly to
their long experience in Africa, whereas the British
army took the field with the notions and traditions
of the Peninsula. But what he conceived to be of
still greater moment to the honour and power of this
country, was the means of raising troops ; for he
held that it is impossible for a country to keep its
ground in the present state of the world without, at

least, the power of raising large armies, and that England is mistaken if she thinks it possible to stand aloof from the affairs of the Continent. On this last point M. de Tocqueville's language is so forcible, and so much opposed to the prevailing opinion of the day in England, that we quote the passage :—

> In general, although it is rather imprudent to speak of a country which is not one's own, I allow myself to say that the English would be wrong to fancy themselves as far separated and apart from the rest of the world as they have hitherto been, insomuch that events of universal interest on the Continent should not affect their institutions. I think, that in the present age of the world, and still more in that which is approaching, no European nation can long remain entirely different from all other nations; and that whatever becomes the general law of the Continent cannot fail to exercise in the long run a very great influence on the peculiar laws of Great Britain, in spite of the sea, and in spite of the special manners and customs and institutions which have heretofore, more than the sea, protected you. We shall perhaps not see the verification of this remark in our own time; but be assured those who come after us will see it; and I should not be afraid to have this letter placed in a notary's office, to be read fifty years hence.

M. de Tocqueville was well acquainted with the English language, with English modes of thought, with English opinions. He says in one of his letters that he can without difficulty place himself at the English point of view on any question, and tell beforehand what an Englishman would think of it.

He entertained the highest opinion of the English intellect, and he attributes to it a marked superiority (in speaking of Mr. Grote's 'History of Greece') over German scholarship. But although he was entirely free from national prejudice, the fact is that he knew English men and English books better than he knew England. For twenty years he never visited it. In 1836 he left it still agitated by the throes of the Reform Bill and, as he supposed, on the verge of a progressive democratic revolution, though a pacific one. In 1857, when he returned to it for the last time, he expressed his astonishment at finding the country so little changed after all, and that, in spite of the Reform Bill and all the incidents of twenty years, it was still just the same Old England. He was himself so well aware of his comparatively imperfect knowledge of this country, that he carefully abstained from writing upon it ; and although some portions of his English journals have now been published, they must be regarded as the impressions of a traveller rather than as the deliberate judgment of a philosopher. We think, for example, that he was wrong in assuming that the English aristocracy is based mainly upon wealth and the acquisition of wealth, though he is entirely right in the assertion that it is not based exclusively on birth. Immense fortunes are daily realised in England which have no connexion at all with the aristocracy; and, on the other hand, the most frequent and beneficial additions to the House of Lords are those which are made on the ground of high legal ability, long public service, or personal eminence, irrespective of mere possessions. Great wealth, unaccompanied with political or personal claims, does not raise a man in England to the peerage; but the peerage of England is unquestionably open to all men who rise by their own ability, in church or state, to the first rank in their professions. That is its real basis and its true power.

Before we revert to the political opinions of Tocqueville, it may not be inappropriate to introduce in this place a letter to one of his friends, whose life has been devoted to metaphysical and theological inquiries. It is a page of general and lasting interest :—

Your last letter contains things on the great questions which occupy you, deeply thought and well expressed. This letter well deserves to be read again, and the subject of it is the greatest, I may almost say the only subject, which deserves the attention of man. Everything else is a bubble in comparison with it. I should have had a passionate love for the philosophical studies which have been your constant occupation, if I could have turned them to more profit; but, whether from some natural defect or from a want of resolution in the pursuit of this design, I have always found at last that all the scientific notions to be acquired on these subjects did not carry me further, and frequently carried me less far, than the point I had reached at the outset by a small number of simple ideas, which all mankind do in fact more or less entertain. These ideas lead easily to a belief in a First Cause, which remains at once evident and inconceivable : to fixed laws which are discernible in the physical world, and must be supposed to exist in the moral world ; to the providence of God, and therefore to His justice ; to the responsibility of man, since he is enabled to discern good from evil, and, therefore, to a future life. I acknowledge, that apart from revelation, I have never found that the nicest metaphysical inquiry could supply anything more clear on these points than the plainest common sense, and this has made me somewhat out of humour with it. What I called 'the bottom I cannot touch' is the Wherefore of the world ; the plan of creation of which we know nothing, not even in our bodies, still less in our minds—the reason of the destiny of this singular being whom we call Man, with just intelligence enough to perceive the miseries of his condition, but not enough to change it. . . . That is the depth, or rather the depths, which the ambition of my soul would sound, but which will for ever remain infinitely beyond my powers of knowing the truth.

In these meditations, which diversified a life devoted to literary labour and to rural pursuits—a philosopher in the morning and a peasant in the afternoon—M. de Tocqueville spent the last years of his life. We fancy, as we read the letters written within a few months of its close, that a tone of increased serenity tempered the melancholy of political disappointment, and a greater power of thought plunged into the future of the world which he was not destined to behold. But though the shadow was already stealing along the wall, with that unconsciousness which is the last happiness of man he still looked forwards to a brighter future.

I see (said he on the 12th January, 1858, to Mr. Freslon) that you do not give way to despondency as to public affairs, and you are right. I too am far from singing a *de profundis* over French society. Only, I am very much afraid that we are not destined to see that personage restored to vitality. The history of the past affords but little light as to the means of resuscitation, because the principles of life within it are different from what they once were. Down to a recent period, the living and active forces of society were in the educated classes. When these had been persuaded, excited, and united in one conviction, the rest followed. Now-a-days, not only have the educated classes become temporarily insensible by the disease of long revolutions, but they are in reality dethroned. The centre of social power, so to speak, has been gradually displaced and at last abruptly changed. It now resides in classes which read nothing, or at least only read newspapers when they read anything at all; and that is the profound reason which leads our Government to reserve its fetters for the periodical press. We academicians are free to cry out as loud as we' please, addressing an academical public; but the least buzz of a hostile thought is suppressed if it is thought likely to reach the ear of the people. Don't tell me then that Voltaire, Rousseau, &c. overthrew by books powers far more durably established. Those powers were better established, it is true; but the force to overthrow them was far more within the reach of writers of books and better within their grasp. They were surrounded by the upper or middle classes, who believed in ideas: but those same classes now-a-days abhor and dread ideas, whatever they may be (as far as they are ideas) and think of nothing but interests. Moreover these same upper and middle classes, whose ears were so open, were still the masters of society. When they were won over, all was done.

I believe with you that these classes may again be persuaded and excited; and I think that when that is done, a great, though still a less, influence may be exercised through them over the people: but this can only be accomplished very slowly, by dint of a multitude of small blows struck successively on the public mind. It is certainly a good, and even a necessary thing to follow this up, and it would be an exaggeration to say that those who do so are losing their time; but it would be a still greater exaggeration to believe in the complete efficacy and prompt effect of these efforts. To change the mind of the nation quickly, instruction less refined and more adapted to the classes who are now all-powerful is requisite; and as the periodical press is not free, it is only by *facts*, and not by ideas, that the people can be enlightened as to the true character of the government it lives under. If this government followed its natural disposition, if it were now to commit the faults by which in the long run absolute governments always fall, the nation would see clearly and at once what its constitution is; and as, after all, the comparisons between our own age and the decline of society under the Roman Empire are inaccurate—as the mass of the people forms neither a corrupt nation, nor a timorous nation, nor a nation enslaved like the Roman mob, on that day when light shall break in upon it the nation will judge.

These extracts are long, but they are taken from a volume little known to English readers. They are not inferior in wisdom and in acuteness to any of M. de Tocqueville's earlier writings, and they bear directly on one of the questions most interesting to the world—the state of opinion and the duration of the Imperial Government in France. Their interest indeed appears to us to be vastly increased by the light cast on them by subsequent events. We shall therefore resume and complete them by adding to them one of the last letters to M. de Beaumont, dated

Tocqueville : 27th February, 1858.

I cannot tell you, my dear friend, how much your last letter has interested me, and how entirely I agree with most of your observations, amongst others with that on the value of liberty. Like you, I have never been more entirely convinced that liberty alone can give to human society in general, and to the individuals which compose it in particular, all the prosperity and all the greatness of which our race is capable.[1] Every day confirms me more in this belief; my own observations, the lapse of life, the recollections of history, the events of the present day, foreign nations, our own, all combine to give to these opinions of our youth the force of absolute conviction. That liberty is the *sine quâ non* to form a great and virile nation, is to my mind evidence itself. On this point I have a faith which I should be glad to have on many others. But how difficult it is to establish liberty firmly in nations which have lost the use, and even the true conception, of it! How

[1] M. de Tocqueville's definition of liberty, given in a fragment of his English journal (vol. viii. p. 374), is as follows :—

'Liberty seems to me to hold in the political world the place of the atmosphere in the physical world. The earth is peopled with a multitude of beings differently organised ; yet all live and flourish. Alter the conditions of the atmosphere, they suffer ; remove them out of it, they die. . . . Change your laws, vary your manners, reform your creed, modify your forms ; if you can attain to this, that man should have full liberty to do whatsoever is not bad in itself, and the certainty of enjoying in peace the produce of what he has done, you have hit the mark. The mark is the same, but there are many ways of attaining it.'

powerless are institutions when they are not fostered by the ideas
and habits of the people ! I have always thought that to make
France a free nation (in the true sense of the word)—that enterprise to which we have devoted our lives to the extent of our small
abilities—I have always thought, I say, that this enterprise was a
grand but a rash one. I think it every day more rash, but more
grand also; and so much so that, were I to be born again, I
should still prefer to risk everything in this hazardous undertaking
rather than to bow under a necessity to serve. Will others be
more fortunate than we have been? I know not; but I ask
myself whether in our time we shall see in France a free nation,
at least what you and I mean by the word. That does not mean
that we shall not see revolutions. Nothing, believe me, is settled.
An unforeseen circumstance, a new turn given to affairs, any
accident whatsoever, may bring on extraordinary events to force
every man from his retreat. It was to that I alluded in my last
letter, and not to the establishment of regular liberty. But what
makes me fear that nothing will for a long time make us free, is
that we have not the desire to be so. . . . Not indeed that I
am one of those who say that we are a decrepid and corrupt
nation, destined to perpetual servitude. Those who, with this
notion, exhibit the vices of the Roman Empire, and complacently
imagine that we are to reproduce them on a smaller scale, are
people who seem to me to live in books and not in the reality of
their age. We are not a decrepid nation, but a nation worn and
terrified by anarchy. We are wanting in the sound and lofty
conception of freedom ; but we are worth more than our present
destiny. We are not yet ripe for the definitive and regular
establishment of despotism ; and the Government will find this
out if ever it attains sufficient security to discourage conspiracies,
to cause the anarchical parties to drop their arms, and to crush
them from the scene. The Government would then be astonished,
in the hey-day of its triumph, to find a stratum of bitterness and
opposition, beneath that layer of obsequious followers who now

seem to cover the surface of France. I sometimes think that the only chance of seeing a strong love of liberty revive in France is in the tranquil and apparently definitive establishment of absolute power. Observe the working of all our revolutions; it can now be [described with great precision. The experience of seventy years has proved that the people *alone* cannot make a revolution ; as long as that necessary element of revolutions works alone, it is powerless. It does not become irresistible till a portion of the educated classes has joined it; and these classes will only lend their moral support or their material co-operation to the people when they cease to fear it. Hence it is that at the very moment when each of the governments we have had in the course of the last sixty years appeared to be the strongest, it caught the disease of which it was to perish. The Restoration began to die the day when nobody talked any longer of killing it, and so with the July monarchy. I think it will be so with the present government. Paul [M. de Beaumont's youngest son, then a child] will tell me if I am mistaken.

Ten years had elapsed since the date at which this letter was written, when the signs of the times, especially in the elections, began to indicate a spirit very different from the apathy of abject submission and indifference which seemed to have emasculated France. On almost every point of the country—in the choice of representatives, in the choice of the *conseils généraux*, and in the municipal elections—the Government found its nominations energetically disputed and not unfrequently defeated. The machinery by which universal suffrage was converted for a time into a toy for prefects and ministers to play with, and an instrument to crush the real intelligence of the people, proved to be worn out. There was once more a voice and a will in the ballot-box; and that voice condemned the Imperial Government. As M. de Tocqueville observed in 1858, it is by *facts* alone, and not by arguments, that the true character of the Government became known—facts such as the state of the finances, the Mexican war, the restrictions of the Press, the prosecution and punishment of electoral committees, were gradually bringing back light to the French nation, and when ' light breaks in, the nation will judge.' In spite of many errors of judgment and of conduct, we do not dispute the services which the Emperor Napoleon III. rendered to France, and his popularity long remained undiminished with the great majority of the nation. But that popularity could not cover all the shortcomings and abuses of his government; and dependent as it was on his personal authority, the idea of the termination of his reign became as much an object of terror to the timid, and of perplexity to the wavering, as the incoherent threats of anarchy. For what would he leave behind him? A Government composed of men for the most part profoundly discredited—a youthful heir—a regent perhaps, who, both as a foreigner and a woman, has hardly had justice done her by the French people,—and, on the other hand, a rising tide of liberal feeling, more and more disposed to demand institutions which should give the nation security for the future and a real voice in its affairs. There was but one course to be pursued with any prospect of security to the Imperial dynasty and of tranquillity to France; and that course was to accept the progress of liberal opinions. It might not have been impossible, even with the institutions of the Empire, to transform the absolutism of the sovereign into a system of government which might have afforded a moderate and reasonable satisfaction to the country. The Imperial Government, though extremely arbitrary, and irresponsible to any organised body in the State, never failed to acknowledge its democratic origin, and to exercise its power with some regard to the prevailing sentiments of the people. It is not by resistance or repression that the Empire could regain the ground it has lost; and if France is again to be saved from another of those periodical convulsions which may even now be approaching, like a storm on the furthest limit of the horizon, it will be by timely concessions to the reviving energy of the nation. At such a moment, the voice of M. de

Tocqueville, in his ardent love of freedom, will not be unheard or without influence, and we shall be curious to learn what answer will be made to this posthumous appeal of a great thinker and a great patriot.

I have retained, with the change here and there of a tense in a verb, this concluding passage because it describes, not unfairly, the views with which the Imperial Government was regarded some years before its fall. These views have been justified by more recent occurrences. Already in 1866 it was apparent that the game of absolutism was played out and that light was breaking in. The Emperor made an attempt to meet this new situation of affairs by concessions to the Liberal party, which seemed at one moment to promise a less perilous solution. But, whether they were made by the Sovereign without sufficient sincerity, or met by the constitutional party without sufficient energy and intelligence, they unhappily failed, and after a short trial the Imperial Government was thrown back in the spring of 1870 into the hands of men the least capable of guiding and controlling a great movement. The failure of this experiment, which dates from the moment when M. Buffet and Count Daru withdrew, on inadequate grounds, from office, left in the mind of the Emperor but one expedient: namely, the possibility of restoring his prestige and authority by a successful campaign. That, as he knew, was his last card: he played it, and lost the game. But there is scarcely an incident in this series of events which had not been anticipated by M. de Tocqueville ten and even twenty years before in the course of his correspondence or his other writings. He predicted, as has been shown in these papers, not only the fall of the Empire, but the manner of its fall; and his remarks are more instructive now, when they have been confirmed by experience, than they were at the time when they were written. [1872.]

AGRICULTURAL FRANCE.

AGRICULTURAL FRANCE.[1]

THE most cursory traveller who is whirled by steam in less than thirty hours from the coast of Picardy to the shores of Provence, can hardly fail to be struck by the diversified aspects of the soil and rural economy of France. He leaves in the Department of the Pas de Calais a soil and climate less favoured by nature than the southern coast of England; he finds in the Department of the Var a region vying in its products with the valley of the Arno or the *huerta* of Valencia. But throughout this vast and varied tract of country, he will, if he has known the condition of France for any considerable period of time, be not less struck by the astonishing marks of agricultural improvement which are everywhere visible. When we, whose lot it is to belong to what must now be called the elder generation, first visited France in the years

[1] The following paper was first published in the *Edinburgh Review*, No. 232, in October 1861, as a review of the work entitled—
Économie rurale de la France depuis 1789. Par M. Léonce de Lavergne, Membre de l'Institut, &c. Paris: 1860.

which succeeded the peace of 1815, the aspect of the land was that of a country impoverished and devastated by a quarter of a century of domestic convulsions and of war. The progress which had commenced under the enlightened ministers of Louis XVI., and the passion for improvement which took possession of the French nation in the eighteenth century, were rudely arrested by the Revolution. Landed property itself was violently transferred from its former owners to a class of men who had for many years neither the confidence, nor the capital, nor the skill to improve the cultivation of the soil. Whatever was beneficial in the former relations of landlord and tenant had been destroyed; whatever is beneficial in the new order of things was as yet imperceptible. The Imperial conscription for the wars of Napoleon had drained the rural population to an excess from which it has not even now recovered in numbers or in physical strength. The appearance of a French village in those days was that of squalid discomfort, in which even the more wealthy of the peasant proprietors were content to live. Their dwellings mere cabins; their farm buildings mere hovels; the church dilapidated from neglect or defaced with whitewash. Carriageable by-roads were unknown : except on the great paved chaussées or royal routes constructed by Louis XIV., the country was intersected by mere tracks, which rendered it equally difficult for the farmer to obtain manure for his fields or to dispose of the produce of his harvests. Stock was extremely scarce and the breed of animals wretched. The only relief afforded to the exhausted soil was by a frequent but unintelligent system of fallows—scientific agriculture, rural machinery, artificial manures, drainage and irrigation were alike unknown. Such was the state of agriculture in France about forty years ago, and if we go back another forty years, we must in fairness add that such was the state of agriculture in England also. Modern agriculture is almost the creation of the present century.

Arthur Young lived and travelled about eighty years ago, and he has recorded with admirable truth and sagacity the actual condition of both countries in his time. It was given him to foresee, but not to realise, the splendid profits and advantages to be reaped from the new era, when the science he professed would regenerate the soil of Europe, and enable it to support with increasing wealth and prosperity countless millions of hnman beings.[1] Few

[1] Arthur Young was sorely tempted in 1789 to purchase the estate of Riaux, within a few miles of Moulins, consisting of a châteu, two mills,

men now alive can be said to have witnessed this
prodigious transformation in England, and the
younger generation has a very imperfect conception
of the agricultural operations of their grandfathers.
A change has been wrought in the land somewhat
more gradual, but certainly not less beneficial than
those which have taken place in manufactures and
in locomotion, though more than half the people of
England are probably not aware of it. But in France
a similar transformation is going on before our eyes.
Owing to the causes we have adverted to it began
much later ; it has proceeded more slowly ; but in
these later years its progress is astonishing, and the
results are the more striking as they are favoured by
a climate in many parts of France very superior to

---

nine farms, &c., in all 3,000 acres of good land. The price then asked
for the whole estate was 300,000 livres, the gross rental being 12,500
livres, and the nett rental about 8,000. The Englishman saw and recorded his conviction that the price was low for 3,000 acres of land
capable of tripling and quadrupling its produce and value in the hands
of a farmer who could handle it ; but he shrewdly adds, ' the state of
the government, and the fear of buying my share in a civil war, prevented me from contracting this engagement at present.' At that time
he was assured that there were six thousand estates for sale in different parts of France. M. de Lavergne has ascertained that this very
estate of Riaux was sold in 1799 by its owner (who escaped the Revolution and did not emigrate) for 201,000 livres ; in 1826 it was again
sold for 315,000 livres ; and at the present time such an estate in the
Department of the Allier is worth about 600,000 livres, or double what
it was in 1826, and triple what it was in 1800. This is a fair example of
the increase of the value of land in France in the present century.

our own. They are indeed apparent to the most superficial observation. A vast amount of building for farming purposes and for the abode of the rural population is rising on every side. Great as the architectural improvements have been in Paris and in all the great towns of France, the enormous increase of domestic rural buildings of solid materials and good workmanship is even more remarkable, for these are the practical, unostentatious results of private wealth and industry. Here and there the old château or the new country-house, surrounded by its park, and restored to the uses of country life, marks the increase of these tastes and pursuits among the upper classes. Roads and railroads have already opened the great majority of the departments.[1] The food and clothing of the peasantry have improved. Fallows are less frequently to be seen; there is an enormous increase of green crops, and a proportionate augmentation of stock; and the whole system of farming is neater, more liberal, and more productive.

[1] There are in France about 250,000 miles of roads, of which about 20,000 are first-class highways, 50,000 second-class, the rest country roads. It has been calculated that twenty-five years would be required to put these all in good condition at the expense of the communes. And, as will be seen hereafter, there is the greatest disinclination on the part of the Communes to rate themselves for this purpose. They were assisted by the Emperor to the amount of a million sterling.

M. de Lavergne has undertaken to relate the course of this economical revolution in the unpretending but highly interesting and instructive volume now before us. We need hardly remind our readers that M. de Lavergne, the author of a well-known book on the 'Rural Economy of England, Scotland, and Ireland' is the most distinguished writer of the day on a science which he has made peculiarly his own, and which we must call, for want of a better name, 'agricultural economy.' The term 'rural economy' is commonly applied in a narrower sense, to the conduct of rural operations, and the management of land. But agricultural economy embraces all the varied and important questions which arise in connection with the production and distribution of agricultural wealth : these are, in other words, precisely the most important questions political economy has to deal with, for the soil is the fertile mother of almost all produce, and the arts which increase and develop that produce have the most direct bearing on all the political and social relations of man. M. de Lavergne is not merely a scientific writer on agriculture, for on that ground we have probably several agriculturists in England who are his equals. But he has brought his agricultural knowledge to bear with great ingenuity and good sense on the whole state of his country. By this key he explains with remarkable lucidity the natural geography of France ; he interprets the national character and the past history of the people ; and he has given us a book of simple facts and sound reasoning, which is an excellent guide to the true state of the nation. It is, in a very portable form and a most agreeable style, a complete topography of the rural districts of France, which are still far less known to our travellers than the remotest corners of Germany and Italy, although to the archæologist, the politician, and, we may now add, the agriculturist, no part of the Continent presents more numerous subjects of interest.

The reign of Louis XVI. is a period in the history of France to which very scanty justice has been done. The tremendous catastrophe which closed the career of that unfortunate sovereign in blood and darkness, seemed to have erased from human memory the preceding fifteen years—from 1774 to 1789—which were devoted by the King and the ablest of his ministers to useful and intelligent reforms. It is not too much to say that the reign which began by M. de Turgot's celebrated ordinances for opening the trade of the country and abolishing the Corn Laws, and which carried into effect in 1786 the Commercial Treaty with England, did in reality anticipate some of the most important economical reforms of the present century. Before Turgot's reforms the agriculture of France lay under a system of close protection. The price of corn, the trade in corn, and even the amount of corn to be sown were regulated by authority. All changes in the usual course of husbandry were prohibited, as if corn could be grown without other crops. Vines could not be planted without the permission of Government. To all these absurdities Turgot gave the death-blow when he declared, in the preamble to one of his laws, 'The prosperity of the country is mainly based on the cultivation of the land, on the abundance and profitable sale of its produce, which is the only proper encouragement of husbandry. This profitable sale can only be the result of the most absolute liberty in buying and selling. It is this liberty which secures to the farmer his just recompense, to the landlord a fixed income, to the industrious labourer regular and proportionate wages, to the consumer what he needs, and to citizens of all ranks the enjoyment of their rights.' This language was used by the ministers of Louis XVI. thirteen years before the commencement of the Revolution. The same enlightened spirit manifested itself in the Provincial Assemblies of 1776, in which many of the great nobles and prelates of France took a most active part. The records of these Assemblies prove that the Church and the aristocracy of France were not, at that time, insensible to the wants of the country ; and that they might, under judicious direction, have laid the basis of constitutional government and national prosperity.

If the Government of which Turgot was the head had had the power to carry three such measures as an Act for the Commutation of Tithe, an Act for the Enfranchisement of Copyholds, and an Encumbered Estates' Act, it is perhaps not too much to assert that the worst effects of the French Revolution might have been averted. But the monarchy, though nominally absolute, had no such power, for absolutism is essentially weak unless it is backed by great military strength. The measures which Turgot did propose were for the most part defeated by a combination of the privileged orders. It became necessary to convoke the States-General to obtain the sanction of the nation to necessary and indispensable reforms ; the States-General overshot the mark, and the whole social edifice was thrown down.

M. de Lavergne doubts whether the abolition of tithes and seignorial charges on land had the beneficial influence on agriculture which has commonly been attributed to them by French writers, and he points to the example of this country to show that great progress may be made in agricultural improvements without any violent invasion of the property of the Church or the rights of the manor. The annual value of the tithes in France before the Revolution was about three millions sterling, to which must be added another million lost in the process of collection[1]; but the maintenance of the ecclesiastical establishments by the State costs at present upwards of two millions sterling. The difference in amount is, therefore, not very large, but the burden is transferred from one class of taxpayers to the whole nation. In addition to the tithes the productive lands and other property of the Church and the religious orders of France in 1789

[1] In the concluding chapter of this work M. de Lavergne states that the tithes of France amounted in 1789 to 133,000,000 on two milliards and a half of gross produce, but this includes the lay impropriations. Tithe in France did not amount to above one-twentieth of the gross produce, and Arthur Young remarked that this charge was proportionately much heavier in England than in France. The whole benefit of the suppression of tithe in France has gone into the pocket of the owner of land, not of the farmer, for rents have risen in the same proportion. It is true that the cultivator is at the same time the owner of the land he cultivates in at least one-third of France.

were worth two and a half millions more. There were then about 17,000 men and 30,000 women in regular orders, so that the average per head was 50*l.* a-year. But, after all, the effects of the seizure and sale of this property are much less important than is commonly imagined. Many of the religious orders have now landed property in France not much inferior in value to what they possessed in 1789; and as for their numbers, it is certain that in 1851 there were in France 29,486 women in religious vows, and several thousands of men.[1]

The value of the lands confiscated from the emigrated nobles was upwards of one hundred millions sterling; and this extent, added to the confiscated domains of the Church and the Crown, amounted to one-third of the whole territory of France. But there was in truth no possibility of disposing, in the then state of the country, of the enormous extent of land thus suddenly thrown

[1] These statements of M. de Lavergne are contested by M. Paul Boitteau, in a curious and instructive volume recently published by him under the title *État de la France en* 1789. M. Boitteau is a far more eager champion of the Revolution than M. de Lavergne, but his book is a careful collection of the statistical records of the time. He estimates the whole income of the French Church in 1789 at ten millions sterling, but we suspect him of exaggeration. Count Montalembert used to say that if France had the law of trusts which exists in England, the disendowed Church of France would be re-endowed by private gifts in half a century.

on the market. The quantity actually sold fetched forty millions sterling; the remainder was restored to the former owners; and, indeed, of the portion sold the larger part found its way back to them. The Restoration allotted forty millions to indemnify the emigrants, and this sum was distributed in 1825. The list of these claims proves how limited the resources of the French landowners really had become before the Revolution. A few names are inscribed for 40,000*l.* and upwards—but a great many for only 40*l.*—and the majority of the compensations paid did not exceed 2,000*l.*; some, indeed, were mere peasants who claimed and got less than one hundred francs. The truth is that the condition of the French landed aristocracy before the Revolution was for the most part pitiable and contemptible. They were the nominal owners of a quarter of the soil of the country, but they were encumbered with debt, destitute of capital, incapable of intelligent enterprise. The higher nobles flocked to the Court to make their way by pensions, places, and court favours; the lower gentry vegetated in their pride and poverty on wretched freeholds, often not bringing in 100*l.* a-year of nett income. It cannot be denied that in a great degree they deserved their fate; though the violence with which their extinction was effected defeated for many years the salutary results which might otherwise have attended a change in the tenure of land throughout France.

The advantages which have resulted from the Revolution to the rural population (except, perhaps, that least honourable class which found means to speculate on the misfortunes of their neighbours), were for a long time doubtful, and always indirect. The same force which tore the noble from his château and sent him to die in exile, tore the peasant from his cabin and sent him and his fellows to die by millions in the armies of the Republic or of the great Emperor.[1] It is false to contend that the regeneration of France could only be wrought by such means. Whatever be the value of the results, they were purchased at an excessive cost, and whatever was most valuable in them might have been attained at no such cost whatever. The period of the lowest depression of France in her rural and popular interests is precisely that when she was covered with military glory and in the full

[1] The ex-director of the conscription under the First Empire, computed the actual loss of men born within the old limits of France and destroyed in the Imperial wars from 1804 to 1815, at 1,700,000. This estimate does not include the wars of the Republic, or the loss of men not born in the kingdom of France.

tide of revolutionary success ; and the evils inseparable from war were greatly aggravated by the stupid legislative prohibitions of the Imperial Government. Thus as late as 1812 a law was passed rendering it penal to speculate in corn, and fixing a maximum price for wheat at thirty-five francs the hectolitre! In 1789 the annual value of the agricultural produce of France was estimated by Lavoisier at about a hundred millions sterling, or rather more than a hundred francs per head of the population of the country at that time. In 1815 the agricultural produce was valued by Chaptal at one hundred and twenty millions, a small increase for a quarter of a century, and one barely in proportion to the increase of the population. This small augmentation of one element of national wealth was more than balanced by the destruction of the foreign and colonial trade.

A few public works, more ostentatious than useful, had been undertaken with great parade by Napoleon. Others were commenced or projected, but without results, as the war devoured all the resources of the country. These exceptional creations of an arbitrary power, glorifying itself in its works, contributed much more, like those of Louis XIV., to the splendour of the sovereign than to the greatness of the nation. France was still, to say the truth, without roads, except some royal highways, without bridges over her rivers, without flourishing ports on her coasts, almost without capital and without men. The frenzy of the Revolution and the ambition of a ruler had successively consumed the greater part of that which the labour of a great people had produced.

In spite of the disasters of a double invasion, peace was no sooner concluded than an immense impulse was given to the resources of France. Since 1815, her foreign trade has quintupled, her manufactures have quadrupled, her agriculture has doubled its produce, under the influence of those three great principles of peace, justice, and freedom, which are the eternal antidote of war, violence, and despotism. Eighty thousand miles of roads have been opened in the country; ten thousand miles of railway have been completed or are now in progress, canals have been made, rivers rendered navigable, ports and docks constructed. The progress of rural economy, especially from 1815 to 1847, kept pace with this great movement, and has not been sensibly thrown back by the unfavourable and extraordinary courses of the last few years, in spite of bad seasons, the potato disease, the vine disease, the mortality of the silkworm, and the disturbed state of the political world. The tenure of land has of course been modified to a considerable extent by the laws of succession established in France, but this change is less rapid and complete than is commonly imagined in England. Taking the area of France at 45,000,000 hectares, M. de Lavergne computes the one-third of the soil is still held by 50,000 large proprietors, possessing an average of 750 acres; another third by 500,000 middling proprietors possessing an average of 75 acres; and the last third by 5,000,000 of small-proprietors possessing an average of 7 acres. This calculation is obviously merely approximative; but it is certain that there are in France 16,000 landowners paying 40*l.* a-year and upwards in land-tax to the State, and about 37,000 landowners paying from 20*l.* to 40*l.*

In the cultivation of the soil it seems that since 1789 about 5,000,000 acres have been added to the productive area of the country; vineyards and orchards and meadows have considerably increased; woods have diminished. In tillage the fallows have decreased by one-half; the growth of wheat, barley, and oats has increased a third; that of rye and the inferior kinds of grain has diminished. Water-meadows have tripled in extent, and the cultivation of roots, which was hardly known in 1789, now covers 5,000,000 acres. But the quality of the crops has risen even more than their extent. The quantity of wheat actually grown has nearly doubled; live stock has also doubled in number and value; the silk crop and the rape oil crop have quintupled. The production of homegrown sugar has come into existence, and the growth of wine has also doubled. From these facts M. de Lavergne concludes that the total value of the agricultural produce of the country exceeds 200,000,000*l.* sterling, or at the rate of about 6*l.* per head of the population. He also infers that rents have risen since 1789 in the proportion of 12 to 30; farmers' profits in the proportion of 5 to 10; outlay in that of 1 to 5; taxes on land and dues have diminished in the proportion of 7 to 5; and labourers' wages have doubled.

The subdivision of the French territory into eighty-six departments, which was preceded by the establishment under the old French monarchy of thirty-one 'generalities,' each governed by an Intendant named by the Crown, and even the prodigious political changes of which that country has been for eighty years the theatre, have not obliterated the ancient provincial landmarks of the realm. The old names of Normandy, Brittany, Burgundy, Flanders, and Provence, insensibly recur when we have to speak of the rural life and national character of these regions, for these divisions are indelibly rooted in the soil; and even the lesser provincial districts of Artois, Le Maine, Berri,

La Sologne, Perigord, &c. may still be traced in the language or manners of the inhabitants and in the produce of the land. For the purposes of his work, M. de Lavergne, not unmindful of these ancient and natural internal boundaries of the provinces, has grouped them in six large divisions, through which he successively conducts the reader. Our limits forbid us to accompany him in this tour of France, but we shall extract some pages, beginning with the north-eastern district, in which he includes the provinces of Flanders, Artois, Picardy, Normandy, and the Isle of France, now forming fifteen departments, less favoured by climate than many other parts of the empire, but by far the most prosperous, wealthy, and civilised part of the country. For these fifteen departments, being one-sixth of the realm in extent, contain 9,000,000 of inhabitants, or a quarter of the population, and these 9,000,000 inhabitants pay nearly 28,000,000*l.* sterling in taxes to the public treasury, exclusive of local dues and rates. It is true that the Departments of the Seine and Paris itself are included in this calculation.

The Department of the North, which opens the ball, is the best cultivated country in France, and one of the best cultivated in the world. I only know the counties of Leicester and Warwick in England, and Hainault in Belgium, which can be compared to it. The average produce of the land over the whole area of the department is 300 fr. a hectare (about 5*l.* an acre), which, deducting the woods and other less profitable parts, gives 450 fr. the hectare of tillage, which is three times the average production of France. The population is at the rate of 213 inhabitants per 100 hectares. If the whole of France were as densely peopled it would contain thrice its present population.

In the sort of microcosm of Europe which is to be found in France, the department of the North represents the Low Countries. The drained marshes near Dunkirk resemble those of Holland; the rest of the country is a continuation of Belgium. The country is generally flat; the climate damp and foggy. The stratum of arable land, a mixture of clay and sand with a calcareous subsoil, is deep and rich; in some places too sandy, in others marshy; but these drawbacks have been corrected by active industry. It would seem that these dark and dreary regions, where water is for ever permeating the air and the soil, are the best adapted to the growth of the human race, since it is always in them that population reaches its maximum.

Such as it is, the agriculture of Flanders has no rival, or at least no superior. Notwithstanding the wealth continually raised by it, the fertility of the land still increases. The reason is that the domestic animals take a large share in this splendid development of life. The Flemish cart-horses are well known. The Flemish cows are some of the best milkers known; this department contains 200,000 of them. Sheep are not numerous, but enormous. Pigs, poultry, and the domestic animals, all in the same proportion.

This multitude of animals produce immense quantities of manure. But the Flemish farmers are not satisfied with this class of manure only: they use the sweepings of the streets, the residue of the oil mills, bones, sea sand, and especially one peculiar sort of application, which no other people prepare and use with equal skill—I mean nightsoil. This manure, which is rejected with disgust by many countries, and especially by the English (who are beginning to think better of it), is a most powerful fertilising element, and to waste it is to throw away a vast amount of wealth. This manure has enabled the Flemish farmers to extend their exhausting crops, without impairing the fertility of their land, and to exceed even the English in productive power. Whilst England devotes three-quarters of her area to the grazing of cattle, Flanders employs only one quarter; yet she has in proportion a larger head of stock: the difference is made up by the application of nightsoil.

This magnificent cultivation is probably the oldest of the kind in Europe, for it was in full activity in 1776, and it was described with enthusiasm by Arthur Young in 1789. Flanders had in fact nothing in common with France, to which it had been comparatively recently annexed, and Arthur Young remarked that the old boundary of the province and the kingdom might still be traced in his time by the good and bad farming.

One highly important element of agricultural prosperity has, however, been added to the province since 1789, which is less familiar to our English readers :—

In the first class of these productions must be ranked one created in the present century, and which takes rank as the finest agricultural conquest of our age,—beet-root sugar. The invention was made in Prussia, and in 1799 a chemist at Berlin had produced some native-grown loaves of sugar. In 1809, during the war, it was introduced into France; the peace of 1815, by reopening the colonial trade, gave it a check, but it has ever since gone on to improve. Of 350 manufactories of home-grown sugar in France, 150 are in the Department of the North.

It might be apprehended, at first, that the production of beet-root sugar would be injurious to the production of meat and corn, by employing and exhausting the best lands. But this apprehension turns out to be unfounded, at least in well-cultivated districts. It is now demonstrated that the manufacture of sugar not only creates a new source of profit, but also augments the other produce of the soil. The extraction of saccharine matter from the root only takes away a portion of its substance; the pulp and the leaves are excellent fodder for cattle, and the profits of the sugar-houses cover the expense of abundant artificial manures. In 1853 the city of Valenciennes, which is the chief seat of this trade, inscribed on a triumphal arch these words :—

'*Growth of corn in the district before the introduction of sugar-works*, 353,000 *hectolitres; head of cattle*, 700. *Since the introduction of sugar-works—corn*, 421,000 *hectolitres; cattle*, 11,500 *head.*'

This piece of statistics may admit of a reply, inasmuch as it is not certain that the increase of corn and cattle would not have been still greater in forty years if the Flemish farmers had applied themselves to those objects exclusively. The English do not grow sugar, but the happy alternation of beef and bread, by the commixture of pasturage and tillage, has also made immense progress in England. In any case, however, this department succeeds, by the extent of its manures, in cultivating 20,000 hectares of beet-root, each hectare bringing in 40*l*., 80*l*., or 120*l*. of gross return. No other crop produces so much in the same area. It is the highest exploit of our rural industry. By dint of a careful choice of seeds, artificial varieties of the beet-root have been created, which produce far more sugar than the old kinds. The famous principle of *selection* may thus be applied to plants as well as to animals, and extend to unknown limits the victories of man over nature.

Oleaginous seeds, rape and others, cover about 20,000 hectares, flax 10,000, giving on an average 40*l.* the hectare ; some flax lands have returned as much as 200*l.*, and even 240*l.* a hectare. The growth of corn per acre is equal to that of England. In the districts of Lille and Valenciennes the average rent of land is at least 150 fr. the hectare (2*l.* 10*s.* an acre); in those of Dunkirk, Hagebrouck, Cambrai, and Douai, 100 fr. Besides sugar, the country has other lucrative rural manufactures, such as the preparation of potato starch, breweries, oil mills, and distilleries. During the late scarcity the Government prohibited distilling from grain,—a measure to be regretted, since the more numerous are the purposes to which corn crops can be applied, the more profitable it is to grow them, and the more will be grown.

Unhappily the highly profitable (small) culture has a radical defect which restores the balance in favour of the English system of husbandry—the excess of the rural population. In spite of these resources of manufactures and trade, those who live by husbandry alone form about half the population, at a ratio of 100 per 100 hectares, which is more than in any other country except perhaps in China. This superabundance of hands is not a necessary consequence of small farming, but it is the natural tendency of it. If Flanders produces more than England in proportion to its extent, it produces only half as much in proportion to its population. There are nowhere so many paupers as in this rich and fertile country. The city of Lille is deplorably distinguished by the fact that *one-third* of its inhabitants are assisted by public charity; and in many of the rural townships the proportion is equally great. This curse of pauperism materially diminishes the splendour of these finely cultivated districts.

M. de Lavergne's testimony on this last point is

the more valuable as he is, upon the whole, a strong advocate for small farms and the subdivision of land, when not carried to excess. But the truth is that the relative merits of small and large occupations depend very much on the nature of the soil and produce. In the mountainous regions of the Jura, of the Doubs, and the Vosges, results have been attained by the cottier system which would probably have been impossible on a large estate. In the Vosges especially, the intelligent reforms introduced fifty years ago by the good Pastor Oberlin in the Ban de la Roche, and imitated by an equally virtuous Catholic priest at Gérardmer, have proved in the highest degree beneficial to the pastoral and industrious population. But in the great plains and valleys under tillage, M. de Lavergne himself quotes numerous examples of farms of from 300 to 600 acres, as the best examples of rural economy in France.

The best test of the success of the cultivation and manufacture of beet-root sugar in France is the contest which the home-grown root has carried on against the cane-grown sugar of the French colonies. In 1830 the whole production of beet-root sugar was ten millions of kilos; in 1840 it had risen to forty millions : but during this period colonial sugar was heavily taxed and home-grown sugar free of duty. The colonies loudly demanded equal freedom or equal protection. A graduated duty was put on beet-root sugar, and in 1847 the two sugars were equally taxed. The question excited the liveliest interest at the time, and amongst the pamphlets written upon it was one entitled 'Analyse de la Question des Sucres, par Louis-Napoléon Bonaparte; Fort du Ham, août 1842.' The revolution of 1848 was followed by the abolition of slavery in the French sugar colonies, and the farmers of Flanders derived no small advantage from the check thus given to their tropical competitors; for the equality of the tax operated unjustly upon the unequal conditions of the rival producers. It was no longer the beet-root sugar growers who required protection against the colonial interest, but the colonial interest which required protection against beet-root sugar. In spite of the inferiority of climate and of the raw material, the industry, the capital, and the science of France produced sugar on terms more advantageous to the consumer than the West Indian planter with his rude agriculture and his scanty means. By the law of 1860 the duty on colonial sugar was fixed for some years somewhat below the rate of duty on home-grown sugar, but the beet-root sugar grower holds his ground; and there is reason to believe that he will continue to prosper, even though the French colonies are fast recovering more than their former productive power, and the French market should be opened ere long, like our own, to the sugar of the world. These are the facts which justify M. de Lavergne in asserting that to the farmers of Northern France beet-root sugar has really been the finest agricultural conquest of our age.

It is a remarkable peculiarity of France that some of the largest estates and the most important farming establishments are in the neighbourhood of Paris. The 'Isle of France,' as it was called before the Revolution, contained the most magnificent endowments of the great abbeys of the capital, some of them dating from the reign of Charlemagne, and in passing into secular hands the traditions of these great ecclesiastical estates have not been entirely lost.

Large fortunes have at all times been made by agriculture in the neighbourhood of Paris, but more especially in the last half century. Some of the farmers have their million of francs, many more their 20,000*l.* or 30,000*l.* Farming is here an art, employing large capitals and returning large profits, especially in that district called FRANCE *par excellence*, because it formed part of the original domain of Hugh Capet. Large estates are here also less divided.

More than 3,000 of the rural assessments exceed 1,000 fr., and there are many landowners having from 2,000*l.* to 4,000*l.* a-year.

The Duc de Luynes is said to have 40,000*l.* a-year in land, chiefly in this district. The estate of Ferrières, near Ligny, now belonging to Baron Rothschild, contains 7,500 acres, the park alone 1,000. Estates of from 1,250 to 3,000 acres are tolerably numerous, especially in Seine-et-Marne, one of the departments of France in which land is least divided. The two aristocracies of birth and of fortune have, at all times, sought to hold large possessions in the environs of Paris, and in spite of revolutions they have succeeded. Most of these estates have changed hands, without much subdivision.

In many of these properties clustering round the royal domains of Versailles, St. Germain, St. Cloud, Meudon, Rambouillet, and Fontainebleau, agriculture has long been held in high honour. Thus, near Rozay en Brie, thirteen leagues from Paris, stands the Château de la Grange, rendered illustrious by the long residence of General Lafayette. The course of events is so mutable that the conduct of public men is open to the most opposite opinions; and different judgments may be formed of the political influence of Lafayette; but no one will contest the nobleness and dignity of his life. On quitting his glorious prison of Olmütz, he took up his residence at La Grange in 1801, and remained there throughout the Empire and the Restoration. The château is a massive building, flanked with five large towers, and surrounded by a park of 150 acres, half grass and half wood; the farm consisted of 500 acres of arable land. There it was that Lafayette, surrounded by his family and his friends, long presented that noble and dignified spectacle, so rare in France, but so common in England and America, of a great public man cultivating his own fields. Like his friend Washington, Lafayette was fond of agriculture, and practised it with success. He contributed notably to propagate the race of merino sheep in the province of Brie.

To this example might be added another of more

recent date. Since the Revolution of 1848, M. Guizot has resided almost continually in the old Augustine monastery of Val Richer in Normandy, which he purchased twenty-five years ago, and the adjacent farms, under the skilful management of his son-in-law, are a model of drainage and dairy farming to the whole country. To speak more generally, the revolutions which have made the most eminent men in France strangers to the contests of the capital and to the seats of ministerial or parliamentary power, have thrown their energy back on country life, and have powerfully contributed to the beneficial change we remark in the rural economy of the whole nation.

The great stream of the Loire, taking its rise to the east of the volcanic mountains of central France, and bending in a mighty curve of five hundred miles till it reaches the Atlantic, may be said at once to divide the northern regions of France from the southern, and the east from the west. From its central course, from its vast extent, from the fertility of the valley which it waters, and from the historical associations crowded on its banks, the Loire is the great artery of France. It was there that in the secular contest of the kings of France with the armies of English yeomen, the monarchy took refuge, and the first exploit of Joan of Arc was the relief of Orleans. Louis XI. passed the greater part of his gloomy life among the pleasant vineyards of Touraine. Charles VIII. was born and died at Amboise; Louis XII. lived at Blois, and that stately palace, once the scene of the splendour, the policy, and the crimes of the House of Valois, was not deserted until after the Wars of the League. The presence of the Court and the generous soil and temperate climate of the country, had raised it, even in those troubled ages, to extraordinary prosperity. The city of Tours, in which St. Martin had reared, ages before, the ensign of Christian civilisation, and which at one time disputed with Paris the first rank in France, had formerly twice as many inhabitants as it now possesses. The banks of the river were crowded with country residences, which still retain abundant traces of the Italian taste introduced into France by the Medicis, and which modern fashion has within the last few years magnificently restored to more than their former luxury. Here, as elsewhere, the Revolution committed acts of devastation and vandalism which sixty years have not entirely effaced; but one of the most gracious acts of the French nation to the Bourbons was the purchase of the

Château de Chambord for the Duc de Bordeaux, though it has served only to give a title taken from the banks of the Loire to another Pretender. If country life is to be found anywhere in France, as we understand it in England, it is on the banks of the Loire, partly on the vine-clad slopes of Touraine, partly in the more remote departments of the west, where the habits and pursuits of the gentry as well as of the peasantry are exclusively agricultural. We shall leave M. de Lavergne to speak of the cultivation of this interesting region :—

The Valley of the Loire is deservedly considered one of the finest parts of Europe. From Orleans to the sea, for a distance of about 100 leagues, a long plain of alluvial soil extends, conquered from the stream by the hand of man, and not unfrequently invaded by the stream from which it was conquered. These lands, of exuberant fertility, have been seized upon, as is always the case in similar instances, by the small proprietors: more and more subdivided into narrow allotments, they fetch as much as 400*l.* the hectare (160*l.* an acre), and present a complete spectacle ot garden cultivation. A whole people of small farmers, who dispose of their produce in the towns adjacent to the river, inhabit a string of villages and cottages on the slopes of the valley, and even on the banks of the stream, protected by dams which are as old as Charlemagne. In ordinary times the Loire drags its idle waters along its sands, or at least, when swollen by rains, respects the dykes which enclose it. Occasionally, however, the river rises to excess, bursts or surmounts the artificial barriers, sweeping away harvests and habitations : but the soil is so productive and the climate so mild, the small farmers are so persevering, and the market so good, that no sooner have the waters retired than the luckless victims set to work again, and the damage is soon effaced.

If the plain of the Loire offers this fine range of cultivation, her chalky cliffs are not less covered with vines. The vineyards of the Loire cover an extent of 250,000 acres, nearly equally divided between the two banks. Rabelais, who was himself a 'Tourangeau' (native of Touraine), boasted of the light wines of his native soil. The annual produce amounts to 2,000,000 hectolitres, chiefly drunk in the country, though some of it makes excellent vinegar for exportation. Vineyards as well as plains are infinitely subdivided. The vinedressers hollow out their dwellings and their cellars in the soft, chalky rock which grows their vines, and when the year is favourable and the liquor good, they live happily in these humble earths. Paul Louis Courier was born amongst these people, and affected the name of 'Vigneron' in his writings; not wrongly, for the name belongs to one of the most democratic sections of the French population. A very small plot of ground, planted with vines, supplies occupation and a competency to a whole family.

To these literary recollections M. de Lavergne might have added that Béranger retired during one of the happiest periods of his life to a cottage on the banks of the Loire, and that some of his most pleasing letters and most cheerful songs were dated from 'La Grenadière.'

The old provinces of Maine and Anjou, which also belong to the western region of the Loire, are now superior to Touraine in point of farming, and rank amongst the most improving departments of

France—especially that of La Sarthe, renowned alike for its poultry and its hemp. But the agricultural progress of this district is closely connected with its political history. It borders on the Bocage and it was the scene of the Vendean wars. In no part of France before the Revolution of 1789 were the relations of the nobles and the peasantry so friendly. In no part of France was the Revolution so ill-received. At the first levy of the conscription the people rose, together with their lords, in defence of the throne and the altar; and it was only by a war of extermination that their resistance was overcome. Indeed, their spirit remained unbroken by the military triumphs of the Empire; and in 1815, the Vendean country gentleman had little change to complain of beyond the sufferings and losses inflicted on himself and on his dependants by that terrific contest. The weapons which have really changed La Vendée are not those of war, but of peace. During the reign of Louis Philippe, roads were cut through inaccessible districts, the market was opened, agricultural produce has risen incalculably in price, the application of lime-dressing to the soil has enabled the farmer to grow wheat instead of rye, four-course husbandry has made its appearance, water-meadows have been introduced with the greatest success in that moist and mild climate, and the Durham breed of cattle has effectually taken root in the country. The proprietors of the soil of Maine and Anjou are principally small resident country gentlemen, farming their own land in conjunction with the peasantry; and M. de Lavergne assures us that, if such a thing as a true French country gentleman can be said to exist, it is here we must look for him; indeed, he goes so far as to add that a Yorkshire squire would here find himself not entirely out of his own latitude. We are convinced that, although agriculturists have fewer opportunities of exchanging their feelings and opinions with those of foreign countries, there is at bottom a genuine interest and sympathy between men in different countries who are engaged in the same noble and honourable pursuits; and we would wish for no better proof of it than the reception given a short time ago by a party of Essex farmers to the Marquis de Vogüé, a great Legitimist nobleman and farmer of France, who came to England for the express purpose of joining one of our agricultural meetings in that county—an event which would certainly have appeared impossible to preceding generations of farmers both in his country and in our own.

In endeavouring to trace the progress of the

agriculture of France, we are embarrassed by the incalculable variety of the products of a soil and climate which include in the same territory all the temperate zones of Europe. We have seen in French Flanders the combination of the careful tillage of the Low Countries; on the eastern frontier, the Vosges, the Jura, and the Alps remind us of the magnificent pastures of Switzerland and the industrious dalesmen of the Black Forest; to the north, in Normandy, we find a reflection of the southern and midland counties of England, large dairy farms, a fine breed of horses, and a peasantry still retaining the shrewdness and strength of their northern descent; farther to the west, the Celtic population of Brittany, inhabiting a granite-bound coast, which owes whatever fertility it possesses to the mild breezes of the ocean, rear an immense head of cattle, compensating in some degree for the imperfect tillage of the soil. But when we reach the south-western and south-eastern regions, in a warmer latitude, the value and variety of the products of the soil become far greater.

Saintonge and the Angoumois have been for centuries the seat of the great brandy distilleries, which, in spite of imitations, give Cognac a monopoly in the world. In good years the brandies produced from these districts are worth three millions sterling, and as the greater part of them are exported, Henry IV. might well call the Charente 'le plus beau fossé de mon royaume.' In these climates every kind of vegetation contributes in different ways to the agricultural wealth of the country—the chestnut produces an abundant esculent crop—the walnut-tree is so valuable that one-third of the oil made in France is prepared from it and rivals the produce of the olive groves, whose grey foliage fringes the bare and burning rocks of Provence. In the valley of the Garonne, the plum trees alone produce a crop of prodigious amount, known all over the world as the 'French Plums' of our desserts: and indeed throughout the South of France, and even in the mountains of Auvergne, the preparation of dried fruits is an important branch of culture and of trade. The mulberry-tree and the vine cover the plains of Languedoc, and as we approach the ancient seats of Roman power at Arles, and of Papal dominion at Avignon, the agriculture, as well as the majestic ruins of those ages, remind us that we are on the confines of Italy.

Everything here becomes Italian; the climate, the crops, the associations of the past, the manners of the people, and almost their language. Near us is Nîmes, that Rome of the Gauls, whose monuments are better preserved than those of Rome herself. Before us is Arles, inhabited by Constantine, and once destined, it is said, to become the capital of his empire. An immense arena, ancient theatres, magnificent aqueducts, attest, on every side, the power of Rome. If from antiquity we pass to the Middle Ages, we encounter at Avignon the greatest institution of Italy and the world, the Papacy; and in earlier times still that Court of Provence which was the harbinger of Italian taste, and the home of troubadours who preceded Dante and Petrarch.

The greater part of the Department of Vaucluse was Papal soil down to the Revolution. Its agricultural prosperity, which is second to scarcely any part of France, is due to one word—irrigation. The crops of Lombardy are justly lauded: the county of Avignon is not less prolific, and for the same reason. The Pontifical Government early introduced the Italian method of distributing water. One of the streams which serve to fertilise the plain in its myriad channels is the Sorgia, springing from the Fountain of Vaucluse, not more celebrated in poetry than for the abundance and utility of its inexhaustible waters.

The olive-tree begins to appear at Montelimart, and increases as we proceed towards the south. But the mulberry becomes more rare. Indeed, although attempts have been made to cultivate the mulberry for the silkworm in many parts of southern France, the production is not entirely successful except in the Cevennes, more especially in the districts of Alais and Uzès in the Department of the Gard and of Argentière and Privas in the Ardèche. The mulberry-tree, to produce an abundance of nutritive leaves at the proper season, requires a cool soil under a brilliant sky: the silkworm requires throughout the months of May and June warmth and pure air. Both the tree and the caterpillar require an infinite amount of delicate precautions, which are only to be obtained from a population long trained to this peculiar operation. But the value of the produce and the value of the land combining these conditions is enormous. Plantations of mulberry-trees have been sold for 600*l.* an acre, and the silk crop of France down to 1853 had reached the value of four millions sterling. In 1854 one of those mysterious diseases which attack the very sources of production began to affect the silkworm. The loss has been at least three-quarters of the crop in France, and as yet no effectual discovery has been made of the cause or the remedy of the evil.

The whole territory of France does not exhibit in an equal degree the signs of agricultural improvement to which we have adverted, and the high table lands or mountain ranges of the central departments, frequently crossed by English travellers on their road to Switzerland and Italy, afford the least favourable aspect of what may in more favoured regions be called 'la belle France.' Yet even here something has been done to reclaim the desolate heaths, and to convert the sandy tracks into roads. Fifty years ago people used to say that the land in La Sologne was worth three livres an acre, *if there was a hare upon it.* Now the large estates of that district are under cultivation. The Emperor himself built a sort of farm-château, where he watched the progress of the works he had ordered: and possibly the interest he takes in that district may have been heightened by the fact that it was the original residence of the Beauharnais family. In the character and composition of that singular man, the blood of the Beauharnais flows as near the heart as the blood of the Bonapartes. There is too, it must be acknowledged, a picturesque charm in those rural districts which modern improvement has not squared and levelled and embellished. Rural life as it existed half a century back was a true picture of the oldest existing state of manners and the most primitive state of civilisation. It has been remarked by a recent traveller in modern Greece, that although you may seek in vain for the gods and heroes, the warriors and orators, of the mythological and historical ages of the Greek commonwealths, the old man with his ass and his faggot—the eagle and the tortoise—and a thousand other unchanged rural traditions still present the living reality of Æsop's fables. M. de Lavergne makes the same remark on the primitive districts of central France.

Berri is the heart of France. It was there that in the English wars the expiring nationality of France took refuge. Charles VII. was at one time only king of Bruges; and to this day no province retains so much of the stamp of ancient France. The manners, the dialect, the accent of the people are those of the seventeenth century. Except on the line of the principal roads, the towns retain the calm and monotonous air of the old *bourgeoisie;* the rural districts still resemble the imperishable picture drawn by La Fontaine of rural France in his day. The shepherd still leads his flock; the housewife still plies her distaff; the woodman brings back his faggot; the horse and the ox are in the same meadow; nature in all her wildness still skirts the cultivated lands; the heron stalks beside the streams; the hare and the frogs, the rabbit and the weasel, are all there; with the fox robbing the poultry-yard and the wolf robbing the fold. This region, half a desert and half cultivated, which lives and speaks by the imagination of the fabulist, has lost nothing of its old aspect. At the corner of a field and a common one might still fancy that ancient colloquy of the wolf and the dog; and the breeze which sweeps over the mere still repeats the dialogue of the oak and the bulrush. This mixture of civilisation and solitude, which takes us back two centuries, cannot last much longer; the wolf, especially, is quite out of date. But these destructive animals still abound in the east and the centre of France, and the sums they cost, partly from the sheep they kill, and partly from the fences and watchers required to preserve the flocks, are enormous.

It is evident that these results of agricultural improvement, which have already doubled the wealth and prosperity of the French people, are due in the first place to the maintenance of peace. They have not acted with equal intensity upon the growth of the population; and it was demonstrated by the last census of the Empire, in 1856, that the augmentation of the population in the rural districts has been incredibly slow and small. In fact throughout France hands are wanting to the thorough cultivation of the country; and as the introduction of farming machinery to do the work of hands can only be the result of time, the value of the peasant-labour absorbed by the military conscription, at the rate of 100,000 able-bodied men per annum, is a heavy loss to the country, and a burden which falls with especial weight on the rural districts. This evil must, of course, be incalculably augmented by any interruption of the peace of Europe; and it may be confidently asserted that France gains much more in all that really constitutes the power and wealth of a nation by devoting her whole strength to the improvement of her internal resources, than she could do by the conquest of the most coveted provinces of neighbouring States. The Imperial Government owed everything to the peasantry of France; and the only political principle to which the Emperor can fairly lay claim, is his theory, not fully confirmed by experience, that a government based ·on the firm support of the masses of the agricultural population can hold its ground, not only against the revolutionary passions of the great towns, but even against the great majority of the educated classes. The peasantry are precisely the class which has most to lose and least to gain by war. The army itself, which is dreaded by some politicians, as a formidable engine for the disruption of Europe, is in reality little more than the peasantry trained to arms; and nine-tenths of these conscripts and soldiers have no higher ambition than to fall back, at the expiration of their term of service, upon the villages and homesteads in which their lives are to be happily and usefully spent.

Of all the measures which the Emperor Napoleon, in his full possession of unlimited power, thought fit to adopt, by far the wisest for his dynasty and the best for the country were those calculated to ameliorate the condition of the rural districts. He said with truth to the peasants of the Allier, that the improvement of the country was a more useful and important work than the transformation of great cities. And, upon the whole, his measures for this purpose were well

conceived. He had learned that the interference
of the Government by way of protection is
rather mischievous than beneficial; he abolished
the sliding scale of import and export duties on
corn; he opened markets by the expansion of
roads at home and by treaties of commerce with
foreign countries; and he evinced an active and
intelligent solicitude for these, the first, interests
of the country. It would be unjust to preceding
Governments, and especially to that of King Louis
Philippe, not to add that the same path was trodden
with no mean success by the ministers of that reign;
and that the vast material improvement in the condition of France is the fruit of measures commenced
under the constitutional monarchy, momentarily arrested by the convulsions of 1848, and vigorously
continued and enlarged by Napoleon III. Whatever
may be the opinions we entertain of the political
institutions of the Second Empire, on the ground
of material improvements it is absurd to deny that
the Emperor rendered great services to France—
services indeed so great that one of the charges
brought against him by his uncompromising opponents is, that these benefits caused the nation
to forget even that loss of freedom by which they

have been purchased. However this may be, nothing is more certain than that the policy which enriched the rural districts and rebuilt the towns of France—which is doubling her agricultural produce, and has more than doubled her foreign trade—was irreconcilably opposed to the policy of aggression and war.

We have dwelt with pleasure on these indications of the agricultural progress of France, because they afford the strongest contrast and the most powerful counterpoise to the revolutionary passions and principles which are described in other pages of these volumes. Under the reign of the Emperor Napoleon III., that portion of the Imperial policy which regarded the rural population was pacific, progressive, and in some respects liberal; but it was diametrically opposed to the policy represented by the great towns and by the spirit of the Revolution, which tended to communism, insurrection, and war. The conflict between these two elements of his system of government proved fatal to its permanence. The rural population were sacrificed to the towns: the conservative to the revolutionary party; the interests of peace to the desperate chances of war. We have seen the result: for the French nation had in reality given pledges to peace, greater than they were perhaps themselves aware of ; and all the true interests of the country have suffered from hostilities with a powerful enemy, in exact proportion to the prosperity they had previously attained, and the yet more brilliant promises of the future.

FRANCE IN 1870.

FRANCE IN 1870.[1]

THE French Revolution has been, for a period of eighty years, the admiration, the terror, and the wonder of the world. The wisest statesmen, the most eloquent writers, have exhausted the powers of thought and language in the attempt to examine its causes, to describe its progress, and to discover its consequences. Burke, Madame de Staël, and Joseph de Maistre were amongst the first and greatest prophets of this new order of things—prophets of evil as well as of good, conscious that the powers and the wrongs of former times were swept away as by a deluge, but incapable of discerning the ultimate results of the changes they witnessed and foretold. Three generations have passed across the stage of human affairs, but the problem is still unsolved.

[1] This article was published in the *Edinburgh Review* on the 15th January 1871. The following books were reviewed:—
1. *La France nouvelle.* Par M. Prévost-Paradol. 8vo. Paris: 1869. 2. *Histoire des Classes rurales en France et de leurs progrès dans l'Égalité civile et la Propriété.* Par Henri Doniol. Seconde édition. 8vo. Paris: 1867. 3. *Monsieur Guizot à Messieurs les Membres du Gouvernement de la Défense nationale.* Lisieux: 1ᵉʳ décembre 1870.

France has not reached that haven of freedom, good government, and peace which has been the object of so many virtuous aspirations and of so many fierce convulsions. Five dynasties of emperors or kings, and two or three republics have successively been proclaimed, accepted, abandoned, and overthrown within living memory. And, at last, we ourselves, in this our time, are witnesses of the most portentous and disastrous of this long series of calamities. The events passing before our eyes— the total momentary extinction of government in France—the occupation of a large portion of her territory by the forces of a triumphant invader—the annihilation of her armies, which reduced the war to a struggle between a highly organised force and an undisciplined people—the captivity of him who was her supreme ruler, of her marshals, and of her whole military staff—the reduction by famine of impregnable cities and arsenals—the disintegration of several parts of the realm—the unutterable confusion or collapse of her national resources—the strange but total absence of men of high character and authority to deal with events of such unparalleled magnitude—are phenomena which will never cease to occupy the philosopher and historian as long as the world endures. These too are incidents in the great tragedy which commenced in 1789. These are at once the results of former revolutions and the causes of future perturbations. And if it be possible to divert our gaze from the startling occurrences which mark every hour of so great and terrible a spectacle, we would endeavour to take a more comprehensive survey of this vast course of events, and to trace in the operation of the revolutionary principles which were let loose eighty years ago in France the true source of the present social, political, and military condition of that gallant but unfortunate people.

The Revolution of 1789 undoubtedly swept away abuses which had become intolerable—the feudal tenure of land, the privileges of the nobility, the prodigality and arbitrary power of the Court, the corruptions of an opulent and intolerant Church; nor do we think that the destruction of these secular evils was paid for at too high a price, great as that price was. The Revolution was unjustly accused by its enemies and detractors of having overthrown institutions necessary to the welfare, perhaps even to the existence, of society. The accusation was unjust, because these institutions perished, not so much by the attacks of the Revolution, as by their own vices and weakness: they were rotten before they fell : it was time they should be hewn down and cast into the fire. Nothing could save them, for they could not save themselves. The question we ask relates, therefore, not to what the Revolution destroyed, but to what it has created—not to what it overthrew, but to what it has established. When the work of reconstruction commenced, it was found that the spoliation of the Church and of the great landed proprietors, whose estates had been forced upon the market at a time when there was no money to pay for them, had called into being an immense class of peasant proprietors, whose small holdings have since been further subdivided by the operation of the Civil Code. It was found that the traditions of hereditary monarchy had received a mortal blow, and that in a country which has never sincerely accepted republican institutions, the succession to the throne has nevertheless in fact become elective. It was found that the aristocracy, deprived of the support and favour of the Court, had no station or authority in the land, but was rather an object of jealousy and hatred. It was found that the destruction of the endowed Church had thrown the functions of the clergy into the hands of a poor and illiterate body of peasant priests, and that the influence of faith and morality had been weakened in proportion to the weakness and incapacity of their representatives in the education of the people. Such were the chief elements of the new social life of the French nation. These elements were successively grasped by military genius which wrung from France the blood of generations, and left her at last exhausted and defeated. They were wrought upon by an unscrupulous and mendacious press; by secret combinations hostile to every established government; by the passion of equality, which means the hatred of rank; by visionary schemes opposed to the laws of property: until by these various causes the national condition of France has become that of a pure social democracy, based, not on the principles of the American constitution of society, but on the destruction of the principal institutions which had hitherto subsisted in European communities.

The question we desire to ask ourselves is, whether this striking change has contributed in the last resort to the power, freedom, and prosperity of France? or whether, on the contrary, the tremendous array of calamities which have fallen upon her may not be traced to causes inherent in her revolutionary career. In the whole range of modern history, no country has been suddenly brought so near to actual dissolution; no modern armies have ever before been sent wholesale into a Babylonian captivity; no capital of the first rank has seen itself beleaguered by countless enemies, relying for its defence on nothing but the spirit of its own citizens, and exposed to all the horrors of famine and war. Wars and sieges conducted on such a scale remind us of nothing more near to ourselves than the incursions of the barbarians, or the capture of Jerusalem and of Constantinople. Sudden and unexpected as these results are, even by those who have brought them to pass, the causes of them must lie deep. No nation could at once have fallen from such a height to such a depth if it had not contained within itself some disease, gnawing its most vital parts. No doubt the Imperial Government of the last twenty years bears with justice the immediate responsibility. The Emperor and his Ministers declared war on a frivolous pretext without any means of carrying it on; they deceived the country, and were themselves deceived, in taking credit for resources which their own folly and prodigality had wasted and consumed; and they left France in her hour of utmost need stripped of every rag of authority and cohesion. But the Imperial Government itself was the offspring of the Revolution. It received, not many months ago, a renewed vote of confidence from seven millions of the people. It was the type of a government created by universal suffrage, and irresponsible by virtue of the power which had called it into being. It was, as the late Duc de Broglie said of it with bitterness not long after the *coup d'état* which had sent him to Mazas, ' the government which the lower classes desired and the upper classes deserved.' Detestable as we conceive such a government to be, it had a basis in the revolutionary theory ; and until its effects were laid bare by the frightful results of its own incapacity and weakness, it seemed so strong that no other form of government could contend with any semblance of success against it. It continued to the last to prostitute authority, to pervert the judgment of the people, to exclude from office every man of independent character and merit, and to pretend to a strength which it did not possess, for nothing is in truth so weak as absolutism or so timorous as personal power. But nevertheless it was the chosen government of democratic France, and especially of that portion of the French democracy, the peasantry, which, though narrow-minded, ignorant, and easily duped, is incomparably more honest and attached to the cause of peace and order than the democracy of the large towns. This con sideration, therefore, brings us one step nearer to the root of the matter. The fatal consequences of the present war, and the revolution attending it, are attributable to the Government of the Empire; but the Government of the Empire was upheld to the last by the votes and confidence of the dominant power in the French nation. Be it from ignorance, be it from corruption, be it from passion, that these evils have sprung, it is to the constituent body, the only true source of power, that we must look for the source of them. It was the pleasure of the French democracy to be governed absolutely. They dreaded and abhorred a more liberal form of government, as tending to anarchy. Experience had taught them the cost of one variety of revolutionary licence; they rushed with indiscriminating vehemence into the other extreme; but that too has thrown them into anarchy and completed the circle of misfortune. 'Un popolo uso a vivere sotto un principe,' says Machiavelli, 'se per qualche accidente diventa libero, con difficoltà mantiene la libertà;' and quoting in the next chapter the example of Rome, he adds, 'Il che nacque da quella corruzione che le parti Mariane avevano messa nel popolo, delle quali essendo capo Cesare, potette accecare quella moltitudine ch' ella non conobbe il giogo che da se medesima si metteva in sul collo.'[1] The inference we draw from these facts is that the dominant power of the French nation has been misplaced by the Revolution, and misdirected by universal suffrage; that the classes invested with the franchise were incapable of discerning their true interests; and that the classes by whom the government of the country might have been safely carried on were paralysed and proscribed by numbers. It may be worth while to trace the operation of these causes in greater detail.

Before we proceed, however, to this part of our task, we pause for a moment to point out the striking contrast to the institutions and social condition of France which is to be found in the institutions and social condition of her victorious adversary. The counterpart is complete. If France is the representative of the most advanced form of European democracy, Prussia is the representative of monarchy in its most complete modern organisation. The King of Prussia is not a tyrant or an autocrat, for he governs in strict accordance with the laws of his kingdom; but the law itself emanates for the most part from the royal authority. The Royal House

[1] Discorsi sopra Livio, i. 16, 17.

of Prussia is the impersonation of the State and the central force of the nation. For two centuries that family has had the good fortune to produce a series of princes, many of them able and brave, some of them great, but all following with exact uniformity the principles of government, of policy, and of war which have raised their kingdom to its present. eminence. They have had the talent and good sense to place themselves at the head of the cause of progress, and though by no means 'liberal' in the sense of a readiness to relinquish any portion of their own regal authority, they have not been slow to adopt every improvement and reform which could increase their own power and ameliorate the condition of the people. In peace and in war they have served their country with extraordinary zeal and energy. In their hands monarchy has never been suffered to degenerate into a thing of empty pageants, luxurious indulgences, or ceremonial forms. It stands erect because it is real.

The constitution of the aristocracy in Germany, and especially in Prussia, has never enabled it to exercise a preponderating independent influence in the State. But it has retained, even now, a very strong tradition of the privileges of birth; it stands aloof from the middle classes and the people; and it regards as its sole profession a devoted service of the State and the Crown. The army, more especially, though raised on the broadest principles of national conscription, is officered and led by the upper classes. Numerous families of noble birth, poor, brave, and loyal, are the natural resource of a military monarchy; and, whatever may be thought of the Junkerdom of Berlin in its politics and its manners, it will not be denied to be an element of strength to the Crown and to the army.

The civil government, which embraces with inconceivable minuteness all the relations of social life, and restrains all freedom of action, is in the hands of a powerful bureaucracy. The representative bodies, more recently introduced in Prussia, have in truth no real control over it. They are not even composed of men capable of carrying it on. On almost all important questions, their wishes and votes have been set aside and trampled on by the Ministers of the Crown with absolute contempt. Of that freedom which consists in the government of the nation by the nation, or in obedience to the will of the nation, there is in Prussia no sign, and not even a pretence. Authority subsists in its severest and most naked form.

But the people, naturally docile and submissive to

acts which would produce a change of Government in England, a revolution in France, and a *pronunciamiento* in Spain, are satisfied that in the long run the policy of the Government is enlightened and just. They know that the administration of the public finances is inflexibly honest and frugal. They see that the Government has by its zeal in the work of education made them the most instructed people in Europe; and they are perhaps unconscious that this education has so moulded their minds and very being that they are trained to habits of obedience, loyalty, and respect, not common in more democratic communities. Even the popular opinions and prevailing sentiments of the day, encouraged by the press, have been skilfully used by the Government to promote the aggrandisement of the monarchy by pursuing objects marked out by national ambition.

There is something of a Spartan character in the institutions of Prussia—the authority of the kings, who are also the commanders of the people—the simplicity and frugality which all ranks have retained in an age of luxury and indulgence—the crushing weight of public authority which shapes everything to its will and extinguishes the individual in the State—and the harsh unamiable manners formed by a life of discipline—belong alike to the ancient and the modern military State ; and these characteristics were united to a stronger sense of duty, of moral obligation, and of religion than could be found amongst the wits and philosophers of volatile Athens. The Lacedæmonians were notoriously the least courteous and hospitable of all the Greek States; art, eloquence, and poetry never flourished on their soil. Training and discipline with a view to regimental preparation and rigid obedience were and are alike the objects of the Spartan and the Prussian lawgivers. Oratory, which plays so great a part in the affairs of more popular States, was and is alike unknown and powerless at Lacedæmon and at Berlin. This silent and self-contained policy gives a rare steadiness to political action, and engenders a hatred of revolutions. The object of the athletic exercises of the other Grecian States, as it is in England, was excellence in games; the exercises of the Prussians, like those of Sparta, are all directed to war. Lastly, it is possible that the land laws of Lacedæmon may have had purposes and results analogous to the great land reform introduced by Baron von Stein.

A State thus constituted on the strictest dynastic principles is the antithesis of France. Accordingly,

Prussia has been the most constant and bitter enemy of the French Revolution. She began the contest of the anti-revolutionary war, which led to results so disastrous to Europe, because at that period France was in all the magnificent energy of her new-born hopes of freedom, and monarchical Europe was in a stage of extreme decrepitude. Prussia more than any other State drank that cup of humiliation to the dregs. It was Prussia who put her hand to the Treaty of Basle, which first made over to France the left bank of the Rhine, since so fiercely contested. It was Prussia that accepted Hanover from the dominator of Europe. She expiated that weakness by Jena, and by seven years of excessive suffering from the French occupation. But in those sufferings her regeneration began. The structure of the monarchy and of the army was laid afresh on a broader and stronger basis. When she took the field again in 1813 she commenced a new life. In 1814 her dominions were extended till they touched the frontier of France on its most sensitive and vulnerable point, and she consented to mount guard there, which she has done with effect for more than half a century. And when the attack was rashly, madly, renewed by France, Prussia uprose with all the ancient hatred of her revolutionary neighbour—with a lively recollection of ancient wrongs which have been studiously kept alive in the hearts of the people—and with a strong faith that the time was come when her Sovereign could claim the first rank in Germany and in Europe. The climax and consummation of this great revolution is to be found in the recent act by which the princes of Germany have been led to place the renovated Imperial Crown of Germany on the head of the King of Prussia. Hohenzollern has succeeded Hapsburg. The reluctant vassals of the Empire have acknowledged their own defeat in the celebration of a national triumph. The crown which was refused by the late King when tendered by a democratic assembly in 1849, has been accepted in 1870 as the symbol of military might. It has been purchased by great achievements in war, attended by infinite misery and suffering; and no doubt it is the dearer to the Sovereign who will wear it, as a pledge of the triumph of the monarchical principles of Germany over the democratic armies of France.

Thus, then, while France has during a lengthened period of time undergone a series of political changes, and been subject to the operation of social causes, which appear to have undermined and diminished her power as a nation, Prussia has been steadily growing under the influence of her monarchy; the supremacy of the reigning House has been raised to the highest pitch; her territories have been greatly extended; her alliances have given her the military command of Southern Germany; her population has largely augmented; her military system and armament have been reformed and carried to perfection; and she finds herself at the head of a people prepared to make enormous sacrifices for the advancement of her political objects. We give Count Bismarck credit for having foreseen these things and their results. He has for many years—that is, since the humiliation of Olmütz and the pitiful conduct of Prussia during the Crimean war—had steadily in view the means by which he could gratify the ambition of his country and his own, by raising her to the first rank of European Powers, and by placing the Imperial crown on his master's head. Such an undertaking involved the overthrow of the Germanic Confederation, the violation of numerous treaties, the destruction of the whole system of the balance of power in Europe, war with Austria, concessions to Russia, defiance of England, and at last a death-struggle with France. It therefore exacted an incalculable sacrifice of human life and property. But the man of 'blood and iron' knew what he meant to do, and he has apparently done it. The end is a great one. But probably no other living man would have had the force of will and the insensibility of conscience to enter upon that blood-stained path. However guilty of recklessness and ambition the French Government may have been in the transactions which were the immediate cause or pretext of the declaration of war, it can never be denied that the disruption of Europe, the change in the relative position of States, and the final overthrow of the great settlement of 1815, were the results of the policy of Prussia in 1864 and 1866, guided by Count Bismarck, and we do him no injustice in supposing that he desired and intended them, and was prepared to pay the cost of them. The passions of men are, after all, but the blind instruments of the Providential government of mankind. The spectacle of human misery and helplessness would be too dreadful but for the belief that even the crimes of nations are working to some beneficent though unseen end, and that there is a plan in the ultimate conduct of human affairs infinitely more vast and just than the schemes of statesmen and the tactics of successful war.

Count Bismarck undoubtedly foresaw in 1866 the relative inferiority of Austria to Prussia in military strength, especially when attacked at once on the Elbe and on the Po; and in this respect he showed a degree of penetration shared by few persons in Europe. Did he in 1870 entertain a similar belief as to the relative strength of Prussia, aided by the South German States, and of France? That is a question to which at present no answer can be given; but it is not impossible that he may have arrived at a similar conclusion. He knew the strength of the German armies; he probably had information that the French could not place above half that number of troops at once on the frontier, and that the French reserves under the law of 1868 were not organised.[1] He knew the character of the Emperor, the weakness of his Government, and the absence of high military talent in the army. But in addition to these personal and military considera-

---

[1] It has now been ascertained that at the moment of the declaration of war there were not more than 150,000 effective combatants in France ready to take the field. About 100,000 men of the active army were absent on furlough (more especially as it was the season of harvest); but these were scattered over the whole territory and engaged in farm labour. They were hastily summoned to join their regiments, but a fortnight elapsed before they could resume their place in the ranks, and then they had lost to some extent their military habits and the knowledge of their officers. The reserves had no existence at all, and had never been called out.

tions, there are numerous facts and arguments arising out of the condition of France herself, which might perhaps suggest the same conclusion to a man of more than common powers of discernment. To these, as they appear to us to be displayed by the unexampled and unforeseen events of the last few months, we now return, and they are the more interesting as they raise questions of general application to the interests of society in other countries at the present day.

It has been said, and the fact will hardly be disputed, that the strong monarchical constitution of Prussia is one great element of her power. Hereditary kingship is as sacred and as valuable in the eyes of the Prussians as if her princes came of the divine race of the Heracleids. In France, hereditary monarchy, by which we mean the indefeasible right of the head of the State to rule by descent, and to transmit his power to his next heir, perished on the scaffold with Louis XVI. Attempts have been made by each succeeding government to revive it. But these have in fact failed. No French sovereign except Charles X., has taken the crown by succession since the commencement of the Revolution; and the right of succession, though constantly acknowledged by the law, has been so often set aside by revolutions, that no reliance can be placed upon it. 'I cannot forget,' said Napoleon III. to Lord Clarendon on the birth of his son in the Tuileries in 1856, 'that no prince born in this house has succeeded his father on the throne.' In fact, the duration of a dynasty in France is from fifteen to twenty years.

What, then, is the true value of hereditary monarchy? Does it conduce to the strength and stability of governments by determining the succession to supreme power, or does it detract from them by the chance of placing that power in incapable hands? The answer of a theoretical reasoner on government might admit of doubt. The answer of practical experience resolves that doubt, and for sufficient reasons. When the succession to the supreme power depends on a popular vote, a legislative preference, or a revolution, the dynastic question is continually paramount to every other consideration in the mind of the ruler. His object is to transmit or perpetuate his power, and to this object the whole policy of his reign is subservient. At any moment the change may occur. At any moment he or his heirs must be prepared to meet it. A king who ascends the throne by even the most legitimate forms of election, as William III. in

England or Louis-Philippe in France, must be prepared to deal with large bodies of his own subjects who dispute or detest his authority. The Jacobites conspired against William; the Royalists and Republicans waged a factious opposition against the House of Orleans. Louis Napoleon was elected by a vast majority of the French people; but the minority, consisting of the best, the wisest, and the ablest men in the country, stood aloof from him and his Government, and were throughout his reign his irreconcilable enemies. An elective sovereign therefore no longer represents the integrity of the empire. The house is divided against itself. Divisions of party on such a question attack and weaken, not only the administrative functions of the Government, but the representative of the State itself. The sovereign therefore regards a portion of his own subjects as his most formidable enemies; and should a crisis of danger occur, which ought to call forth the united action of every citizen, that is the very moment his adversaries or rivals will select to overthrow him. Francis I. after Pavia was not the less King of France in a Spanish prison. Napoleon III. after Sedan is a nameless fugitive in a foreign palace, and the State drifts in total anarchy to the verge of dissolution. The hereditary rights of the Valois were unassailable; those of the Bonapartes are a jest.

Even in the United States of America, where the periodical renewal of the supreme magistrate by election is established by law and peacefully conducted, the presidential election weakens the authority of the State and of the Ruler. It was a presidential election which caused the civil war. Another election ensued in the heat of the contest; the Americans very wisely kept Mr. Lincoln in his place. Every American president is mainly occupied with the desire of procuring his own re-election, or, if his second term of service is nearly over, of procuring the election of one of his adherents. General Grant at this moment is in the former position, and his policy is governed by it. The policy of his opponents is equally governed by the hope of defeating him and taking his place. Hence personal interests largely control and distort public measures. There is now, we are sorry to say, a party in the United States who would not scruple to plunge their country into war with England, if they thought that measure would give them a majority at the next presidential election. The fault is not so much in the men as in the vicious institutions which hold out such temptations to faction.

In this country, if by any misfortune the principle of hereditary monarchy were shaken, we have no doubt that the people of England have sufficient experience of freedom and sufficient respect for the law of Parliament to conduct peaceably their own affairs. But the golden bond which holds together the British Empire would be broken. The central force, which makes this nation so great a power in the world, would be dissipated. The symbol, which is recognised alike by the free settlers of Australia and by the dusky natives of Hindostan, would be lost. The outlying realms of British rule would recognise no allegiance to the elected ruler of the English people, who might be good enough for us, but who would be nothing to them. In our Parliament they are not represented; in our councils they have no voice. It is the authority and style of the Sovereign as Head of the Empire which alone unites them to us and makes us one nation. As it is, whatever may be the defects of our political and social institutions, Great Britain may boast that for more than one hundred and eighty years the course of law and the tranquillity of the realm have been unbroken, and that, enjoying as much freedom as any people in the world, she has also enjoyed a degree of internal peace, order, and security to which no other nation can lay claim.

These examples may illustrate the value and the strength of what we mean by the principle of hereditary monarchy; and however seductive the theory of republican election may be to some minds, we defy them to replace it. All other principles of supreme government are contested and contestable, and this especially at the most critical moments. Dynastic law and tradition alone place the representative of the supreme power above every accident except that of the extinction of his race. The French Revolution in striking down the monarchy of a thousand years destroyed the tradition, and it has not been restored. They have substituted for it the ideal of 'France'—and no doubt in a country so homogeneous and so patriotic, the name is a name of power. But France not represented by any efficient lawful sovereign, or represented by a committee of declamatory lawyers carried to the Hôtel de Ville by a Parisian mob, is in fact as helpless as an idol of wood or stone. Who speaks with authority in her name? Who controls the passions and interests of her provinces with an equal hand? Who protects her? Who defends her? Who can ever direct aright the course of her policy towards the enemy or the passionate self-sacrifice of her sons? Who can make peace? Who can contract in her name? In nothing is the contest with Germany more fearfully unequal than in the fact that it lies between the most powerful monarchy of Europe, governed with absolute clear-sighted authority by its king, and a headless State, torn as much by internal dissensions as by foreign invasion. Prussia, too, has had her days of humiliation. After Jena, the king retreated to the Niemen and hardly found a refuge from the oppressor within the verge of his own dominions. But, wherever he was, there was the Crown, there was the Sovereign, there was the State. Nothing was irrecoverably lost as long as the vital principle of the monarchy was preserved. To France, unhappily, by the results of her revolution that resource is denied; and anarchy, save where it is locally controlled by the wisdom and courage of a few scattered and spontaneous leaders, presents her defenceless to the enemy and unprovided for the future.

The decline and fall of the French aristocracy, as a political body, dates from a period long anterior to the Revolution of 1789. To find a race of nobles and landed proprietors leading an independent existence on their estates, and playing an independent part in the affairs of their country, we must go back to the sixteenth and seventeenth centuries, and to the time when a large portion of the best blood in France held the Protestant faith. The civil wars, the proscriptions of Richelieu, the bigotry of Louis XIV., and the corrupt Court of his successor, established the ascendancy of the Crown, of the Catholic Church, and of Versailles. That important element in society which, in this country, has so often fought the battles of freedom against the encroachments of prerogative, perished in France; or if it retained its own privileges and possessions, these were rendered odious to the people, because they had ceased to be held for the general good. In the reign of Louis XV. the income of the noble consisted chiefly in the revenue he could draw, under various names and pretences, from those who held under him, not in the shape of rent but of charges on every form of rural labour. His agents harassed the tenants with fiscal rapacity, and were constantly at war with the customs that formerly protected the cultivators of the soil. The landed interest was everywhere poor. Nobles, ecclesiastics, ennobled citizens, and purchasers of fiefs were alike overwhelmed with debt. The rate of usury was enormous. Their condition was described by Forbonnais as that of men 'reduced to extreme penury with immense nominal possessions.' Accordingly, wherever sales of land could be made, it was purchased with avidity. In 1760 it was computed that a quarter of the soil of France was held by the peasantry, a quarter by the *bourgeoisie*, two-tenths by the clergy, and three-tenths by the nobles. The subdivision of land was regarded as the best remedy for the deplorable condition of the country, and the creation of a peasant proprietary was already advocated as the panacea of the nation. D'Argenson, for instance, in a work published in 1740, which Voltaire described as the best book he had read for twenty years, insisted upon the expedient of 'reconstructing the edifice of society, shaken by bad laws, by the creation of a class of individuals who should be morally and economically independent.' His ideal was that the land should belong to those who cultivated it. We shall see in another page of this inquiry, what are the political and military results of this system. Suffice it here to say that it was loudly demanded at the outset of the Revolution by all classes of the community, that the nobles themselves abandoned their feudal rights as untenable, and that the change of tenures was accomplished. To this hour, this is the result of the Revolution which is most loudly applauded by French writers of the greatest learning and authority, as, for example, by M. Doniol (now Prefect at Grenoble), from whose instructive history of the rural classes in France we have borrowed the foregoing facts. It is equally admired by those English writers who seek in the democracy of France the model of the reforms they desire to introduce into this country in the tenure of property and the organisation of society. We may, therefore, assume that this state of things is regarded as highly beneficial, and so undoubtedly it has proved in the improvement of the condition of the peasantry, when liberated from feudal burdens, which have happily no parallel amongst ourselves. But our object at this moment is to point out, as a simple fact, that the change involved the extinction of the social and political influence of the upper classes; for the abuses of the feudal tenures and the vices of an aristocracy, identified by its sources of revenue and its habits of expenditure with the Court, had engendered throughout France a fierce hatred of social inequality, which has gone on increasing to this day, though the causes in which it originated have long disappeared. The services, therefore, which may be rendered to a nation by a class of educated proprietors and capitalists, by the performance of the public duties of their station, by the improvement of cultivation and rural administration, and by the local influence of men solicitous for the common interest of those around them, are in a great measure lost to France. There is no 'public spirit,' to use a most emphatic and characteristically English term. Even on the larger estates in the hands of those who are capable of discharging the duties of a resident gentry, the good offices of the wealthy are regarded with suspicion and hostility, as great perhaps as when those duties wore the invidious shape of feudal privileges. The result has been, to a considerable extent, to displace the educated classes from their natural position as the leading servants of the public in local and political affairs. There is a chasm between them and the surrounding peasantry, which is rarely crossed ; and the peasantry would certainly refuse to recognise in the gentry the champions or representatives of their own interests.

It was one of the boasts of the authors of the French Revolution that they had destroyed the spirit of *caste*, and had substituted for it that Equality and Fraternity which are still inscribed on the ruins of Paris. By *caste* is meant certain divisions in society, based on religious or social observances, which are absolutely exclusive and self-contained, and arrogate to themselves a superiority which their fellow-creatures and fellow-countrymen are forbidden to share. In India, for example, all contact with persons of an inferior caste is contamination, and no man can shake off the imprescriptible conditions of his birth. Inasmuch as the ancient nobility of France and the priesthood formed castes, they have perished. They are reduced in all respects to the common level of society, and if any distinctions still survive among their descendants — as for example, in the matter of intermarriage—these are merely retained by the force of tradition in their domestic manners. In England we have, and always have had, classes, but never castes; because our classes and ranks have always been open to free competition. The nobles and statesmen of Henry VIII. and Elizabeth, the true founders of our modern aristocracy, were, like most of their successors, men born in the middle classes whose merits raised and ennobled them; and many of their descendants have fallen back into the ranks of the people again. But the spirit of caste is not confined to nobles, or priests, or lawyers. It may exist just as strongly, and spread over a broader area, in the ranks of the people. We say, then, that it does exist, and with great intensity, in modern France. The Revolution, which destroyed the upper castes of society, created the lower—quite as exclusive, quite as intolerant, quite as tyrannical. The peasants of France form a dominant caste in the rural districts. The workmen form a dominant caste in the towns. Neither of these bodies of men will endure the slightest interference with their notions of privilege. Neither of them will look beyond the interests and prejudices of their own order. Both are alike jealous of each other, and of any other kind of superiority. Both regard any departure from their own peculiar habits and pursuits as a derogation from their own dignity. They act together among themselves as long as their interests are identical, and as long as there is a perfect equality between them; but as soon as any man is in a condition to play a more conspicuous part in the country, he ceases to be one of themselves and they no longer trust him. They regard him, on the contrary, with envy, jealousy, and aversion. This is precisely the spirit of caste in its most odious and mischievous form; although the democracy of France would probably be surprised if they knew that we laid to

their charge precisely the same vice of exclusiveness
which they imputed to the old aristocracy and
the nobles.

We think this fact, which is due partly to the
spirit of the Revolution and partly to causes anterior
to that event, explains in some measure the extraordinary deficiency of men capable of leading,
governing, and guiding the nation at this great crisis.
That many such men exist in so intelligent a country
as France is certain; but their position is singularly
unfortunate, for they have been proscribed for the
last twenty years by a Government they refused to
serve, and yet they are not accepted as leaders by the
people. The dead level of equality has passed over
their heads, and as none are conspicuous, none great,
the country has no tried or natural chiefs and rulers
when it most requires them We have the astonishing fact before our eyes that at this moment,
with the exception of three or four great reputations
surviving from the period of parliamentary government, there is not known to be in France a general,
a statesman, or an orator of the first rank. There
is not a man on whom the eyes of the whole community rest with the confidence and deference paid
elsewhere to high rank, to tried honour, and to
genius. Society, and especially the society of the

Empire, is barren. Nor is that of the Republic more fertile.

It will no doubt be said that the Revolution of 1789 was singularly prolific of great men. A generation of extraordinary energy burst forth at the call of freedom, and filled the world for fifty years with their exploits and their renown. They sprang alike from every rank and class of society. But the men whom the Revolution called into action were not its children. They had been born, reared, and educated under the old order of things. We have now before us the descendants of the revolutionary period in its third generation—men educated in its maxims and subjected to its social discipline. These are its true descendants and its legitimate heirs. Has, then, the influence of the Revolution raised or lowered the character and capacity of Frenchmen? Has it enlarged their sphere of action? Has it strengthened those ties between the upper and the lower classes of society without which national action is paralysed? Has the growth of democracy, to the exclusion of every other element, given greater union, force, and power to the nation and to the State? Down to a very recent period it was believed, and would have been maintained by all French writers, that these results had been attained. But we leave our readers to answer for themselves these questions.

It is a melancholy reflection that but little has been done by modern democracy to dignify and exalt mankind. The area of human happiness has certainly been extended by the diffusion of freedom and knowledge, and we rejoice in that result. But the creative genius and power which enlarge the boundaries of thought and action thrive not upon that level plain 'on which every ant-hill is a mountain, and every thistle a forest-tree.' Democracy, it may be, bears with it the destiny or the doom of civilisation; but nowhere as yet has it been favourable to greatness. Even in the United States, where it reigns without control, no man since Washington, who was certainly no democrat, can be said to have risen to true eminence, even under the pressure of a great crisis. The growth or manifestation of intellectual force bears no proportion at all to the spread of population and wealth. In like manner, France never was at any former time so populous, so rich in all material gifts, and apparently so prosperous as in the later years of the Second Empire; but never in all her varied history was she so destitute of greatness, whether in counsel or in arms. The same observation might be addressed to ourselves. Great Britain in 1805 had not half the population, probably not one-fifth of the wealth, and far less material culture, education, and freedom, than we enjoy at the present day. But we cannot boast that our age is more prolific of great men in statesmanship, war, literature, law, and science than the first decade of this century; and there are those who think, we trust erroneously, that the relative strength of the nation as compared with that of some foreign States has declined.

The turning point in the history, both of England and in France, lay in the sixteenth century, which gave the one to the Protestant, the other to the Catholic cause—the one to free inquiry, free institutions, and the virility of self-government; the other to the Romish creed ingrafted by a Latin form of civilisation on a Celtic race. Upon a comparison of Catholic and Protestant nations by the test of social development, the advantage does not rest with the older creed; and even though that creed may have lost much of its ancient authority and intolerance, the soil in which it has flourished long gives signs of exhaustion. Nevertheless, the Church of France, the Church of Bossuet and Fénelon, of Pascal and Arnauld, of Port-Royal and Saint-Maur, fills a glorious and imperishable page in the annals of that nation and of the human race. The Gallican clergy maintained their rights against the Ultramontane pretensions of Rome. They were the depositaries of the learning and the piety of the realm. They upheld with eloquence and fidelity the noble principles of Christian morals in presence of a corrupt Court and a pleasure-loving people; and they discharged with no mean results their important function of the educators of the nation. The Revolution swept all this away. It was impossible to attack the Church (says M. de Tocqueville in one of his letters) without touching every fibre of the State. In losing their endowments they lost their independence. The connection between the clergy and the higher classes of society was broken. They became a stipendiary priesthood, without the advantages of an establishment and without the energy of free denominations. Their numbers are recruited chiefly from the ranks of the peasantry, who seek in holy orders a means of escape from military service, or a means of transferring to the rest of the family another parcel of the patrimonial estate. The modern parochial clergy of France are a virtuous and devout class of men. But they are narrow-minded and ignorant to excess. They are the tools of the most bigoted Ultramontane doctrines, even against the judgment of their own prelates. Their influence is confined to women and devotees, and they have almost entirely lost their control over the higher education of the country. The consequence is that the education of the upper classes of men is strangely divorced from a high system of moral and religious principle, based on the accountability of man to God, and that in place of it a course of secular instruction, regulated by the Imperial University, and based chiefly on the exact or natural sciences, has trained the minds and characters of modern Frenchmen. It is not true that the French are an immoral and irreligious people, as is too commonly supposed by those who take their notions of French life and society from the garbage of French literature, the novels of the day. In the towns and cities, and in the army, there is undoubtedly a great laxity of practice, arising from many causes. But we hold very cheap the pretensions of those who thank God they are not as those Sadducees. In the great mass of the rural population there is as much rectitude, chastity, and sobriety as in any other country. But they are a people who have lost their guides. A plain standard of faith and duty is not brought home to their doors and hearths. Their conception of duty is based on notions of filial piety and mutual interest. The sense and love of truth has been painfully weakened among them. They afford a speaking example of what an intelligent people may become when education is severed from religious principles and when the standard of those principles is lowered or obscured.

We make these remarks with diffidence and regret, for it is a most invidious task to comment on the failings of a neighbouring people, when we are conscious how far we ourselves fall short of the highest rule of life. We know how hard it is for education to combat the materialist tendency of the age, the density of population, the pressure of a thousand social ills. But though we fail—as all must fail—to reach the lofty ideal of a Christian people, we are not ashamed to avow our conviction that the greatness of a nation depends in no small degree on the visible standard of faith and duty set before it. Take away the Bible and the activity of the Christian ministry from the people of this island, and what would they become? Yet that is to some extent the condition in which a large proportion of the people of France find themselves. The defects of such a society are precisely those which might be anticipated in a community in which the religious sanction of moral law has lost its power. A recent

theological writer[1] who has investigated with
acuteness the causes of the corruption and decay of
the Roman people under the Emperors, sums them
up in one expressive phrase—the separation of
religion and morality. There was religion in Rome,
but it was the religion of paganism : there was
morality, but it was the morality of philosophers.
The two great elements of social law were disunited.
Something of the same kind may perhaps be traced
in France, and the condition of the country presents
obvious and striking resemblances to that with
which we are familiar in the pages of Roman
historians and Roman satirists.

We have now cursorily noticed the most important
of the ancient institutions of France, swept away by
the Revolution. Let us proceed to consider what
the Revolution has substituted for them. It has
conferred upon the people equal civil and political
rights, extending to universal suffrage, and these are
occasionally exercised directly and in the last resort,
so as virtually to supersede the representative
system. It has established a system of administration, in all departments of government, which
derives its strength from the central authority and

[1] Irons' *Bampton Lectures* for 1870, p. 8.

not from the people. It maintains a large permanent army raised by conscription. It applies to the upper classes a system of education of which the École Polytechnique is the type; and it methodises in a high degree all the other steps of distinction and advancement in life. It encourages small landed property, and discourages large estates, by the operation of the Civil Code in subdividing property. The Civil Code, which is the true root and fertile parent of the democratic social condition of France, limits the testamentary power, and virtually divides a man's property between his offspring in his lifetime, by the indefeasible recognition of their share in it; it renders almost impossible the accumulation of wealth in a family for several generations; it proscribes, prohibits, and defeats all trusts, settlements, entails, and limitations of real and personal property; and it favours the two prevailing passions of the people—the passion for equality and the passion for the acquisition of land. Under the operation of these causes and motives, the soil of France is greatly subdivided. Four or five millions of citizens and their families live by the cultivation of their own parcel of land and in the enjoyment of the political rights connected with it. They form a numerical majority in the State, and as they present an extraordinary degree of uniformity of taste, habit, and opinion throughout France, the probability is that without concert they will all act in the same manner. It was thus that, hating the Republic in 1848, they made Louis Napoleon their candidate, and ratified the *coup d'état* of 1851 by their votes. On broad principles of republican equality and universal suffrage, the peasantry are and ought to be the masters of France; and as they are vehemently opposed to the revolutionary doctrines of the great towns, the rural vote is, of the two, the basis of legality and order. That, however, is all that we can venture to say for it. It has been frequently contended that peasant proprietors are the best guarantee against wars and revolutions—that they have everything to lose and nothing to gain by such convulsions—and that France ought therefore of all countries to be the most exempt from them. Even so acute an observer as Lord Palmerston remarked, during a visit to France he made just before the Revolution of July 1830, that 'there were too many millions of owners of land and funds in France to let it be possible, that anything should happen endangering the safety of one property or the other.' A natural inference, but one totally confuted by experience. There is no question that the millions of French proprietors of land and *rentes* detest revolution and dread war. It is equally true that they are nominally invested with supreme power in the State by their votes. Yet they cannot avert revolution or resist war, nor even, as it seems, oppose a bold front to them when they occur. By all accounts this hapless peasant—this unit of French society—this individual of small possessions and absolute rights, might be a very happy and inoffensive member of society, if the world were always undisturbed; but throw him into perilous and critical circumstances, and he is as chaff before the wind. And this brings us nearer to the causes which appear to us to have contributed to this marvellous collapse of a great people. The action of democratic laws and habits seems to have pulverised and disintegrated the French nation—to have destroyed at once both the strength and cohesion of its elements—and to have given birth to a race of beings too small to deal with great emergencies, and too much divided to combine to meet them.

To render this novel state of things more intelligible to the English reader, let us contrast it with the institutions familiar to ourselves. Everything in England is organised to give permanence and perpetuity to the relations of life and property. Property is held by one man under innumerable limitations for the benefit of others not only in the present generation, but in generations to come. Few men dispose absolutely of what they possess, unless it be self-acquired. All the relations of life are based on the principle of *interdependence*—all classes, ranks, and individuals are bound each to each by mutual duties. The land is worked by a combination of the labouring man, the farmer, and the landlord. Each of them is indispensable to the other. The labourer draws his wages independent of the variations of prices and seasons ; the farmer is enabled to farm 300 acres with a capital which would not purchase thirty acres of his own ; the landlord is the chief capitalist, who in the long run bears the main risk of the adventure. He has his duties to his tenants, duties to his family, duties to the public. The public funds, and all sorts of securities, are held to an immense amount in trust under family settlements, by which the immediate interest and power of the individual are checked and circumscribed by the interests and rights of others. This mutual dependence, which exists with reference to property and its uses, runs through every branch of English social life : it is the basis of our credit :

it is the secret of our enormous power of association : it is the breath of public life, for it begets a sense of duty to others on the one hand, and a sense of reliance on others on the other hand.

All this is reversed by the laws, manners, and social institutions of modern France. The Civil Code prohibits all the varied forms of limitation of the right of property. It recognises but one form of property, which confers absolute ownership. No man holds anything subject to the claims of another; no man has reversionary or other claims over the possessions of another. One consequence of this state of things is, that although the upper classes of France and America are less rich than those of England, they spend what they have more freely; they have in fact more to spend, because their capital, as well as the income derived from it, is at their own disposal : just as we see in England that newly-enriched persons spend their money more freely than old territorial families. In the lower classes, the desire to obtain a certain possession is increased by the sense of absolute property in it. But the owner of a small parcel of land becomes selfish and self-contained in proportion to this sense of individual power. The land suffices to maintain and employ himself and his family. If he keep clear of the neighbouring money-lender, he is sole master of it. He owes nothing to the landlord; he asks nothing of the labourer.[1] His wants, his desires, and his sympathies are bounded within the limits of his own fields. No doubt some advantage from this state of society is to be found in the self-reliance and independence it confers. But this advantage must be set off against the indifference it begets to the wants and claims of others. It engenders, therefore, a high degree of selfishness, accompanied by dislike and distrust of everything that interferes with it, and an indifference to more enlarged interests. To give a striking example of the effect of this state of society. The Civil Code, as is well known, compels a man to divide his land and other property equally amongst his children. The French peasant regards the extreme partition of his possessions as an evil only to be avoided by limiting the number of his descendants. He therefore restricts himself to two children. The most imperious of human passions is

[1] In the villages of Auvergne, where the soil is entirely divided between small proprietors working on their own land, the last remaining landlords or large holders have been compelled to sell their estates because they find no labourers to cultivate them. With the exception of a few smiths, carpenters, and masons, who are useful to themselves, the peasant proprietors will not allow persons not of their own class to dwell in their villages: the superfluous population, for whom there is no land, are driven away to seek employment in towns.

kept in check by this consideration. The interests of morality suffer, and the numerical strength of the population is stopped in its natural growth by a sordid view of personal interest. The effects of this check to the rural population are sufficiently obvious. Even the physical growth of the race is stunted by it. It can be arithmetically demonstrated that the conscription drains off the whole natural increase of the country, and the rural population of France is therefore almost stationary. The population of the towns tends, on the contrary, rapidly to increase by the immigration of a certain class of persons from the rural districts.[1] But this class consists of those who, not being holders of land, and not choosing to accept the condition of agricultural labourers, are driven away by their own families and by the custom of the country to seek employment in towns. They are therefore the most discontented portion of the nation. They readily adopt the loose habits and the loose social theories current amongst French *ouvriers*: they form what is termed the *prolétariat*

[1] In Paris alone this immigration is calculated at three or four hundred thousand men in the last twenty years. Their fate has been singularly unfortunate, for after having laboured with their hands to rebuild the capital of France with unexampled splendour, it has devolved on them to defend it, and an immense number of them perished in the siege of Paris, and under the disastrous reign of the Commune, in the ruins of many of the edifices they had themselves raised.

of France, and, having no stake in the country and no interest in maintaining its institutions, they readily become the turbulent partisans of republican, and even revolutionary, principles. It is amongst this class alone that the republic has any hold; by the mass of the people it is not only not desired, but dreaded and abhorred. Yet these are sufficiently numerous and powerful in the towns to overthrow many an established authority, and to make the establishment of a stable and free government a task of great difficulty. The democracy of the provinces is conservative. The democracy of the towns is destructive. But these opposite results arise from the same cause—an intensely selfish interest.

This selfishness of the small proprietor has been described by the best writers as *individualism*. Individual property, individual independence, individual gain, is the basis of democratic institutions. Let anyone observe an assembly of French peasants on a market day. All equal, all alike, all sharing one class of interests and passions, intolerant to excess of any superiority of intelligence, wealth, or power, they resemble the atoms of which a floating mass may be composed. In ordinary times their lives are industrious and contented. But they are wholly unprepared to meet an emergency: they are governed by no public spirit or sympathy with public objects.[1] Beyond their own narrow field of vision, they see and acknowledge nothing but the power of the Government. Such a people is trained to live under an absolute authority; and accordingly, if their opinion is asked on the subject, it is in favour of absolute authority that their votes are given. Should that absolute authority fail in the discharge of the public duties devolving upon it, there is nothing to protect such a people from anarchy or subjugation. The life of man is so short and the powers of a single generation so limited, that it is only by adding together the efforts of several generations and by securing permanence and perpetuity to the results of human labour, that great institutions are created. Trusts and settlements which give permanence to family property, endowments, chartered corporations, and hereditary rank, are all legal contrivances for the purpose of securing and perpetuating the

---

[1] To cite another illustration from Auvergne. The communal or parish roads in France are made by the Commune, which levies so many days' statute labour on its own members for the purpose. In Auvergne the communal roads are detestable, sometimes hardly exist. The reason given is that no man will consent to tax himself for a benefit he would share with his neighbours. The roads made by the State and the Department are, of course, excellent, but they are not under the control of the peasantry.

benefits of labour and success. They give strength and stability to society by creating interests and powers more lasting and comprehensive than those of the present time. They are to the moral energy of man what mechanism is to force, by preserving and applying what it cannot produce. But to all institutions of this permanent nature the spirit of democracy is opposed. It views with a jealous and hostile eye everything that it cannot control. It resists permanent and collective obligations as an encroachment on the unlimited personal freedom of the individual. It therefore weakens the traditional elements of society and readily sacrifices the past and the future to what is supposed to be the interest of the present. By one system men are raised to the power and duration of institutions; by the other institutions are reduced and contracted to the individual weakness of man. Democratic power is an essential and useful check to the abuses of authority, but it is a feeble or violent instrument of government, and the collective strength of a nation may be sensibly diminished by it.

Even the sentiment of patriotism, the feeling which ennobles the humblest members of a community by making them share the triumphs, the greatness, and the pride of its most illustrious ornaments, is weakened by democracy, and may eventually be destroyed. Patriotism takes its origin in a grand historic conception of the dignity and power of the country to which we have the honour to belong. It makes the poorest peasant or beggar participate in some degree in the glories of a mighty State, and it dignifies the obscurity of his individual lot by the sense of a common greatness, and the strength of common interests. But as the sense of individual interest increases, and the sense of common interests declines, the source of patriotism is dried up. Men are less willing to sacrifice their lives and their property to a national cause. The idea of national greatness loses half its influence when the symbols of that greatness are broken. The sympathies of the people are contracted within a narrower horizon; and thus a sort of local or petty patriotism survives long after the national sentiment has decayed. The French have been for several ages an intensely patriotic people. Their attachment to the name and glory of France was proverbial. It is scarcely possible to conceive that so powerful a passion should have subsided. But if the truth must be told, the events of the late war and the present condition of the country denote a perceptible decline in the patriotic sentiments of the

French people. They are incomparably less ready than the ardent volunteers of 1792 to sacrifice everything for the glory of France and of the Revolution. If they must choose between the broad interests of the State and the narrow interests of their province, their commune, or their homestead, they will prefer the latter. The revolutions which have so often shaken the State to its foundations, and destroyed all faith in its power, have engendered a closer attachment to local and domestic concerns; and the call of the country in danger, which roused a dozen armies from the soil at the outset of the great European war, was comparatively powerless in 1870, when twenty-six French departments were occupied by a victorious invader.

We had already written these remarks, when it occurred to us to turn to a half-forgotten passage in which M. de Tocqueville has described with his wonted sagacity the same distinction, and traced its consequences. The page is so remarkable, and so apposite to the present state of things in France, that at the risk of forfeiting our own credit for originality we transcribe it :—

Aristocratic institutions have the effect of closely binding every man to several of his fellow-citizens. As in aristocratic communities all the citizens occupy fixed positions, one above the other, the result is that each of them always sees a man above himself whose patronage is necessary to him, and below himself another man whose co-operation he may claim. Men living in aristocratic ages are therefore almost always closely attached to something placed out of their own sphere, and they are often disposed to forget themselves. It is true that in those ages the notion of human fellowship is faint, and that men seldom think of sacrificing themselves for mankind; but they often sacrifice themselves for other men. In democratic ages, on the contrary, when the duties of each individual to the race are much more clear, devoted service to any one man becomes more rare; the bond of human affection is extended, but it is also relaxed. Amongst democratic nations new families are constantly springing up, others are constantly falling away, and all that remain change their condition : the woof of time is every instant broken, and the track of generations effaced. Those who went before are soon forgotten; of those who will come after no one has any idea; the interest of man is confined to those in close propinquity to himself. As each class approximates to other classes and intermingles with them, its members become indifferent and as strangers to one another. Aristocracy had made a chain of all the members of the community, from the peasant to the King: democracy breaks that chain and severs every link of it.

Again, after pointing out that freedom, and the habitual performance of public duties by the power of association, as in the United States, are the only correctives of this selfish individualism and isolation, M. de Tocqueville proceeds, in another chapter :—

Aristocratic communities always contain amongst a multitude of persons, who by themselves are powerless, a small number of powerful and wealthy citizens, each of whom can achieve great undertakings single-handed. In aristocratic societies men do not need to combine in order to act, because they are strongly held together. Every wealthy and powerful citizen constitutes the head of a permanent and compulsory association, composed of all those who are dependent upon him, or whom he makes subservient to the execution of his designs. Amongst democratic nations, on the contrary, all the citizens are independent and feeble : they can do hardly anything by themselves, and none of them can oblige his fellow-men to lend him their assistance. *They all, therefore, fall into a state of incapacity*, if they do not learn voluntarily to help one another. If men living in democratic countries had no right and no inclination to associate for political purposes, *their independence would be in great jeopardy*, but they might long preserve their wealth and their cultivation : whereas if they never acquired the habit of forming associations in ordinary life, *civilisation itself would be endangered*. A people amongst which individuals should lose the power of achieving great things single-handed, without acquiring the means of producing them by united exertions, *would soon relapse into barbarism.*'

This last sentence states with admirable precision the whole pith of our own argument.

Unhappily, but not unexpectedly, it was in these *débris* of the French Revolution, and amongst a people upon which democracy had exerted all its disintegrating power, without the correcting influence of freedom and self-government, that Imperialism struck root. And Imperialism, as it was understood and practised by the late Sovereign of France, aggravated all the' evils of democracy and indeed lived upon them. The nation sank under the influence of a corrupt personal Government, which became the sole depositary of power, and promised the people in exchange unbounded material prosperity. The press was fettered. The right of association for political objects was denied. Even the material progress of the country was purchased at the price of higher interests, and proved a perishable commodity, and (to quote another phrase of M. de Tocqueville) 'the more enfeebled and incompetent the citizens became, the more active the Government was rendered, in order that society at large might execute what individuals could no longer accomplish.' There lay the delusion. There can be no strength in a Government other than the strength of the nation; and if the nation sinks in energy, morality, and independence, sooner or later the Government must share the same fate.

No example of this truth can be more striking than the condition of the French army at the outset of the war, for the army is the youthful strength of the nation, trained by the Government itself and under its immediate control. We are certain that the peasant population of France had no desire for war. They knew the price of it too well, and all their interests and tastes were opposed to it. If a *plébiscite* could have been taken on the question, the votes would have been ten to one for peace. But they were powerless even to make known their opinions; utterly powerless to check the Government in its course. The Emperor appears to have supposed (perhaps erroneously) that the army did wish for war and was prepared for it. The warning voice which had come from the ranks in the last *plébiscite* had startled and alarmed him. But even the army was infected by the disease which had struck so deep into the community—no respect, no power of combination, no discipline, luxury among the officers, discontent among the soldiers, most of whom were longing to return to their parental fields. Taken from the population, the army shared the peculiar feelings of the population, and its military character was decomposed by them. In no other manner can we account for the unexampled spectacle of the rapid dissolution, after two or three indecisive battles, of large bodies of disciplined troops.

The world saw in 1794 of what might be capable an army, hastily raised, but burning with the fire of revolutionary patriotism and hurled against the antiquated battalions of Germany. But nothing differs more from that enthusiastic and victorious levy than the late army of France, raised by conscription frnm a people intent on their own interests, relaxed by a long peace, trained in part by irregular warfare against the tribes of Africa, officered by men

who owed everything to their military rank and had
no social importance. Seniority is, of course, the
strict rule of promotion in democratic armies. The
consequence was that all the superior officers of the
French army were elderly men; their average age
was from 60 to 64; the average age of the revolutionary generals of 1794 was 30.[1]

It was undoubtedly supposed that the natural
valour and pugnacity of the French soldier would
break forth with an irresistible impetus in face of
the enemy on the Rhine. But this expectation was
disappointed. The *dynamical* force of the army was
wanting. It displayed no power of cohesion; after
the first reverses, the defeated corps collapsed into a
rabble; acts of astonishing insubordination marked
the whole line of march; and at the last extremity,
both in Sedan and Metz, there was no disposition to
adopt the heroic alternative of desperate, and perhaps
unavailing, resistance. These facts are so much at

[1] Even in point of numbers it would seem that the armies of
modern France have not increased in the same ratio as the population. On the 1st January 1678, says M. Camille Rousset in his invaluable *Histoire de Louvois* (vol. ii. p. 477), Louis XIV. had under
arms 279,610 men. The population of France probably did not at
that time exceed seventeen millions. In 1870, with a population of
forty millions, the number of effective French troops in the field
was apparently not much greater than it had been nearly two centuries before. It is true that France suffered cruelly from the exhausting levies of Louis XIV.'s wars, and that in the course of his reign
the population declined.

variance with the past history and character of the French army, that we cannot but infer from them that the social and political condition of the nation had debilitated the army. They appear not to be the same race of men as those valiant conscripts, mere boys, of 1814, who, in numbers not exceeding 40,000, barred the road to Paris against the Allied armies; twice broke the ranks of Blücher; and nearly decided Schwarzenberg to desist from the invasion. All democratic institutions are possessed of an intense energy at their origin and commencement. They are animated by popular enthusiasm and revolutionary power. But when these transitory elements of strength wear off, they have far less of tenacity, perpetuity, and endurance than the institutions of monarchical and aristocratic States. This observation seems to apply to their military as well as to their civil condition. Again, no armies are less likely to be animated by an intense military spirit than those which are raised by conscription from a people of peasant proprietors. Every recruit joins the army by compulsion, not to seek in it the profession of his choice, but in obedience to the law which obliges him to quit his natural position in life for several years, and tears him from the cultivation of his own or his father's homestead. He is therefore a reluctant soldier, and, far from regarding the barrack or the camp as his home, he desires nothing so much as to return to his village. The conduct of the French, both in the field and as prisoners of war, warrants the belief that these feelings had more weight with them than the passion of military glory or even the sense of military duty. The existence of a vast multitude of peasant proprietors is probably beneficial as an element of peace, but it certainly does not augment the military power of the State. No one can doubt that the late reverses of the French armies have inflicted a tremendous blow on the national pride of the people and on their absolute faith .in the invincibility of their arms. But this shock does not appear to have called forth a corresponding effort on the part of the population. Everybody has noticed with surprise the surrender of populous towns to small parties of invading horsemen. The enormous lines of communication of the Prussian armies have seldom been assailed. And the travellers who have crossed France during the war have been struck by the submissive acquiescence of the peasantry under a calamity which appeared to them to be irresistible. We know very well what they feel. We can guess the fierce exe-, crations with which they dog the track of the invader.

But personal and local interests are powerful restraints on national action. The defence of Paris is heroical, and amongst the gallant chiefs of the Army of the Loire may be reckoned many of the best names of France; but the general attitude of the people has hitherto been that of despair rather than of enthusiasm.

It would be unjust to the Provisional Government of Defence and to the nation, not to admit that prodigious exertions have been made to repel the enemy, not without hopes of ultimate success. It would be ungracious to criticise their language, or to question the wisdom of their actions, under so many difficulties, when we are perfectly convinced of the sincerity of their patriotism. The remarks we are making are not aimed at any particular persons or parties; but at the general tendency and result of that state of society which has obtained the mastery over France by the Revolution. Nothing can more completely illustrate that tendency than the fact that in a supreme crisis of fate, France finds herself governed by two or three second-rate lawyers, who owe their notoriety to readiness of speech. The country has been fed upon falsehoods, and was never suffered to know the truth until it was too late to act upon it, because there was no man bold or strong enough to tell the truth to the supreme democracy, which shares with absolute kings the privilege of being approached with 'bated breath and flattered into ruin. To this hour, this poor stricken people is addressed in the language of courtiers, as if its ministers and journalists were its slaves; and it is hard to say who will assume the invidious duty of breaking the spell.

The Government of National Defence in France is represented by two men, General Trochu in Paris and M. Gambetta at Tours. No man has a higher character for personal rectitude and virtue than General Trochu. Unambitious, he has never sought the terrible responsibility which has been thrust upon him; and he could give no greater proof of patriotism than his honest resolution to serve his country and to defend the capital in conjunction with men whose political opinions have nothing in common with his own. Whatever be the result, he is one of the heroes of duty. We doubt not that he has performed a most arduous task with conscientious devotion; but he has shown no signs of the inspiration of military genius, and nothing in his past life had given him any opportunity of displaying it. M. Gambetta is a man of a different mould. He has the energy of revolutionary times. He

probably shares the opinion—we think an erroneous
one—that the cause of the Revolution was saved in
1794 by the violent measures of the Terrorists; and
though we believe him to be entirely free from their
execrable indifference to bloodshed, like them he
would not hesitate to resort to almost any means of
promoting his ends. The Terrorists were men who
believed in the strength of violent governments, and
who held very cheap the restraint of law. In the
name of liberty they claimed to exercise the most
arbitrary and unlimited power. This race of politicians is not extinct in France. In some of the
great cities they are formidable by numbers, and
when the war is over they will still present a formidable obstacle to the re-establishment of a regular
government in the country. The first step to the
re-establishment of such a government would evidently be the election of a National Assembly,
empowered to re-constitute the State on a legal
basis. To that measure, however, M. Gambetta is
strongly opposed. He has done all he can to induce
his colleagues to postpone it. He apparently distrusts his own ability to retain the power, conferred
upon him by the mob of Paris, in presence of the
representatives of France; and he prefers to exercise,
as long as he can, a power which is unlimited because

it has no legal character or basis. Nothing can be more absurd or more akin to the conduct of the Republican *commissaires* of the first Republic than M. Gambetta's interference with the military commanders who still remained to France: and his language throughout has been systematically mendacious. The ascendancy of such a man at such a time, who supplies the want of statesmanlike wisdom by declamatory energy, and aspires to be a Danton without the scaffold, is singularly characteristic of the revolutionary state of the country. He too is a child of 1792, destined probably to found as little as his predecessors, and not to equal either their momentary greatness or their unforgotten crimes.

M. Guizot, in whom age does not chill the fervour of patriotism or shake his faith in parliamentary government, has recently addressed a letter to the members of the Government of National Defence, in which he does ample justice to their exertions to save the country. But he proceeds in these remarkable terms:—

> Beware of illusions : in the present state of affairs, and of yourselves, you are not equal to your task. The present war has. and can have, for us, no other object but peace; and you are doubtless well aware that the country desires peace, when it can be obtained with honour. But the enemy, in order to treat for peace, and the neutral Powers, in order to second us in obtaining it,

require to have before them a complete and effective Government with a serious prospect of duration, and one which may be relied on to execute the treaties it may sign. You have neither that strength nor that character. You are an incomplete and provisional power. You have even been obliged, by the investment of Paris, to cut your Government in halves—one for Paris, the other for the provinces; and these two fractions of Government, materially severed from each other, have not always exhibited the same political aspect, whatever may be their mutual good-will : the spirit of order predominates in that of Paris ; the spirit of concession to disorder in that of the provinces.

Nor can it be denied that under this government, by reason of its division, the most important questions are decided—resolutions of peace and war, levies of the people, and national loans— by one or two persons, without debate, without publicity, and by the sole authority of this or that individual. What is this but another form of personal government, without responsibility subject to the control of debate, and without any pre-existing securities to the country?

Evidently nothing but a National Assembly, freely elected by the whole country, can put an end to a state of things so imperfect, so irregular, so precarious. Such an assembly can alone, by its debates and its decisions, realise and cover at the same time the responsibility of those who are in power, and give the Government the union, the support, and the strength which it requires—requires at home and abroad, for peace and for war. What is now desired, what is now demanded of the Republic, as it was formerly demanded of the Constitutional Monarchy, is the government of the nation by the nation. No negotiation can be carried on without it. Where, but in a National Assembly, capable of transporting itself to any part of the territory and causing the influence of its presence and the sound of its voice to be everywhere felt and heard—where else, I say, shall we find that common centre and source of action necessary to give effect to the will of the nation ?

We cordially concur in these sentiments; and we would fain cherish the hope which M. Guizot expresses, that such an Assembly will again bring forth from obscurity into light and power those estimable and able men who once formed the nucleus of the Government of France — men who are not fitly described by the name of any dynastic party, but who are at once conservative and liberal, asking nothing of the Government but to restore peace and order, the authority of the law, and a certain measure of freedom. Unhappily, M. Guizot himself admits that this worthy portion of the community has almost always shown itself too timid or too submissive to offer an effectual resistance to those who either trample on liberty in the name of order, or sacrifice order to what they term liberty. The history of the French Revolution has been the history of the conflict of these two extremes. The *juste milieu*, as M. Guizot perseveres in styling his own party, has fared but ill between them. And even now, for the reason we have given at some length in this article, we entertain but a faint expectation that the moderate and intelligent men of the middle classes will recover strength and energy enough to rescue the country from the grasp of the ignorant and the violent. Yet that is the problem to be solved before France can be restored to permanent peace, prosperity, and freedom.

We shall now leave our readers to draw their own inferences from these phenomena, and to answer as they please the questions—Is not France, as she now exists, the true child, in the third and fourth generation, of the democratic Revolution of 1789? Is not her present failure to be traced to permanent causes, even more than to temporary accidents, which indeed must themselves spring from such causes?

But ere we conclude we cannot but express the profound sorrow with which we witness even the momentary eclipse of the brightest planet in our system. With all the faults of her rulers and the failings of her people, France remains incomparably the most original, ingenious, and vivid of the Continental nations. When we remember what her literature has done for the world in the last three centuries; with what depth of insight and keen edge of discernment she has sounded and dispelled a host of errors; with what sagacity she has pursued every path of scientific research; with what lively skill she has popularised the arts; with what energy she has advocated the liberties of mankind,—her conquerors of the hour are no more worthy to be named beside her than the Macedonians were to rival the glory of Athens. She may indeed have been overeager to assert a political influence in Europe; but the influence of her language, of her tastes, of her genius, of her sympathies, and even of her manners, reached and will reach from the Tagus to the Volga.

It cannot be forgotten in this country that the joint influence of France and England in the Western Alliance has been for forty years the mainstay of the Liberal cause in Europe. 'Paris,' said Lord Palmerston in one of his happiest moments, 'is the pivot of my foreign policy.' It has been the good fortune of the generation to which we ourselves belong to root out those sentiments of mutual aversion and hostility which had subsisted between the two countries for so many ages. That alone has been by far the greatest and most important fact of this age, for to it we owe, till the present time, the peace of the world and the peace this country still enjoys. In that period of time, a multitude of difficult questions have arisen. They have almost all been solved in the sense desired by the Liberal Government of Great Britain with the active concurrence of France; and without that concurrence we should have found ourselves called upon to withstand alone the policy of the Northern Courts, which has been almost invariably opposed to ours. Thus it was that Belgium was constituted; that, by the Quadruple Treaty, the succession to the Crowns of Spain and Portugal was fixed in the constitutional line; that Greece was protected against Russian ascendancy: that in South America the River Plate was opened; that the rights of European nations were defended in China by the allied armies, and commerce placed under the guarantee of political treaties; that peace was restored in Syria; that the great contest against Russia was carried to a successful issue in the Crimea, and the Black Sea neutralised by the Treaty of 1856; that the independence of Italy was established by the arms of France, but with the cordial concurrence and moral support of this country; and that our own commercial relations with France were opened and extended by a treaty which has been a beacon of free-trade to the world. During the Indian Mutiny, far from taking any unfriendly advantage of our difficulties, France gave her cordial good-will to us in that battle of civilisation against barbarism. During the American Civil War the identical policy and conduct of the two States was strictly regulated in concert, and in the affair of the 'Trent' France declared promptly and unequivocally in our favour. Nor can we forget in this enumeration, that the two countries have repeatedly expressed in common, though unfortunately in vain, their conviction that the destruction of Polish nationality has been the cause of lasting evils to the best interests of Europe, which are apparent in the politics of the present hour.

Occasional differences of policy have at times arisen. France stood aloof from our Syrian intervention in 1840, and from our proposed Danish policy in 1864; she detached herself from us in the Spanish marriages and the Mexican expedition. We think that in each of these cases she was wrong; but these differences produced no permanent evil results, whereas the acts of joint policy we have just enumerated stand and remain for the benefit of the world. In all of them we have had the active cooperation of France. We have not had the cooperation, or the good wishes, of any other European Power.

It would be the height of ingratitude if we could now forget these mutual services, which do honour alike to the Government of Napoleon III. and to the Governments which preceded him. But there is too much reason to believe that we shall not be allowed to forget that the blow which has struck down France, has deprived England of no inconsiderable part of her influence abroad. The maritime strength of this country, when combined with the military strength of France, had a prestige and a force which proved fatal to the strongest autocrat of Europe, and were not to be openly resisted by his successors. That fortunate combination is for the present paralysed in one of its limbs, and those who suffered by it are not slow to take advantage of the change. Already the diminution of the force which supported the treaties maintaining the independence of the Ottoman Empire, has been supposed to warrant an arrogant demand to set them aside. It is presumed that public law has lost its authority, since the aid of France can no longer be invoked in support of it; and .whatever power Great Britain may put forth in defence of what she conceives to be just and right, she has for the present lost the support of her most efficient ally.

In spite, however, of all that is past, France has still the moral energy to carry on this great contest for national independence. Victory is the prize of those who can make war longest: and if aught of her ancient spirit remains, she will not treat as long as a stranger treads her soil.

This article was published on the 15th January 1871 at a moment when the contest between France and Germany was not finally decided, although the chances of success were obviously in favour of the Prussian armies. It was not, however, till four days later, on the 19th January, that the final attempt was made, and made in vain to break through the Prussian lines. With the forces at General Trochu's disposal, its success was not possible. Yet, it was not till that date that General Moltke felt his position to be really secure, and the fall of Paris certain. He himself said so.

I am aware that the concluding lines of the foregoing essay were thought at the time to express a hope which subsequent events did not justify, and which, even when it was published, could not be justified. But although France might doubtless have obtained somewhat easier terms of peace from her invaders after the capitulation of Sedan, if the Government of the Emperor Napoleon had not been overthrown by the revolution of the 4th September; yet I confess that I am still one of those who hold that the effort made by France to carry on the war for five months longer, though the result was disastrous, is the one fact which in some degree redeems the honour of the nation. She displayed at least a certain amount of moral energy and physical vigour in that part of the contest; not enough to save her from defeat, but enough to wipe out a portion of the stain on her national character and her honour. This was the sentiment which dictated the concluding lines of this essay; and the reluctance with which she was brought to submit to an oppressive and humiliating peace was the last proof she could give that something of her long greatness still remained in the hearts of her people. I therefore leave the expression unchanged.

COMMUNAL FRANCE.

COMMUNAL FRANCE.[1]

THESE books are not of very recent date; but they are the better suited to our purpose. Imperfectly informed of the true history of the extraordinary events which have recently occurred in the capital of France, and still more ignorant of the future which awaits that country, it is to the past alone that we can look for light upon its condition and its destiny. The scenes of the French Revolution are not so varied or so diverse that we cannot trace in them the operation of uniform causes, and very often a repetition of the same results. Indeed, we think it can be shown that there is a marvellous

[1] This article was first published in the *Edinburgh Review*, No. 273, for July 1871, as a review of the following works :—
1. *Histoire du Droit municipal en France sous la Domination romaine et sous les trois Dynasties.* Par M. Raynouard. Deux tomes. 8vo. Paris : 1829. 2. *Essai sur l'Histoire de la Formation et des Progrès du Tiers État, suivi d'un Tableau de l'ancienne France municipale.* Par Augustin Thierry. 8vo. Paris : 1853. 3. *La Commune, l'Église, et l'État dans leurs Rapports avec les Classes laborieuses.* Par Ferdinand Béchard. Paris : 1849. 4. *De la Décadence de la France.* Par M. Raudot. Paris : 1849. 5. *Histoire de la Terreur* (1792-1794) *d'après des documents authentiques et inédits.* Par M. Mortimer-Ternaux. Sept tomes. 8vo. Paris : 1866.

resemblance between incidents which have occurred under very different circumstances and at a distance of three quarters of a century. These contemporary events give to the history of the Revolution in its earlier years an intense reality which brings the whole tragic spectacle again before us; the lurid light of another conflagration lights up the ruins of the ravaged city. For ourselves, we are free to confess that as one hour of ocular observation frequently teaches more than a century of books and written records, so the events of this spring have given fresh strength and truth to our knowledge of the whole Revolution. The figures of the Commune and the Reign of Terror start once more from the canvas and live—degenerate, indeed, contemptible, obscure by the side of their nefarious prototypes, but animated by the same passions, and performing with unabated fury the same parts. We turn then to these records of the past, to seek in them the explanation of the present. M. Raynouard and M. Béchard are two of the writers who have treated most ably of the municipal institutions of France, M. Augustin Thierry is perhaps the most learned and conscientious of French historians, and M. Mortimer-Ternaux is a trustworthy narrator of the Reign of Terror, because he writes not for effect but for truth, and every statement is corroborated by authentic and original documents of the period. We regret to learn that in the autumn of 1871 this estimable writer died, and that the great work for which he had collected such abundant materials remains at present incomplete.

The military disasters of France in August 1870 were followed, as it was evident they would be, by a political revolution; for the legislative body existing on the 3rd September was restrained by the opposition of the Empress from taking the necessary steps to meet the emergency by any legal provision. The consequence was that what had not been done by law was done by force; and on the 4th September, a self-constituted Government, deriving its principal strength from the mob of Paris, and composed of the leading members of the late Parliamentary Opposition, installed itself at the Hôtel de Ville. Pressure from without, in the shape of the Prussian invasion, gave to this Provisional Administration a slight degree of stability; it assumed the modest and appropriate title of the Defence Government; M. Jules Favre was enabled to negotiate, though with signal incapacity, at Ferrières; General Trochu retained for some time, through his high moral qualities, a degree of respect to which his military talents hardly entitled him ; M. Gambetta proceeded in his balloon to rouse the nation by revolutionary means; and M. Picard succeeded in rescuing his colleagues from the first insurrection of the Commune of Paris on the 31st October. But whilst these authorities carried on with indifferent success their hopeless contest against the organised military power of Germany, they were themselves training in the streets and suburbs of Paris an army still more formidable to themselves and to France. The first step of the Government of the 4th September had been to give arms to the people, and whilst the siege of Paris lasted the whole male population was drilled, prepared to fight, and taken into the pay of the State. Against the Germans, these raw and ill-disciplined troops were powerless : but upon the conclusion of the peace, M. Jules Favre having most unwisely refused the offer of Count Bismarck to disarm the National Guard of Paris, the city remained in the possession of legions of armed citizens, well provided with rifles, cannon, and ammunition. Never at any period of the entire Revolution had the insurrectionary forces of Paris been so well prepared for a mortal struggle. They were in possession of all the stores accumulated for the defence of the capital against a siege of unprecedented magnitude. The population was exasperated by deception and humiliated by defeat. All the ordinary pursuits of life and industry had been suspended by the siege and superseded by military service. Large numbers of the floating revolutionary population of Europe flocked to Paris: larger numbers of the tranquil and terrified residents in that devoted city had hastened to escape from it. It seemed as if the moment, long foreseen in the fevered dreams of the democratic regenerators of mankind, had actually arrived, and that the Universal Democratic Confraternity of Nations was about to be enthroned in the first city of continental Europe. The experiment has actually been made; and deeply as we deplore the ruin and bloodshed caused by this protracted contest, it cannot be denied that some good results may be anticipated from this demonstrative example of what the Government of the Commune is worth. We have no desire to exaggerate either its follies or its crimes. We will acknowledge that it was at first less sanguinary and less addicted to plunder than its enemies had anticipated. But it has been supremely arbitrary and supremely stupid. In the name of liberty, it destroyed every condition of freedom: in the name of the common interests of the city, it reduced that city to the depth of ruin, drove away the wealthier classes and pauperised the lower, extinguished all productive industry, frightened away credit and capital, and, at last, food itself would have been wanting if the population had not been enormously diminished. On economical principles alone, putting aside its military and political absurdities, the Commune of Paris could not fail to reduce one of the first cities of the world, in a few months, to a wilderness and a solitude. The interruption of productive labour and the cessation of the means of exchanges, by which the commodities indispensable to the support of life are procured, must bring about this result. An earthquake, or the eruption of a volcano, would not be more fatal and scarcely more prompt in its effects. For as the wants of all classes of society in great cities are necessarily provided for from day to day, and cities themselves produce none of the first elements of life, the moment the mechanism of their highly artificial system is stopped they begin to perish. Immense numbers of human beings are driven to seek the means of subsistence elsewhere. All that constitutes the strength and wealth of a great capital — the presence of the supreme rulers of the State, the authority of law and justice, the studious population of the schools, the galleries of art, the pursuit of pleasure, the influx of strangers, the relations of society, the steady financial circulation which is the life of trade, the power of universal exchange, the investment of capital, the employment and security of labour, and all the myriad ramifications of demand and supply by which the wants of mankind are provided for—all these things may cease to be. Under the terrible stress of war and revolution, we have seen them cease to be; but the Commune has far more to answer for than the arms of the enemy, for what the German forces overthrew was but an army and a state : the revolution of the Commune shook to its foundation the whole structure of society. The creed of the members of the 'International Association' is simply this—that the old social order must be destroyed, and destroyed by their hands. A power formed by the overthrow of law is itself devoid of law. The members and servants of this ephemeral Government were themselves ephemeral, rising to the surface from the dregs, and bursting when they reach the outer air, like bubbles from the depth of some boiling pool. If any higher intelligence existed to direct the acts and policy of the Commune, it was mysterious, secret, and carefully withdrawn from observation and control. Meanwhile, the people, in whose name these things were done, were incited, bought, or compelled to spend their lives in a hopeless and desperate resistance, for some cause which has not been defined, and some leader whose very name is unknown. Victory itself over such antagonists leaves it equally difficult to conciliate and to subdue them; they can only be destroyed. If they began as fanatics, they ended as incendiaries, assassins, and thieves.

As a means of government the Secret Committee of the Commune was odious and contemptible, but as an engine of social war it was terrific, for in the frenzy of despair it let loose all the powers of destruction. We shall not attempt to describe in detail what no words have yet been found to describe—the appalling spectacle of Paris as it appeared in the month of May 1871, an awful prelude to the most tremendous catastrophe in the history of man. The streets and avenues looked large and vacant, for in place of the gay and busy crowds once wont to throng them, a few bands of rude and drunken soldiers made the solitude more desolate. Half the combatant army of the Commune was believed to consist of fugitives, adventurers, and criminals from every sink and every jail in

Europe. Their courage was inflamed by liquor and rewarded by debauchery. Such indeed was their state of physical gangrene that every blow was fatal, and the wounded were outnumbered by the dead. These demons of misrule held entirely at their mercy all that still existed in the city. Terror was everywhere. Terror reigned. A mysterious power, whose source was as unknown as its name, seemed to direct at will the fury of these myrmidons, and certainly carried on an intrepid resistance without the walls. But they were the ministers of public and private vengeance. Whatever spoke to them of the obligations of religion was an object of abhorrence; whatever spoke to them of the past glory of their country was an object of scorn; they polluted the churches, they trampled on the Cross, they cast down the Column; they defied alike their country and their God; insomuch that those of the city who witnessed these things exclaimed, in their anguish, that assuredly the Ancient Curse, the curse of Rome, of Jerusalem, of Babylon, had fallen upon themselves and upon their children.

But the darkest forecast was exceeded by the doom and destruction of the chief buildings in that great capital. The world had yet to learn what crimes may be committed by a democracy without veneration and without law. In that supreme paroxysm of blood and fire, the passions of man did their worst. In those dreadful days the Revolution still triumphed ; but its triumph annihilated the very seat of its own power. All ties and all traditions were sacrificed. Ruin passed in a torrent of fire over the city. The murder of the hostages—guiltless men torn from the altars and the seats of justice to perish for the guilt of others—was a crime equalled only by the martyrdom of the Carmes and the Abbaye in 1792 ; and it was punished by a sanguinary and indiscriminating massacre of the insurgent populace. If any doubt or disbelieve the tremendous force of self-destruction which lies in the lower strata of great communities and may burst forth with volcanic fury, this example is given them to be a record for ever. If any can witness such events and such calamities, doubting and disbelieving that the world's history is governed by eternal justice and almighty power, 'neither will they be persuaded though one rose from the dead.'

> Well roars the storm to those that hear
> A deeper voice across the storm,
> Proclaiming social truth shall spread
> And justice, e'en tho' thrice again
> The red fool-fury of the Seine
> Should pile her barricades with dead.

> The fortress crashes from on high,
> The brute earth lightens to the sky,
> And the vast Æon sinks in blood
> Encompassed by the fires of hell.[1]

Such was the climax of the history of the Commune of Paris.

Why is it, then, that the very name of the Commune of Paris is a name of terror and turbulence, whilst that of the City of London is synonymous with good order and ancient unambitious civic administration? How comes it to pass that municipal freedom and government either exist not at all in France, or exist for purposes, and in a shape, incompatible with the very existence of the State? When an Englishman is told that the citizens of Paris were contending for the right of electing their own magistrates, and for the civic freedom which the Empire denied them, he naturally sympathises with a cause so nearly allied to his own rights and experience. But in no respect are the two countries more widely different than in the nature of their municipal institutions. That difference is vast and important enough to account for much of their entire political and social history; in order to sound it, it is

[1] Tennyson's *In Memoriam*, cxxv.

necessary to go back to the very root of their social constitution.

The answer, then, we have to make to this question is, that it may be shown from the history of the French people that they have never possessed or practised, either by law or tradition, those established municipal rights of self-government which have been the basis of freedom and civilisation in the chartered cities and municipalities of Italy, Germany, Flanders, England, and even Spain; that what were termed the municipal rights of France have served alternately, either to disguise the action of the central power of the State, or to disintegrate the kingdom; that the municipal forces, which have at times broken out with revolutionary violence in French history, have commonly originated in spontaneous military movements of the citizens, placing them in opposition to the law and not in subordination to it; lastly, that the tendency of these armed Communes has invariably been to overleap the proper bounds of municipal authority, to challenge the State itself by claims of sovereignty, and in the end to make war upon it. The Communes of France have alternately proved to be instruments of despotism or centres of sedition. The all-important element of political life which municipal freedom can alone supply, by attaching men to the conduct of their own public affairs, and by educating them in the discharge of public duties, has in France been wanting for centuries ; and this may not unreasonably be regarded as the chief cause of the repeated failures of the French nation to establish a system of constitutional government. If these propositions are true and can be established by historical evidence, they appear to us to throw a beam of light upon the history of France, and more especially upon the history of her great Revolution from 1789 to the present day. The Commune of Paris of 1871 is no novelty in the annals of France. It is the recurrence of a well-known drama—burlesque, arbitrary, desperate—when acts of government become the acts of maniacs, and all the horrors of bloodshed, ruin, fire, proscription, anarchy, are let loose upon the great city by those who call themselves her chief magistrates. We propose to trace the mischief to what we conceive to be its source.

The municipal law of France, as described by M. Raynouard, was based upon the ancient right, established by the legislation of the Roman Empire, which authorised the inhabitants of a city to choose their magistrates and to administer their affairs. The oldest cities of France were in fact the municipalities of Gaul. They were copies on a small scale of Imperial Rome; and in this shape they were anterior to the grant of any municipal charters by the Crown, though such charters were subsequently granted in and after the twelfth century to define their powers or confirm their privileges. Thus the cities of Perigueux, Bourges, Marseilles, Arles, Toulouse, Narbonne, Nîmes, Metz, Paris, and Reims were all undoubtedly Roman *civitates* governed by consuls, or a senate of *boni homines*, elected by their fellow-citizens. But their rights far exceeded what are now understood by municipal or civic franchises; they were in many respects sovereign communities; they levied troops, made peace and war, concluded treaties, and administered justice in their own name. Thus, for example, it was provided by the constitution of Perigueux that the 'civitas sit libera, et nullius jurisdictioni subjecta,' and that ' ad voluntatem vel dispositionem consulatûs ibit universitatis exercitus et ducetur.' The earliest act of homage of the citizens of Perigueux to the kings of France took place in 1204.

The city of Paris never solicited or accepted any charter of incorporation, and M. Raynouard argues (we think unwisely) that she stood in no need of any such safeguard. 'Before Cæsar's conquest,' says he,

'Paris had enjoyed municipal liberty. Her *Nautæ*, authorised or at least protected by the institutions of Rome, became her most useful citizens. They had influence enough to unite the rights and interests of the municipal magistracy to the interest and right of their powerful company, and the symbolical Galley, which still figures in the city arms, as well as the old title of Provost of the Water Traders (*Procurator mercatorum aquæ*), borne by the chief magistrate, attested this change.' 'Most of the cities of France,' he adds, 'never had charters of incorporation. Their own municipal right sufficed to them. They claimed no other safeguard.' It was a *jus ante omnia jura natum*, or, to use an English expression, it was the common law of the country.

From this definition of the municipal rights of France we draw two inferences: *First*, the Crown, when not bound by charter, could, and did, revoke the municipal liberties of the people, when a city happened to displease the Court, as for instance, Philippe de Valois suppressed the corporation of Laon, and Charles VI. suspended the municipal government of Paris in 1382. *Secondly*, the powers of corporations not being defined by charter but by usage, were, so to speak, self-evolved; they were sometimes narrowed and sometimes extended to excess; they were not under the control of a judicial authority or even of the legislature; therefore in times of subjection they were contracted within the limits of servitude, in times of revolution they expanded to absolute sovereignty.

It might be shown, by a careful examination of the principles and history of the Gallo-Roman and the Teutonic or Anglo-Saxon municipalities, that there is this radical difference between them—the former tending to a partition of sovereignty, and consequently to the alternative of federalism or civil war, as was exemplified by the Italian republics of the Middle Ages and by the cities and provinces of France until they were overpowered and absorbed by the Crown—the latter aiming at no sovereignty at all, but confined to the discharge of strictly municipal functions in loyal subordination to the State from which they drew their powers. Dr. Brady has shown, in his Essay on English Boroughs (which is the best authority on the subject) that 'all free-burghs in England *had their beginning from charter;* for a free-burgh, in the true sense of the word, was only a town of free-trading, with a merchant guild or community, without paying toll, pontage, or other royal dues.' The English borough charters first made the citizens free men; then conferred liberty of trade, fairs, and markets; then acknowledged the power of assessing the tenths or fifteenths granted to the Crown by Parliament; and they were called upon in many cases to elect and return members to Parliament—a privilege which was regarded as onerous. But of direct political or executive power there is no trace whatever in their history; and this essentially distinguishes them from the communes of France.

This distinction has in fact been drawn with prodigious erudition and searching discrimination by M. Augustin Thierry in his well-known letters on the History of France and in the 'Tableau de l'ancienne France municipale,' annexed to his 'Histoire du Tiers État'—a work which well deserves to be studied as a masterpiece of historical criticism. M. Thierry has shown in his writings that the municipal constitutions of the towns of France were extremely diversified. They retained traces of the ten or twelve states which were ultimately absorbed in the unity of France; and he divides them into distinct classes or zones. In the towns of the south the municipal institutions were of Roman origin; their magistrates were styled Consuls; and they enjoyed a very high degree of sovereignty and independence, extending, says Thierry, 'even to the plenitude of a republican constitution.' In the north the cities were formed by the association of guilds, under the pledge of a civic oath; and their condition resembled that of the free towns of Flanders. In the central regions of France the sovereignty of the communes was more limited. In Normandy and Maine they resembled the early municipalities of England. In the cities of Eastern France, which had formed part of the Germanic Empire, the Teutonic form prevailed—that is, their powers were restricted, because, says Thierry, 'the emperors of Germany were systematically hostile to municipalities created by the revolutionary mode of insurrection or by that of mutual associations.' They were in fact corporations like our own, exercising no powers but those which had been conceded to them by the Crown. They were expressly inhibited from framing or claiming any rights 'sine domini sui assensu.'[1] It is impossible for us, in this place, to follow out in detail this very intricate subject. For our present purpose it suffices to point out, in the words of Thierry, in his essay on the 'Affranchissement des Communes,' that 'les plus anciennes et

---

[1] See the 'Henrici regis sententia contra communiones civitatum,' in Pertz' *Monumenta Germanica*, tome ii. p. 279.

les plus considérables *s'établirent spontanément, par insurrection*, contre le pouvoir seigneurial ;' their very basis was insurrection ; and so it has been throughout the history of France. It is obvious that this fact explains, on the one hand, the tendency of the communes to disintegrate the State, and, on the other, the extreme jealousy and hostility of the State towards municipal institutions of so formidable a character. These two conflicting elements appear to subsist down to the present day, and the recent civil war between the Commune of Paris and the representatives of the nation is the last manifestation of them.

To quote at once a striking example of this French conception of municipal liberties :—at the very outset of the Revolution, on the 23rd July, 1789, when the name of the city of Paris was heard for the first time in the Assembly after the taking of the Bastille, Mirabeau exclaimed : ' Municipalities are the more important as they are the true basis of public happiness, the most useful element of a good constitution, the everyday resource of society, the safeguard of every home, and, in short, the only mode of interesting the whole people in the government, and of extending rights to all classes of the community.' But upon Mounier's asking whether he proposed to leave each town to frame its own municipal institutions (*de se municipaliser à sa manière*)—adding that he thought it would be too dangerous for the Assembly to create states within the State, and to multiply sovereignties—Mirabeau replied emphatically that his intention was that the Assembly *should not* organise the municipalities; that every corporation ought to be subject to the great principles of national representation; but, provided these were complied with, the details of municipal government ought to be left to the townspeople to settle for themselves, as they please. We shall shortly see the fruits of this principle.

It should also be borne in mind, though this part of the subject is too extensive to form part of our present inquiry, that the old constitution of France was remarkable for its Provincial Estates and Provincial Parliaments. In thirty provinces which were successively annexed to the Crown of France in six centuries and under fifteen kings, the old constitutional representation of the people by the three Estates existed. These assemblies all survived till the sixteenth century; it was not until the middle of the seventeenth century that the system of government by royal intendants was established over the generalities of France; and down to 1789, eight provinces, comprising a quarter of the kingdom, were still *Pays d'États* and had preserved some traces of provincial independence. But this fact, though of great importance to the history of France, is distinct from the proper civic or municipal rights of the towns, to which we are now addressing ourselves. In the *plan de réforme*, secretly prepared by Fénelon in 1711 for the Duc de Bourgogne, the revival of the Provincial Estates, on the model of the Assembly then still subsisting in Languedoc, was proposed for the regeneration of the country. Upon the accession of Turgot to office the same idea was resumed in his 'Mémoire au Roi sur les Municipalités' with greater precision. Each parish was to have had an elective board for the purposes of rating, roads, and the relief of the poor; the votes were to be in proportion to the rateable income of the tax-payers. Necker, who succeeded him in office in 1776, zealously adopted and partially applied these views, and in 1778 an edict was passed to revive the Assembly of the province of Berri. It was afterwards extended to Dauphiné, Montauban (Haute-Guienne), and the Bourbonnais. These experiments were highly successful; but it did not escape the penetration of Necker that there was great danger of these bodies *aiming at political power*, and in a secret memoir to the King written in 1778 he used these remarkable words: Ils s'y prennent comme tous les corps qui veulent acquérir du pouvoir, en parlant au nom du peuple, en se disant les défenseurs des droits de la nation . . . . il faut donc se préparer à des combats qui troubleront le règne de votre Majesté, et conduiront successivement ou à une dégradation de l'autorité ou à des partis extrêmes dont on ne peut mesurer au juste les conséquences.'[1]

In our own political constitution there never was anything corresponding to these Provincial Assemblies. England was represented and taxed from an early period of her history by the Parliament of the realm for affairs and charges of state, and by chartered civic corporations for municipal purposes. The Provincial Estates of France were an intermediate representative power; they were long of great utility and importance to the freedom of the nation; but they never acquired the authority of the

---

[1] See M. de Lavergne, *Assemblées provinciales sous Louis XVI*, which gives from authentic sources an accurate picture of the provincial and municipal condition of France just before the Revolution.

An excellent Memoir on the History and Organisation of the Provincial Estates of France was also read by M. Laferrière to the 'Académie des Sciences morales et politiques' in 1860, and is published in the eleventh volume of the Transactions of that Academy.

Parliament of England, because the States-General of the kingdom (which consisted of delegates from the Provincial Estates), were rarely convoked ; nor did they supply the want of true municipal government, because they aimed rather at a share of sovereign power. Indeed they were used as a substitute for the States-General, and as a check on the democratic spirit of the towns. Thus the Dauphin Charles V. felt the necessity of resting his authority on the States of the Langue d'Oc and other provinces against the States-General of Paris and of the Langue d'Oil. He successfully played off these Provincial Assemblies, which were essentially aristocratic in their character, against the turbulent democracy of the Paris Assembly, which broke out in the daring enterprises of Marcel and the trades' unions of that age ; hence arose the extension and even the general adoption of Provincial Estates in all parts of France.[1]

It is curious to trace so far back as the fourteenth century the germs of that latent federalism of France which the absolutism of the Crown for the last two centuries was supposed to have annihilated, and to mark, even at that remote period of history,

[1] Laferrière's *Mémoire*, p. 355, and Michelet, *Histoire de France*, cap. 4.

indications of parties not very dissimilar from those which at this moment divide and distract the French nation. A parallel may be drawn between the condition of France in 1356 after the loss of the battle of Poitiers, and the condition of France in 1871 after the capitulation of Sedan. In both instances the French army was destroyed, and the sovereign taken prisoner. King John was removed to Windsor, where he was received with royal honours. Such was the terror inspired by the victorious forces that the French peasantry fled at the sight of an English man-at-arms. Whatever remained of France was within the walls of Paris, where Stephen Marcel, Provost of the Trades, still held his ground and dictated terms to the Dauphin. The red and blue hoods of the citizens then first appeared in political history—for those are the colours of Paris—one day to be allied with the white cockade of the Bourbons in the tricolor of France. The power which conceived and imposed the conditions of the celebrated ordinance of 1356 was essentially the municipal, though revolutionary, strength of Paris. 'The dream of Etienne Marcel and his friends,' says Thierry, ' was a confederation of sovereign cities having Paris at their head and governing the country through a diet under the sovereignty of a king.' Those words might almost have been written yesterday; but, no doubt, the designs of Marcel embraced all the chief ends of constitutional government, accomplished by the democratical dictatorship of Paris acting by means of terror, in the name of the common good, over the rest of France. The struggle lasted nearly three years. The Dauphin's chief officers were slain; the Dauphin's troops driven out of Paris; but the movement failed because Paris stood alone against the forces of the kingdom, and the discouragement of the people.[1] 'Paris,' says M. Michelet, 'se chargeait de gouverner la France. Mais la France ne voulut pas.' The Jacquerie broke out in the provinces. Marcel himself was overpowered and killed by the partisans of the Dauphin, and in him perished, to use the somewhat hyperbolical language of the same historian, 'the representative of Paris against the kingdom, and the last champion of a narrow communal patriotism.' The treaty of Bretigny followed, and ended the war —the most disastrous compact to which a French-

---

[1] Marcel's insurrection ended in August 1358. In November 1358 it was for the first time declared by the Crown that no Commune could be constituted without the royal assent, and that all communal and consular towns were *ipso facto* under the Crown as their feudal superior. The abuse of municipal power led as usual to its restriction.

man ever put his name, until that which was signed the other day at Versailles.

But we revert to the more limited subject of the civic institutions of the country. The expression of Mounier in the National Assembly, that the towns were to *se municipaliser à leur manière*, is singularly descriptive of their history. Whenever they have played a considerable part it has been as the leaders of a military sedition, directed against the supreme power in the State. In the insurrection of Marcel (1356) just referred to, M. Michelet says: 'On sent la verve révolutionnaire et en même temps le génie administratif de la grande Commune.' We know not how far the latter member of the sentence is applicable at the present day, but the 'verve révolutionnaire' has not been wanting in any age, and thus it came to pass that the municipality of Paris was viewed with dread and disfavour by the Crown. Thus in the earlier years of the reign of Charles VI., before the gay young soldier had sunk into a gloomy monomaniac, Paris rose in one of its secular tumults, the Maillotins [1] pillaged the abbeys, broke open the prisons, and defied the King; but the young con-

---

[1] The *maillets* they bore were strong iron maces or mallets, whence their name. The City of Paris sent forth a well-equipped army of 30,000 men, who met the King before Montmartre.

queror of Roosebeke was not slow to turn his victorious arms against his own capital, and rode down the armed citizens with merciless severity. Heavy requisitions were levied on the richer classes; heavier taxes were imposed on the sale of all commodities. The liberties of the city were crushed by ordinances, 'statuentes' (says the monk of St. Denis) 'ut officium præpositruæ exerceret qui regis auctoritate et non civium fungeretur.' 'Il n'y avait,' says M. Michelet, 'plus de ville, plus de prévôt, plus d'échevins, plus de Commune de Paris.' The suspension lasted for twenty-nine years, and when the liberties of the city were at length restored in 1412, a fresh explosion ensued. The Duke of Burgundy, who reigned under the name of his unfortunate nephew Charles VI., was disposed to favour and rely on the popular party, and by his influence the old municipal rights of Paris were restored in that year—'liberè urbis antiquam libertatem restituentes,' were the words of the royal decree. The first result of popular election was to place the butchers of the great butchery of Ste. Geneviève at the head of the corporation, supported by their formidable band of journeymen, the Ecorcheurs, or flayers of the shambles. Simon Caboche was the hero of this fresh municipal revolution; but although the University took part with the butchers, and the Bastille itself was attacked, as it was in 1789, the affair ended in a compromise.

So again, to quote another of the 'great days' of Paris, when the Duc de Guise entered the city on the 10th May, 1588, against the express commands of his sovereign, he was received with tumultuous applause by the Commune, which became from that moment the heart of the League. The irresolute king hesitated to act against his formidable vassal. The next day the burgher-guards began to go over. The fierce populace collected on the Place Maubert, and in a few hours barricades were thrown up across the principal streets. It was the identical story which has since been so often repeated—thrice in our own recollection. The royal troops were paralysed by inaction. The people triumphed. 'You must give me these soldiers as a present, my friends,' said Guise to the townspeople. And so the Swiss, French, and German troopers and infantry were marched out of Paris, led by an officer of the suite of Guise, who commanded them with a cane. The king fled; and Paris remained for about six years in the hands of an insurrectionary government. The Secret Committee of the League and the authority of the Seize were, as has recently been pointed out

by an able historical writer, the prototypes of the
Commune of 1792 and the Committee of Public
Safety; they have again been reflected in the events
of the present year. The pulpits and preachers of
the League were the clubs and journalists of the
sixteenth century. Fanaticism of a different kind
has succeeded to the frenzy of religious bigotry;
but it is not less fatal to the prosperity of the city
and the liberties of the people; for once more,
though from different causes, the forces of the nation
have been compelled to besiege, attack, and reduce
the capital. This military character of the French
Commune was one of its peculiar features, and
adhered to it as long as it retained any real independence. Thus one Millotet, who was *Vicomte
Mayeur* of the city of Dijon, and has left memoirs,
relates that when the Duc d'Épernon returned from
the siege of Bellegarde in 1651, this gallant magistrate met him at the gates of Dijon, armed at all
points, with a feather in his cap and a pike in his
hand, with 6,000 citizens behind him, all well armed,
good men and true. His address to the general
was, 'Monseigneur, you perceive by the condition
of the inhabitants of this place that they are ready
to lay down their lives for your service.' The
mayor was followed by a guard of twenty-four men-

at-arms, and he had his own city artillery, which Louvois only succeeded with great difficulty in wresting from the corporation.

The influence of the Crown in France was constantly employed to lower and destroy the municipal franchises of the towns. Louis XI. was a ready grantor of municipal charters, but M. de Tocqueville, who had carefully examined those which were bestowed on the towns of Anjou, Maine, and Touraine, affirms that they were all conceived in a spirit hostile to the rights and dignity of the people. The King used the middle classes to pull down those above them and to crush those beneath them. He was equally anti-aristocratic and anti-democratic; heaping titles of nobility on the principal persons of the towns to lower the value of rank, and destroying the whole popular and democratic character of the administration of the towns, by restricting the government of them to a small number of privileged families.[1] Nevertheless, down to nearly the end of the seventeenth century, some of the towns of France continued to be small democratic commonwealths, electing their own magistrates, and proud of their independence.

[1] Tocqueville, *France before* 1789, note S, p. 428. See also chapter iii. p. 75.

But in 1692, a still more fatal blow was struck at municipal freedom. The civic offices were then regularly put up for sale, that is, the King sold in each town to certain inhabitants the right of governing their townsmen. Subsequently these purchased rights were not unfrequently resumed, in order to be resold to other competitors. This was done seven times in eighty years, and done for the mere purpose of raising money. These municipal officers were usually unpaid; but the mayor was frequently ennobled; the échevins enjoyed a certain civic rank, and the whole corporation was indulged with exemption from taxation and the billeting of troops, with an allowance for wax candles, sometimes with apartments. A strict line of distinction was drawn between the *notables* of the town and the *burghers* or tradesmen. The notables were almost all public functionaries. The whole corporate body was under the control of the Royal Intendant. Thus at Angers, it was expressly provided that 'the corporation never consults the inhabitants generally, even on the most important subjects, except in cases in which it is obliged by special orders to do so.' M. de Tocqueville has left us a masterly sketch of the municipal government of France during the eighteenth century, in the third chapter of his last work on 'France before 1789.' But it is too long to quote, and too full of matter to be abridged; we must content ourselves with referring our readers to it.

But badly as the municipal institutions of France had been treated by the old monarchy, they fared far worse under the Revolution. The National Assembly was pleased to regard the privileges and traditional rights of the towns as aristocratic privileges; these, therefore, were swept away at a blow. The Convention subsequently confiscated all their property by the law of 1793, and forbade them to exchange, or borrow, without the assent of the Government. The Communes of France have never recovered that measure, although one of the first acts of the Constituent Assembly was to pass a law for the regulation of all the municipalities of France, from the hamlet to the city, on one identical plan, followed by copious instructions (Law of 6th December, 1789); and four months afterwards (May 1790), another law equally minute was passed for the organisation of the municipality of Paris. These laws contained in them, as we shall presently show, the fruitful germs of political and social revolutions; but they did not create anywhere a

true municipal government. M. Béchard wrote in
1849 :—

Our Communes are the shadows of what they were in the days of absolute government, for they have been stripped, in the name of liberty, of everything but their name. The Minister of the Interior is the *ex officio* tutor and supreme administrator of the 37,000 communes of the kingdom, and all public establishments depend on him ; that is the summary of our municipal law.

The administrative monarchy of the last thirty-four years has effaced the last vestiges of municipal government in France.

For, to quote a speech of one of the representatives of the people in the Council of Five Hundred, which conveys the doctrine of the Revolution on the subject :—

France is a Republic, one and indivisible. Is it to be borne that this Republic, which is formed of the combined will and interests of the nation, should comprehend a multitude of endowed corporations, interposed between the State and its members, so as to subdivide the great associations into as many petty governments as there are villages and hamlets, and to foster that fractional and municipal spirit which the constitution has sought to destroy? We have done all we could to extinguish all these bastard authorities.[1]

Such was the view of municipal freedom and independence taken by the men who called themselves the champions of liberty and of the immortal

---

[1] Speech of M. Delpierre quoted by Béchard, p. 73.

principles of 1789. They, like their predecessors, confounded the proper functions of municipal government with a subdivision of sovereign power; and they opposed the exercise of civic rights with as much energy as the boldest supporters of despotic authority. *Ex unitate libertas* was the motto of the Revolution, and it held that provincial and municipal independence only led to civil war, anarchy, and servitude. It is true that events had occurred to give some colour to this delusion. The root of the matter seems to lie in the fiftieth article of the law of 1790, on the municipality of Paris, which is in these words :—' Elle aura deux espèces de fonctions à remplir : les unes propres au pouvoir municipal, *les autres propres à l'administration générale de l'État, qui les délègue aux municipalités*.' The moment the municipalities were thus converted into political bodies, exercising a fraction of direct sovereignty, and even superseding the executive authority of the Crown, they became not the useful servants of the State, but its most formidable antagonists. Moreover, there has never existed in France, as far as we can discover, anything analogous to one of the most essential parts of our own constitutional system, namely, the power of the Court of Queen's Bench to restrain by judicial authority the municipal and executive officers of the Government within the limits of their proper functions, compelling them to do their duty, and allowing them to do no more than their duty. It is this judicial authority which determines in England the place and function of each institution; but in France, especially in modern France, no traces of that controlling judicial power are to be discovered.

No sooner was the municipal law of 1790 passed, than the whole nation was called upon in every commune, not only to establish its own local government, but to create by election a fraction of the entire administration and executive system of the kingdom. Whatever had hitherto been done by the officers of the Crown was henceforth to be done by the elect of the people—magistrates, tax-gatherers, militia officers, judges, even parish priests, were all to spring from the same source. The Commune had superseded the King; and in every commune the Revolution—with all its clubs and its cabals—its hatred of the past and its dreams of the future—was implanted. Hence the Revolution was everywhere, and the reign of anarchy prepared the reign of terror.[1] This

[1] We have before us in Frochot's Memoirs, recently published by M. Louis Passy, his grandson, a faithful account of the little commune of Aignay-le-Duc in Burgundy, and of the city of Dijon, during the Revolution. On a small scale, every one of the elements of disturb-

fact of the subversion and absorption of all executive authority by the communes of France in 1790, has not, we think, been dwelt upon as much as it deserves. It is now, in our eyes, the one decisive fact that accounts for everything else. It tore the sovereignty of France into thousands of fragments; the law itself was left without instruments and without protection; nothing but a despotic and revolutionary power of irresistible force could have restored authority over chaos. The inevitable consequence was a violent reaction. The Convention itself, by the organ of St.-Just, declared that the exercise of municipal functions and revolutionary power imposed on the communes two incompatible duties; and proceeded to restore the authority of the government by the decree of the 4th December 1793, and by a law of the 16th April 1795. The same policy was completed by the Constitution of the year VIII. and the First Consul. But with their exorbitant authority the communes of France lost their independence, and became, what they have ever since continued to be, the slaves and tools of the central government.

ance existing in Paris was reproduced, and with precisely the same results. Probably the same thing took place in every part of France, for, as Mirabeau had predicted, 'the constitution of the executive power was such that the total disorganisation of the kingdom could not have been better devised.'

We think it has been shown by what has already
been said, that the municipal institutions of France
have never enjoyed or received their proper functions, namely, the independent control of local affairs
by elected magistrates in subordination to the
general laws of the kingdom ; and that whatever
power they did possess in the Middle Ages had been
gradually subverted by the Crown, and was finally
destroyed by the Revolution. But one of the effects
of the destruction of legitimate municipal power has
been that, in the absence of a traditional and organised control, based on usage and law, the popular
forces of the Commune have made themselves felt
in a violent and irregular manner at all periods of
social commotion, that they have at once assumed
military power, and usurped a supreme authority in
direct opposition to the sovereign will of the nation
and the State. Some examples of these insurrections we have already cited from earlier periods of
French history. But by far the most signal and
instructive instance of this tendency is to be found
in the Revolution itself, which, from 1789 to the
present day, has periodically convulsed the French
nation. Lord Acton has remarked in a lecture
recently delivered at Bridgenorth on the late
war, which is a masterly and impartial summary of

these great events, that one of the traditions of the French Revolution is the institution of a permanent and irresponsible body *holding the power of insurrection*, and using it for the purpose of controlling the organised authorities—a secret despotism veiled by constitutional forms. At Paris this office was discharged by the Commune.' We even venture to assert that this is the leading and dominant fact of the Revolution itself, and that almost all its most prominent and terrible incidents resolve themselves, upon a close inquiry, into this prolonged and ever-recurring contest between the Commune and the nation. There is a resemblance, amounting to identity, in each of these periods. The actors are changed, for they disappear with marvellous rapidity—even the passions and the war-cry are not the same; but the elements of the strife are unaltered and unappeased. There is always the same impulse to 'se municipaliser à sa manière' on the part of the Commune, and always the same 'verve révolutionnaire' to carry it into effect.

From the 25th July 1789, down to the passing of the municipal law for Paris on the 21st May 1790, the capital was a prey to anarchy. Each of the sixty districts of the city had constituted itself into a separate body, claiming both legislative and execu-

tive powers; and all these bodies were at war with
the electors of 1789, and with their own legal delegates. Bailly, the mayor, had unfortunately said in
a letter to the districts (afterwards called the
Sections), 'The legislative power resides in you. It
is your business to make laws for this city. You
have the intelligence and the power.' This doctrine
was condemned by Sièyes, by Mirabeau, and by the
Assembly, who argued that this was to create sixty
communes in one city, and to perpetuate anarchy.
It was loudly supported by Danton, Robespierre,
and the revolutionary party, who argued that the
sovereignty of the citizens was inalienable. Upon
this (April 1790) a report was made to the Assembly by Desmenniers in the following terms :—

The Committee has seen with regret several communes of the
kingdom misapply the principles of constituent and legislative
power, seeking their strength in themselves instead of in the constitution and the unity of the nation. This would be to imitate
the cities of Greece, as if France could become a federative
government without dissolution; but they have not ceased to act
as if they had for the present and the future the right to regulate
and govern, not confining themselves to municipal power, but
usurping the sovereign authority of the nation and the power of
the legislature.

Mirabeau opposed and denounced these doctrines
of the communes as subversive alike of power and
of liberty. He clearly foresaw that Paris, and the

Commune of Paris, was the greatest peril of France and of the Constitution. ' Paris m'attire,' said he to his friend Frochot ; ' c'est le sphinx de la révolution.' ' It is impossible,' he added on another occasion, to Count de la Marck, ' to endorse this popular dictatorship. Society would be annihilated if the multitude or rather the populace of Paris continues to interfere with the authority of the laws. Paris is lost if it be not called to order and constrained to moderation.'

The position of the Court and of the National Assembly in June and July 1789, was not very dissimilar to that of M. Thiers and the present Assembly in March and April 1871. They occupied Versailles, and they represented the supreme authority of the nation. The irony of events placed the aged but energetic historian of the Revolution in a situation which may not unfitly be compared to that of Louis XVI. himself, which he had judged with so much severity in his earliest work. M. Thiers was head of the executive power of France. He was supported by the majority of the Assembly; but he had been compelled to withdraw his troops from Paris, lest they should fraternise with the mob. The executive power was extinguished in the capital —save by the occupation of Mont Valérien, a modern fortress more impregnable than the Bastille. Thiers was himself suspected and accused by the revolutionary party of designs hostile to the revolutionary cause. That was also in many respects the situation of Louis XVI. and his government at the outset of the Revolution; but with the important difference that the Bastille was taken by the insurgents, and Mont Valérien was not, and that M. Thiers was prepared and enabled to make war on Paris, which Louis XVI. had neither the means nor the resolution to attempt.

In Paris itself the resemblance is still more striking. The first scene of the Revolution is thus described in No. 21 of the 'Moniteur,' to which no subsequent historian can in fact add anything :—

> Citizens of every rank, order, and age, and all Frenchmen in the capital are inscribed as soldiers of the country, and take the green cockade.[1] It is enacted that each district shall form patrols to protect the city, and that these are to be incorporated with the mob (*qu'on s'incorporera avec les brigands*) in order to disarm it without difficulty, and that the Prévôt des Marchands shall promptly provide small arms and munitions of war. Upon this the town flags were hoisted, cannon was fired to give the alert, ditches and barricades were dug and constructed, posts were formed, and in less than thirty-six hours Paris presented the aspect of a fortress, garrisoned by 100,000 men, who were divided into

[1] The green cockade was immediately abandoned, and the old red and blue colours, which had been borne 400 years before on the hoods of Marcel's followers, reappeared next day.

companies, named their own officers, and watched for the tranquillity of the city.

One sees in these arrangements a vestige of the old municipal train bands, but within a few hours they became a revolutionary army. On the 13th July (for that is the date) 'the electors decreed,' that a 'Permanent Committee should be established, composed of persons to be named by the Assembly, but augmented by the electors as they may think fit;' and that the whole armed force of the capital should at once be enrolled as the *milice parisienne*. This permanent Committee was instantly named, apparently by itself, and certainly without any reference to the National Assembly or to any legal authority; and the luckless M. de Flesselles, the last of the Prévôts des Marchands, was placed at the head of it. The first exploit of this self-constituted army and authority was the taking of the Bastille, the murder of its governor, followed by the murder of Flesselles himself, because he was suspected of thwarting the anarchical designs of the people. When called upon for arms, he had in fact sent for some chests, which were found when opened to contain old linen.

It was with reference to these events that Mirabeau said in the Assembly :—

The first and principal cause of the disturbances in Paris is, that no acknowledged authority exists in the city. The chiefs have seized the reins of the administration, under the pressure of urgent necessity, and formed a Permanent Committee without the formal assent of the people; but the effect of this body is absolutely null, because both its creators and those it has created are only private citizens without the trust or character of representatives. This Council will, therefore, organise a *municipality* which will ensure subordination and peace.

Everyone knows how these predictions were fulfilled. The horrible tumult of those days has been described a thousand times, but nowhere with more force than in the contemporary record of the 'Moniteur.' The 'Permanent Committee' itself was in imminent danger of instant death. Flesselles was killed; numerous acts of atrocity were committed; no authority but that of the 'electors' existed in the capital; all trade and industry were suspended; and the Committee resorted, for the first time, to the fatal expedient of issuing daily pay to the citizens 'employed in the service of the country.' The conciliatory weakness of the Court and of the Assembly terminated the crisis, and a deputation consisting of Lafayette, Bailly, the Archbishop of Paris, M. de Clermont Tonnerre, and other eminent persons, entered Paris to compliment the citizens on their victory. It was on that occasion that Lafayette himself was proclaimed by acclamation Commander-in-chief of the National Guard of Paris, and Bailly Mayor of Paris.

Au même instant toutes les voix ont proclamé de même M. Bailly Prévôt des Marchands.

Une voix s'est fait entendre et a dit: '*Non pas Prévôt des Marchands, mais Maire de Paris.*'

Et par une acclamation générale tous les assistants ont répété, '*Oui, Maire de Paris.*'

It was considered a stroke of policy to take the power out of the hands of the anarchists and place it in those of men like Lafayette and Bailly; and no doubt they were capable of rendering services in that capacity. They attempted to do so, though with small success, on the 5th and 6th October at Versailles. But the very fact was a departure from all *municipal* principles. These were political appointments. The Commune of Paris became and remained a political institution. It was a political power in the capital, which proved itself, after a long and unequal contest, superior to the lawful authority of the Assembly and the nation. From July 1789 to September 1792, when in fact the triumph of the Commune was consummated by the dissolution of the Legislative Assembly, the overthrow of the Monarchy, and the election of the Convention, the history of this contest is the history of the Revolution. This usurpation of political power by municipal bodies, backed by organised mobs and armed bands of civic troops, who held first the Court and afterwards the Legislature at their mercy, is the distinguishing characteristic of the whole period. These irregular municipal authorities sprang into life, as we have seen, armed, and one of their fundamental principles was that they should retain armed possession of the capital, uncontrolled by the forces of the State; in other words, that the State and the laws of the State should be divested of the sanction of military force in the very seat of government and legislation. The consequence was that the laws and resolutions of the State became powerless; while the laws and resolutions of the Commune were enforced alike by physical strength, by numbers, and by terror. The next step was to appropriate money to the purposes of the Commune, in order to provide for the daily stipend of their sicarian bands, and this was done partly by pillage of public buildings of which no account was rendered, partly by requisitions, partly by excessive taxation of the rich, if in those days any man was rich. The next step was to assume judicial authority—to establish tribunals for the trial of offences against the State, and to inflict even capital punishment by acts which prefigured the Reign of Terror itself. When the military, financial, and judicial power over the property and lives of citizens had been thus usurped, not content with this despotic administration of the capital, the Commune of Paris sought to give laws by its emissaries to other parts of France. What wonder that the power and independence of the National or Legislative Assembly waned before it?

The debates of that Assembly down to the close of its brief and unhonoured existence are full of protests against this new form of tyranny, expressed in terms of indignant eloquence. It was there that Mazuyer exclaimed :—

> The Commune is carrying on that system of terror which is its chief method of success. The prisons are once more filled, without our knowing for the most part who signed the warrants of arrest; the wealth accumulated in the houses of the *émigrés* and in the Tuileries is abandoned to pillage; everything that can tempt the avarice of a subordinate agent is seized and no trace of it can be found on record; valuable resources are wasted without profit to the natives; the means of defence are annihilated; Paris and France are given over to the most extravagant absurdities and the most insatiable rapacity. *The law must decide whether the French nation or the Commune of Paris is sovereign of the country.*

It was there that Vergniaud raised his voice with still more ardent eloquence against

' those hypocritical and ferocious beings, who are the advocates of scandalous delations, of arbitrary arrests, of the contempt of law, and of general anarchy—against the men who make an aristocracy of virtue and a democracy of vice, to ruin the one and defy the other. The citizens of Paris,' he continued, 'dare to call themselves free. They may not be the slaves of crowned tyrants, but they are the slaves of the vilest and wickedest of men. It is time to break these shameful chains—to crush this new oppression. It is time that men who have made the virtuous tremble should tremble in their turn. Tell it to Europe that, in spite of the calumnies which have been heaped upon France, there is still, amidst the temporary anarchy in which these brigands have plunged us, some virtue in our country.'

The chief value of M. Mortimer-Ternaux's 'History of the Reign of Terror' consists in the demonstrative evidence he has produced in support of this proposition. He makes no pretensions to the dramatic eloquence of Michelet or Lamartine; he has none of the party views of Thiers or Louis Blanc. But he proves better than any other writer that the crisis of the Revolution was the result of the misdirected energy of municipal power at war with the sovereignty of the nation. This view of the Revolution is the more interesting and instructive at the present moment, because it has just been reproduced and imitated by the Commune of Paris of 1871 under our own eyes.

But we have been led by these considerations to anticipate, and we have yet to show by what errors these fatal consequences were brought about. The

Constituent Assembly had been led, as we have seen, by the disturbances in Paris to regard the establishment of municipal authority as one of the most pressing duties of the authors of the new Constitution of France. Accordingly, when in December 1789, the scheme for a new distribution of the territory of the kingdom and for the execution of the necessary administrative powers was brought under discussion, municipal government formed a part of it. It formed so much a part of it, and was nevertheless so erroneously conceived, that it became in some respects the basis of the political constitution. Thouvet and Mirabeau had both presented plans, founded mainly on the ideas of the Abbé Sièyes, for a mathematical division of the kingdom; these, however, were modified on the proposition of Barnave. France was to be divided into from seventy-five to eighty-five departments; each department was subdivided into from three to nine districts, and each district into cantons; each department and each district was to have a council and an executive board, to be elected by the people or rather by electors named by the whole population. Each city, town, and parish was to have a municipal government of its own, with a mayor and also a syndic, whose duty it was to defend the interests of the

Commune. This complicated system of agents and powers composed the whole fabric of the executive authority, and in that capacity was subject to the king, but the king had no power to remove or control his own agents. To complete the anarchical confusion of the scheme, it was provided, and this is important, that the municipal authority should *alone have the power of calling out the military force for the repression of disorder*. The plan was adopted by the Constituent Assembly in a summary manner, after a very few days' discussion, though in fact the whole future government of France was at stake. The true nature and the inevitable result of it had at once been detected and described by Mr. Burke, when he called it 'the ladder of representation by which your workmen ascend from their parochial tyranny to their federal anarchy—the project of turning a great empire into a vestry, or into a collection of vestries, and of governing it in the spirit of a parochial administration—senseless and absurd, in any mode or with any qualifications.'[1] The primary object of the whole scheme was to grind down and parcel out the whole territory with absolute uniformity, so as to efface the distinctions

[1] Burke's Letter to a Member of the National Assembly (January 1791), pp. 3-5.

and traditions of provinces and cities, and to confer upon every parish or township the same right and form of government which was adapted to the largest communities. Such was the origin of the boasted uniformity of France, which has never been violently and openly attacked until the insurrection of the Commune in the present year. But within a very few weeks it became sufficiently apparent that the result of the Constitution of, 1791 was total anarchy. The Directory of the Department of Paris, as it was termed, was a well-constituted, liberal, and loyal body. The Duc de la Rochefoucauld was its chairman ; Rœderer was Procureur-Syndic. This body was sincerely desirous to restrain the excesses and treachery of the municipality of Paris, the Commune, of which Pétion had, on the retirement of Bailly, become mayor. When the dreadful disturbances of the 20th June, 1792, began, this 'Directory' took active measures to require the Commune to act against the insurgents. Rœderer's letters to Pétion, published by M. Mortimer-Ternaux, prove it. But whilst the mob was marching against the Tuileries, Rœderer himself held that the 'Directory' had no legal power to proclaim martial law, and that this could only be done by the Commune. But the Commune were themselves on the side of the assailants. Pétion was playing into their hands. So that, by this strange inversion of all authority, neither the heads of the department nor the Ministers of the Crown could give orders for the defence of the Sovereign, and the command of the military forces of Paris was in the hands of the leaders and instigators of the attack. This *reductio ad absurdum* has been forcibly pointed out by M. Duvergier de Hauranne in the introduction to his ' History of Parliamentary Government in France' (vol. i. p. 250), a work of high authority in the elucidation of these problems, which, notwithstanding eighty years of experience, France has as yet failed to solve.

The constitution of the Commune of Paris by the special law of 21st of May, 1790, was extremely curious and complicated. It has been accurately described by M.. Mortimer-Ternaux in a note to his first volume. Before 1789 Paris was divided into twenty-one quarters. The decree of the 13th of April, 1789, made for the purposes of the elections to the États-généraux, divided the city into sixty districts. These were afterwards reduced to forty-eight sections, and this distribution was retained (under the old name of *quarters*) until 1860, when Paris was extended to the outer line of the fortifications. The 'active citizens,' as they were termed, consisted of all Frenchmen assessed to a direct tax equivalent to three days' pay; these were the primary electors, convoked in their respective sections. Each section named the secondary electors, in a proportion of one per cent. on the numbers entitled to vote. These secondary electors were persons assessed to a direct tax equivalent to ten days' pay. There were at first in Paris about 82,000 primary electors, and consequently 820 secondary electors. The latter elected the deputies to the Legislative Assembly, the executive officers of the department, the bishop, and the judge of the district. The corporation of Paris thus elected consisted of a mayor, sixteen administrators, thirty-two common councillors, and ninety-six notables, with some other officers. The mode of election was by a most intricate combination of open voting and balloting for lists. These offices were held for two years.

Two or three obvious observations are suggested by this strange constitution. In the first place, it was based on a complete confusion of political and municipal functions, or rather the municipal character was swallowed up in the political. A similar confusion existed between the elective and administrative rights of the people—in fact, the sections, which were intended to be mere electoral wards, soon assumed the character of permanent political and military bodies. In each of them debates were continually carried on, and resolutions passed which overruled the corporation and the Assembly. By a decree of the 19th of August, 1792, the former battalions of the National Guard were superseded by 'armed sections;' that is, the citizens of each district formed an armed band, acting under the orders of the commander of each section, and were subdivided into companies of 126 men. This was the application of the theory of the Jacobin Club that 'the people, and each portion of the people, and consequently each section, has the right to use its own share of sovereign power as it thinks fit.' Municipal government, so understood and practised, became simply the negation of all law. The central power of the State was totally extinguished. It had in fact no power but that of suspending public officers who failed to do their duty. But, although the whole authority and control over the capital was thus thrown on the constituencies, the electors never could be prevailed upon to vote in large numbers. At the very first election when Pétion was chosen mayor in place of Bailly, only 10,000 citizens voted. In 1792, the number of electors was doubled by the abolition of the qualification of three days' pay; they then amounted to 160,000; but at the election for the mayoralty, which took place in October 1792, not *one-tenth* of that number could be prevailed upon to *vote at all;* 14,137 electors voted on the 4th of October, only 9,361 on the 8th of November. Of these not above 5,000 belonged to the Jacobins. In many of the sections composed of two or three thousand citizens, not more than fifty or sixty would appear; the most important questions were decided by 150 or 200 voters. Well may M. Mortimer-Ternaux exclaim, after recording these figures, that 'the culpable indifference and stupid apathy of the population of Paris' were as much to blame for the result as the irresolution and weakness of the Legislative Assembly itself. The history of the French Revolution is the history of a triumph of a truculent minority over a timid majority by means of terror. There is not one of the bloody days of this long conflict which might not have been averted by a prompt and determined exercise of lawful authority. But the law itself was paralysed and disarmed by the institutions we have just described, and by the inconceivable inertia of the bulk of the population. It further deserves to be remarked that the Constituent Assembly which had created this Frankenstein, had provided no means of controlling it. The Commune subsisted by virtue of the constitution. It was therefore removed from the competency of the legislature to remodel or suppress it, because in fact it had the same constitutional origin as the Legislative Assembly itself. The whole subject of the municipal policy of the Revolution is so ably described by M. Mortimer-Ternaux that we are tempted to quote his remarks on it :—

This exorbitant municipal power was not vested in the hands of magistrates who might have been personally responsible for the use of it ; but it was entrusted to boards. By this wretched expedient the wire-pullers could remain in the shade, while they worked their puppets as they pleased. Everybody gave his advice ; nobody acted. But, when circumstances called for a prompt decision, the lowest municipal officer would brace on his official belt, and, without a shadow of rightful authority, would give the most important, and sometimes irreparable orders. It would have been impossible more effectually to organise anarchy if they had wished it.

But in the special institutions of the City of Paris, the Constituent Assembly, it must be confessed, reached the acme of absurdity. The whole administration of this great city was bristling with wheels within wheels, which checked and sometimes stopped the general movement. The corporation consisted of 144 members, of whom 48 were selected, and these elected 16 of their own body to form five administrative boards, each sovereign in its own department. At the head of this body was placed a mayor, who could do much mischief and little good—free to sanction disturbances by his presence, but almost incapable of arresting them. This mayor was a sort of idol offered to the adoration of the cockneys of Paris, but an idol resembling one of those Indian deities which are made to nod and speak—which are carried in state through the streets on high holidays—but are consigned to the obscurity of the temple and to clouds of incense on the day of danger.

The complexity of the organic law of the municipality of Paris interfered with the true working of the elections, and disgusted the orderly electors, till, in fact, they ceased to vote. But, when the ultra-revolutionary sections had resolved upon the overthrow of the throne, these artificial barriers fell like a house of cards in the night of the 9th August, at the first blast of the insurgent democracy.

The sittings of the municipal and departmental councils were both declared to be public, and they were consequently abandoned to the incessant and furious pressure of the galleries. Although it had been intended that the 48 sections into which the capital was divided should not remain assembled after an election, and not meet again until they were convoked by the Commune, another clause of the law provided that this convocation of the 48 sections should take place whenever it was demanded by eight of their number. To exercise this right a Permanent Committee of 16 had been established in each section. Thus with inconceivable imprudence the Constituent Assembly had established in Paris 48 centres of perpetual agitation, and framed, as it were, all the rights and privileges of sedition. In each section a knot of leaders had been formed, who were continually calling meetings, and making the most unconstitutional and incendiary motions, which went the round of Paris in a few hours. In fact the sections had become almost permanent, even before the law recognised their permanence.

Such was the constitution of the Commune of Paris at the outset of those fifty days, from the 20th

June to the 10th August, 1792, which comprised the stormy transition of France from the Monarchy to the Republic—'days,' said Mr. Croker, who knew them well, 'which have already had, and will probably continue to have, a greater influence on the destinies of mankind than any other fifty days in the history of the world.'[1] But the contest which marked those days with so much horror, infamy, and blood, was nothing more, and nothing less, than a struggle between the Jacobin party, which wielded all the resources of the Commune and the sections, and the Feuillans or constitutionalists of the Assembly. The Legislative Assembly must for ever bear the stigma of the crimes which it allowed to be committed and to remain unpunished. It was a feeble and foolish, but not a sanguinary or a lawless, body. The great majority of its members abhorred the violent and ferocious policy of the Mountain. Robespierre, Collot-d'Herbois, Marat, and all the band of miscreants who figured in the Convention, had no seats in the legislature which subsisted from October 1791 to September 1792. Danton took his seat in it because after the 10th August he became Minister of Justice, or what was

---

[1] Croker's *Essays on the French Revolution*, p. 161.

called so. It was in the Commune and the Jacobin Club that the real authors of the excesses of the Revolution had established their stronghold. From that fortress of illegality and arsenal of crime proceeded the arbitrary measures and atrocious conspiracies which overthrew the Constitution of 1791, the Throne, and the Assembly itself. It was the Commune that organised in April 1792 the ridiculous fête in honour of the Swiss of Chateauvieux, convicted traitors to their colours, who had gone over to the mob in the disturbances at Nancy, and been sent to the galleys, from which they were rescued by popular enthusiasm and brought back in triumph to Paris, where the Assembly itself was outraged by decreeing honours to the violators of law. It was in the Commune that the whole atrocity of the 20th June originated, when the mob forced its way into the Tuileries, and thrust a red cap on the head that wore the crown of France, to the imminent peril of the Royal Family. Panis and Sergent, two of the city officers of police, were the prime movers in it. Santerre, the commandant of the battalion of the district of the Enfants-Trouvés, was its leader. Pétion, on whom as mayor the duty of maintaining order chiefly devolved, equivocated, disobeyed the requisitions he received from the

Council of the Department, and defeated the measures of defence he ought to have been the first to command. On that fatal day the head of the municipality of Paris was the guardian and protector (such were the strange results of an anomalous constitution) of the royalty of France; but, unlike the gallant Walworth, Lord Mayor of London, who stood by the side of Richard II. to hew down Wat Tyler, Pétion was a Judas who betrayed his king. In spite of the indignation which these outrages excited in the Assembly and throughout a great part of France, the men of the Commune persevered.[1] If they remained unpunished for such acts as these, greater crimes might be committed with impunity.

And they were committed. The 10th August followed by inevitable steps the 20th June. The same authority remained at the Hôtel de Ville. The same audacity pervaded the sections. The

[1] It was at this time that the celebrated petition of the 20,000 was presented to the Assembly against the culpable inefficiency and collusion of the Municipality of Paris. Subsequently, under the Convention, to have signed that petition was in itself a crime punished with instant death. Pétion and Manuel were suspended from office by the Council of the Department, though afterwards restored by the deplorable rashness of the Assembly. Six weeks later the Duc de la Rochefoucauld, Chairman of the Council, paid the penalty of that courageous action with his life. He was murdered on the road from Rouen to Paris.

same tricks were employed to paralyse the defence of the palace. M. Mortimer-Ternaux has analysed and dissected the authentic evidence of what took place on that memorable day with consummate ability. The story has been related a hundred times; but it has been overlaid with whole strata of invention and lies. The true narrative is to be found in the *procès-verbaux* of the forty-eight sections of Paris and the records of the Commune— documents which are still in existence, and which M. Mortimer-Ternaux has carefully examined. We can cite but one trait of this curious picture of municipal government in France.

It happened that on the 9th and 10th August, the command of the legions in Paris devolved by rotation on one Mandat, a civic officer, favourable to the Revolution, but a man resolved to do his duty, to protect his king, and to execute the laws. On the first appearance of disorder Mandat had taken precautions, by doubling the military posts about the Tuileries and preparing an energetic resistance. He was supported and approved by a majority of the Common Council. But these measures occasioned the most violent animosity in the sections and amongst the leaders of the conspiracy in the municipal government. Upon this they determined on a *coup d'état* against their own colleagues and representatives, and promulgated the following order :—

> The Assembly of Commissioners of the majority of the sections, being united, with full powers to save the commonwealth, has resolved that the first measure required by the public safety is to resume all the powers which the Commune had delegated, and to deprive the military staff of the influence which it has hitherto exercised in a manner so prejudicial to liberty. Considering that this measure cannot be adopted without provisionally suspending from its functions the municipality, which can never and in no case act save in accordance with established form, it is decreed that *the Common Council of the Commune is suspended*, and that the mayor, the procureur, and the sixteen administrators are to continue to perform their duties.

We do not remember to have met with a more perfect specimen of revolutionary hypocrisy and despotism. The Common Council protested, and were laughed at. Mandat was at once ordered to be transferred to the prison of the Abbaye. He had already nobly refused to revoke the military orders he had previously given for the defence of the Tuileries. But before he reached the prison, he was dragged from that of the Hôtel de Ville by a band of assassins, who blew his brains out with a pistol-shot on the great staircase. From the room in which they were sitting, 'the Assembly of Commissioners of the United Sections' could hear the groans of their victim and the ferocious shouts of his murderers; but they cared not to interrupt the course of their deliberations, and they continued to complete their orders and arrangements for the insurrection of the morrow.[1] The result of that morrow, the 10th August, so fatal alike to legal authority and constitutional liberty in France, was again due to the ascendancy of the Commune over the intimidated Assembly.

A complete usurpation of executive power by the insurrectionary Commune was the immediate result of the 10th August, for when the throne was destroyed, the Commune, and not the Assembly, assumed the supreme authority. The Convention itself, with all its crimes, was, comparatively speaking, a legal power; and the interval between the 10th August and the election of the Convention is the very darkest spot in the annals of the Revolution. Hostages were seized in their houses by the agents of the Communal police, women and children were cast into abominable prisons, and devoted to massacre, to answer for their husbands and fathers. The right of petition was turned into an instrument of proscription. That liberty of conscience which had

[1] Mortimer-Ternaux, vol. ii. p. 283.

been proudly inscribed among the rights of man was violated by consigning the clergy wholesale to death or deportation. The liberty of the press was annihilated by a decree which suppressed all journals attached to the cause of monarchy—their presses were seized and their editors arrested. Municipal delegates took possession of the post-office, stopped the mails, and opened the letters. All powers, in short, were usurped by a single band of ruffians, who called the ministers, the magistrates, and the executive officers of the State to their bar. Paris, and the leaders of the mob of Paris, were absolute, not only within the walls of the capital, but beyond them. The National Assembly was a mere instrument to register their edicts. One of its first acts was to vote a monthly subsidy of 850,000 francs to be spent by the Commune at its pleasure. A new law of general police voted on the 11th of August, charged the *municipal* authorities with the detection and prosecution of crimes against the State, and gave them full powers to detain and arrest all suspected persons. This act alone placed the whole population at their mercy.

The next step was the creation of what was termed the *Comité de Surveillance* of the Commune, or, as it was termed at the Hôtel de Ville, with ominous reality, the *Committee of Execution.* The nature of their functions may be inferred from the following extract from their records :—

23rd August, 1792.

Upon hearing the Procureur-Général of the Commune, the Common Council orders that the guillotine shall remain standing until further order, with the exception, however, of the knife, which is to be removed after each execution.

24th August, 1792.

The Common Council authorise the manufacturer of machines for decapitation to furnish one of these for the department, to be paid for by whom it may concern.

The Commune hastened to present at the bar of the Assembly an address, proceeding from the pen of Robespierre, and read by the mouth of Tallien, in which they boldly asserted that they alone had saved the country on the 10th of August by the exercise of their revolutionary powers. The Assembly, not yet entirely vanquished, replied by its President Lacroix that 'the formation of the provisional Commune of Paris was contrary to law, and that it was a disgrace to the Revolution to exhibit a single Commune in open defiance of the general will, struggling against the National Assembly.' One of the leaders exclaimed, 'The people are waiting at the door for your answer. The people is free, and you deprive it of liberty.' To which Lacroix rejoined, 'Are *we* then free?'

The day which followed this scene was that on which the leaders of the Commune, Marat, Danton, Robespierre, Manuel, Hébert, Billaud-Varennes, Panis, Sergent, Fabre d'Eglantine, Camille Desmoulins, and a few others, prepared and consummated the most atrocious of their crimes — the general massacres of the *détenus* in the prisons of Paris from the 2nd to the 5th of September. It is impossible to resist the evidence that every one of these persons was privy to this abominable action. Danton desired and encouraged it. Robespierre, by the admission of M. Louis Blanc, did not prevent it. Manuel, Hébert, Billaud-Varennes were present in one or other of the prisons. The last-mentioned patriot paid the hired murderers their hard-earned blood-money of 10 or 12 francs a day. M. Mortimer-Ternaux has seen the receipts, which are still in existence.

The Committee of Surveillance even prepared warrants for the arrest of Brissot, Roland, and thirty of the Girondins—but their time was not yet come. In the Section of the Faubourg Poissonière the following decree was proposed and carried :—

Considering the imminent danger of the country and the infernal machinations of the priests, it is RESOLVED :—

1. That all the priests and suspected persons confined in the prisons of Paris, Orleans, and elsewhere shall be put to death.

2. That the wives and children of *émigrés*, and of persons who are missing, shall be placed in line in front of our volunteers on the frontier, so as to protect these brave sansculottes from the blows of the enemy.

At the Luxembourg, where Joachim Ceyrat was in the chair, the following resolution was carried :—

1. The motion of a member to purge the prisons by shedding the blood of the *détenus* of Paris having been adopted, three commissioners are named to convey this resolution to the Common Council, *in order to act with uniformity.*

On the following day, whilst the streets of Paris ran with blood, and 1,368 mutilated corpses of innocent men, women, and children (that seems to have been the exact number of the victims), were carted off to the lime-pits, the following circular was issued by the Commune of Paris to the departments :—

The Commune of Paris hastens to inform its brethren in all the departments that a portion of the ferocious conspirators, confined in the prisons, have been put to death by the people—an act of justice which appeared indispensable to restrain by terror the legions of traitors hid within our walls, while we are marching against the enemy ; and no doubt the whole nation, after the long series of acts of treachery which have led it to the edge of an abyss, will hasten to adopt a measure so necessary to the public safety; and all Frenchmen will cry with the Parisians, 'We are marching against the enemy, but we leave behind us no brigands to immolate our wives and our children.'

> The Members of the Committee of Surveillance, Administrators of the Public Safety, and adjunct Administrators.
>
> P. J. Duplain, Panis, Sergent, Lenfant, Jourdeuil, Marat (*l'ami du peuple*), Deforgues, Duffort, Cally, Delegates of the Commune at the Hôtel de Ville assembled. Paris, 3 September, 1792.

A last attempt was made by the Assembly after this unparalleled outrage to crush the Commune, and to wrest from these maniacs the power they abused. Cambon exclaimed, ' If you choose that the Commune of Paris should govern the empire, as Rome did, let us submit and lay our heads on the block. But you have sworn to defend the people and to die at your post. Keep then your oath and assert the authority of the nation.' But, as is well known, these efforts were vain. Even the decree which broke the Commune was evaded. Its power was irresistible, and within a few days it attained, what Cambon had called its secret object, which was to overthrow the Assembly and name a National Convention. From that moment, and for nearly two years from that time, the leaders of the Commune were, under another name, the rulers of France, and the Reign of Terror was established. The elections to the Convention were of course made under their direct influence. The Convention itself, in which the majority still belonged to the moderate party, was overawed by the Commune. The Commune pointed the cannon of Henriot on the 31st May, locked the doors of the Assembly on its own members, and exacted the surrender of the twenty-two chiefs of the Gironde.

Here we pause. It is not our object to relate again these dreadful and too famous scenes. Our purpose was merely to demonstrate by what means the Communal authority of Paris overthrew the supreme power of the lawful legislature and subjected the nation to its will. The striking resemblance between these occurrences and those we have just witnessed, does not require to be pointed out.

But it will be said, the Commune of 1871 did not resort at first to these extreme measures. It burnt the guillotine, and it reserved the massacre of its prisoners for the dreadful moment of its own final destruction. In the place of a feeble and defenceless Assembly within its grasp, the representatives of the nation were at Versailles disposing of an army of 100,000 men. Civil war therefore superseded mere terrorism and assassination, and though it may cause even more bloodshed and misery than a Reign of Terror, we infinitely prefer an open contest to be fought out in the face of day to a system of delations, organised seditions, secret persecutions, and judicial murders. If law is suspended by revolution, the authority of arms is the only defence of right. We doubt not that when the truth comes to be known, it will be found that this extraordinary power over the great city was exercised by a very small number of desperadoes and fanatics, who had summoned all the revolutionary agents of Europe to their assistance, and contrived to possess themselves of the town as much by their impudence as by their strength. Acts of lawless violence and dishonesty they did not for a moment scruple to commit. They arrested crowds of innocent persons, up to the Archbishop of Paris and the President of the Court of Cassation, whom they eventually murdered; they proscribed and persecuted the clergy, and profaned the churches with infernal ribaldry and pollutions; they extinguished the liberty of the Press; they created exceptional courts of justice, in which the functions of jurymen were vested in the ' Delegates of the National Guard '—the modern form of the old sections; they imposed forced military service on the whole population between nineteen and forty, on pain of imprisonment, if not death ; they raised money by wholesale robbery and by private pillage ; and they boast of an insane vandalism against public and historical monuments which are the pride and glory of France. All this, we suppose, is what M. Délescluze (who was one of the thinkers among them) meant, when he said on the 22nd April, ' We are for revolutionary measures, but we wish to observe forms, and to respect law and public opinion.' When, however, the supreme hour arrived, and the defence of Paris by revolutionary means became impossible, they threw off all disguise, and proceeded to commit acts of vengeance of so diabolical a character that even the crimes of the Commune of 1792 pale before them. They at least were committed in the name of liberty and national defence; these are the mere extravagances of demons intent on social revolution. An insane hatred of capital and the rights of property was superadded to the political passions of the first Revolution.

Yet we will do the members of the Commune the justice to suppose that some at least among them had a theory of government and political rights, for which they conceived it to be worth while to risk their lives and to wage war against their native country. The energy of their protracted defence implies a conviction that they conceived themselves to be fighting for some just and necessary cause. What was it? The theory of the Commune, as far as we are able to collect it from its own declarations, is that, whereas an absolute Imperial Government had been imposed on the whole of France by the exercise of universal suffrage throughout the territory, and, in short, the country outvoted the towns; so now, the Empire being overthrown and the Republic proclaimed, each town should assume and retain absolute independence, extending to the sole command of its own police, military forces, and administration of justice. The following passage from the official declaration of the 19th April deserves to be preserved. It is an answer to the question, 'What does Paris demand?' and it was probably written by Délescluze, who perished behind a barricade on the 25th May.

> The recognition and consolidation of the Republic, and *the absolute independence of the Commune extended at all places in France*, thus assuring to each the integrity of its rights, and to every Frenchman the full exercise of his faculties and aptitudes as a man, a citizen, and a producer. *The independence of the Commune has no other limits but its rights.* The independence is equal for all Communes who are adherents of the contract the association of which ought to secure the unity of France. The inherent rights of the Commune are to vote the Communal budget of receipts and

expenses, the improving and alteration of taxes, the direction of local services, the organisation of the magistracy, internal police, and education; the administration of the property belonging to the Commune, the choice by election or competition, with the responsibility and permanent right of control and revocation of the Communal magistrates *and officials of all classes*, the absolute guarantee of individual liberty and liberty of conscience, the permanent intervention of the citizens in Communal affairs by the free manifestation of their ideas and the free defence of their interests, guarantees given for those manifestations by the Commune, who alone are charged with securing the free and just exercise of the right of meeting and publicity, *and the organisation of urban defence and of the National Guard, which must elect its chiefs and alone watch over the maintenance of order in the city*. Paris wishes nothing more under the head of local guarantees on the well-understood condition of regaining, in a grand Central Administration and Delegation from the Federal Communes, the realisation and practice of those principles; but, in favour of her independence, and profiting by her liberty of action, she reserves to herself liberty to bring about, as may seem good to her, administrative and economic reforms which the people demand, and to create such institutions as may serve to develop and further education. Produce, exchange, and credit have to universalise power and property according to the necessities of the moment, the wishes of those interested, and the *data* furnished by experience.

Our enemies deceive themselves, or deceive the country, when they accuse Paris of desiring to impose its will and supremacy upon the rest of the nation, and to aspire to a dictatorship which would be a veritable attempt to overthrow the independence and sovereignty of other Communes. They deceive themselves when they accuse Paris of seeking the destruction of French unity, established by the Revolution. The unity which has been imposed upon us up to the present by the Empire, the Monarchy, and the Parliamentary Government, is nothing but centralisation, despotic, unintelligent, arbitrary, and onerous. The political unity, as desired by Paris, is a voluntary association of all local initiative, the free and spontaneous co-operation of all individual energies with the common object of the well-being, liberty, and security of all.

In spite of the vague and ill-translated language of this document (which we have not seen in the original), it is evident that this idea of communal government is based on communal sovereignty. Instead of municipal power being derived from the State or from the State Legislature, the State itself is to become 'a voluntary association of all local initiative'—instead of being subservient, the Commune becomes supreme. The tie uniting these independent sovereignties together being voluntary, is, at most, a slender Federal contract. The authority of the State would therefore be extinguished. The towns would become the centres of political power, but they would be disunited; and the country would, we presume, be held like the *terra firma* of Venice, or the rural districts of the Republic of Florence, in subservience to the urban authority. The Girondins of 1793 were proscribed for their attachment to what was called 'Federalism,' which only meant that they denied the central dominion of Paris, and thought that the National Assembly ought to be protected against Paris by the forces of France. But the Girondins never propounded a scheme which would, like this, disintegrate the territory, depose the Government, and annihilate the collective authority of the law. By a curious inversion of the parts taken in this Revolution, the Conservative Assembly at Versailles is now defending the 'one and indivisible' commonwealth of France, whilst the descendants of the Mountain would pulverise it into a thousand fragments. They propose to carry the French municipal theory of divided sovereignty to its extreme limits, and the consequence will probably be that in the end municipal institutions will be more discredited than they deserve.

It is certainly one of the most curious results of the aberration of the human mind, when it has freed itself from the restraints of faith, law, and experience, that such schemes as these should be propounded for the regeneration of France and described by British democratic writers as 'the finest political conception of the age.'[1] To us the scheme seems somewhat deficient in originality, but for the purpose

---

[1] The expression was used by Mr. Frederic Harrison; for the Commune of 1871 finds apologists and even admirers among a certain class of persons in this country.

of destroying the social and political existence of a nation it is no doubt admirably adapted. It would in fact bring France back to the condition she was in, under the feudal system, in the eleventh century, as described by the most eminent of her own historians: 'Le caractère propre, général, de la féodalité,' said M. Guizot in 1829, 'c'est le démembrement du peuple et du pouvoir en une multitude de petits peuples et de petits souverains; l'absence de toute nation générale, de tout gouvernement central.'[1] The Republican Commune aimed at recovering precisely the same isolated, turbulent, and destructive power which was exercised in the darkest of the Middle Ages by the feudal nobility. The excess of centralisation in France has no doubt given birth to this protest against central authority—that nation, once proudest of its national gifts, and now humbled by the loss of them, was to be taught to renounce alike national authority, national strength, and of course national pride—the empire builded up by the conquests of a thousand years was to be shattered by the workmen of Paris and their inspired guides into communities about the size of the Swiss Cantons; for that is, according to

---

[1] Guizot, *Histoire de la Civilisation en France.* Cours de 1829-30, Leçon i. p. 6.

M. Comte, to be the form of government of Western Europe—and the social life of one of the wealthiest and most industrious of cities was to be placed under new conditions by the expulsion of capital and the extinction of credit—the reign of privileges was to be restored in the land of equality, but they were to be the privileges of the towns over the country, of the needy over the rich, of the turbulent over the peaceful population—lastly, universal suffrage was to be deposed and repudiated because it affords too firm a foundation for the will of the majority, and the minority is to claim its right of directing the revolutions of the world. To these wild pretensions there is but one answer. As they would within a very short space of time annihilate, not only all political power and order, but the very means of existence, and reduce mankind to a second and more brutal barbarism, it is absolutely necessary to resist them by force. Society is, indeed, already resolved into its primitive elements when it is called upon to take up arms in defence of the first principles of life, property and liberty. That is unhappily the state of France, but it is the result, as we endeavoured to show in the preceding paper, of the protracted influence and action of the false doctrines sanctioned eighty years ago by the authors of the Revolution. We traced it then in other forms : we have traced it now in the erroneous conception of municipal power. With these materials the result was long ago foreseen and predicted. That identical result is now before us— no sovereign, no allegiance to the ruler or to the law, no undisputed authority in the representation of the people, no certain peace between the regular and the civic forces of the country, and a chaotic state of society, in which the evils of foreign occupation and the burden of an enormous tribute to a victorious enemy are almost forgotten in comparison with the internal calamities of France.

Gloomy as this prospect is—and we hold it to be the most awful spectacle that the world has witnessed since the invasion of the barbarians—it has not been entirely unforeseen even by the most patriotic Frenchmen. More than twenty years ago, M. Raudot, then a member of the Legislative Assembly, published an essay entitled 'De la Décadence de la France,' which we have placed at the head of these pages, to show that if our prognostications are dark, they are not conceived in any spirit of national rivalry, but have already been anticipated by some reflecting and patriotic Frenchmen. M. Raudot first established by figures that the Revolution had cost France all her great colonies, and that her population had increased by about one-sixth, while that of England and of Germany had doubled. 'Si la dissolution des deux grands royaumes de la Prusse et de l'Autriche,' said he, ' doit enfanter l'unité de l'Allemagne, la puissance relative de la France sera encore bien plus faible. Un, état compacte, plus grand que la France d'un cinquième et peuplé de quarante millions d'Allemands, rejetterait la France au second rang, et pourrait, en s'alliant à l'Angleterre, causer sa ruine complète.' This was published in 1850. He then examined the state of her forces, of her wealth (which has since enormously increased), and the physical diminution of the standard for recruits. If the standard of height which was in force before 1789 were still required, half the population would be rejected; it has in fact been lowered more than three inches. Thus he arrived at the conclusion that France was declining and would decline under the influence of her system of centralisation, which caused the nation to regard the State and Paris as the only vital portions of the country. At the close of this remarkable paper he wound up the subject by pointing out that the subdivision of landed property was tending more and more to give the peasantry exclusive possession of the soil—that the peasantry must therefore soon find themselves at variance with the classes who seek to draw their existence from the State, since the former pay, and the latter receive, the taxes—that the increase of luxury tended to waste the substance of the upper classes, and that the towns were peopled with multitudes of men who lived chiefly by ministering to this expenditure—that the concentration of power led men to look to the State as the sole source of activity, and even as the sole rightful owner of property—that if the life of a great people is arrested, the increase of poverty is such and so sudden that despair drives men to pillage and civil war—that in such a state of things the foundations of the edifice are upon a quicksand, which may be shaken at any moment by a popular convulsion—and that the army alone remains; but as an army can only exist with subordination, discipline, and obedience, its power depends on the maintenance of those conditions (which are now lamentably wanting), and on the other hand the burden and expense of large armies is an additional grievance to the people. Our readers will judge for themselves to what extent these far-sighted observations have been realised. To us it appears that the Revolution has very nearly reached its ultimate consequence by the repeated overthrow of the State and the attempted destruction of the capital ; and ·that if the same principles were to continue to operate for another half-century they would end in the annihilation of the country. But we are not without hope that the tremendous severity of this last paroxysm may work a salutary change. For the first time in the course of the Revolution, Paris has been overpowered and crushed by the nation. Great as the disaster is, we are assured that the abasement of Paris is not regarded as an unmixed evil by the provinces. 'Let Paris perish,' is their cry, ' if she is to be to us for ever a hotbed of revolution or a seat of despotism.' The moment is approaching—perhaps it is come— when a great creative genius might construct in France a system of government on entirely new principles, or rather on old principles revived, and entirely opposed to the revolutionary centralisation of the last eighty years ; but the whole edifice must be built up from the foundation, and the strength of the base is of more importance than the form of its architecture or the name of the superstructure. But who is equal to so great an enterprise ?

EPILOGUE.

MARCH 1872.

SOME MONTHS have elapsed since the publication of the last of these Essays. But the end is not yet. Nothing has occurred to give stability or legal authority to the institutions of France. The future form of those institutions is itself completely dark. The representatives of three dynasties and two republics are in the field on equal terms ; and the only ground assumed by the present provisional Government is that it excludes them all alike. They appear, in fact, to be all equally powerless, and the next cast which may for the present decide the game belongs probably rather to fortune and adventure than to the deliberate judgment and resolution of a great people.

Of the National Assembly we desire to speak with respect, for, in spite of its faults and imperfections, it consists of the most honourable, intelligent, and patriotic men in France. A large proportion of its members are young and inexperienced, but all are animated by the most sincere desire to serve their country. But they do not know how to do it. And if they did they would have to encounter invincible obstacles from the obsolete convictions and the personal pretensions of the Chief of the Executive Power. They are therefore placed in the dilemma of assenting to measures which they know to be pernicious, or of upsetting a Government which they believe to be necessary. It is but too probable that this hesitation between two opinions will prove fatal to their own authority, and that an Assembly not doing what it desires to do, and doing what it does not desire to do, will cease, at no distant period, to be an Assembly at all. Their refusal to return to the capital leaves the chief seat of power open to the intrigues of their enemies; and it is obvious that the army will, when it pleases, again give the law, and perhaps a ruler, to France.

To those who, like the writer of the foregoing pages, have constantly looked forward to the establishment of a Constitutional Monarchy in France, as the natural termination of the Revolution, nothing can be more depressing than the present aspect of affairs in that country. But the disappointment is the same which has pervaded every stage of the Revolution, and blasted the fairest hopes at the moment when they seemed nearest to their fulfilment. For the causes of these miscarriages are constant and uniform, and may be traced, as we have endeavoured cursorily to trace them, through every year and every page of this strange history.

A nation may have wealth, territory, population, genius, industry, even above its fellows ; but if it have not Government the results may be desolation and ruin ; and when the traditions of national life and authority have been repeatedly broken, the task of reconstructing a permanent Government becomes the hardest labour in the world.

THE END.

LONDON : PRINTED BY
SPOTTISWOODE AND CO., NEW-STREET SQUARE
AND PARLIAMENT STREET

39 Paternoster Row, E.C.
London: *September* 1871.

GENERAL LIST OF WORKS
PUBLISHED BY
Messrs. LONGMANS, GREEN, READER, and DYER.

...TS, MANUFACTURES, &c.	12	MISCELLANEOUS WORKS and POPULAR METAPHYSICS	6
TRONOMY, METEOROLOGY, POPULAR GEOGRAPHY, &c.	7	NATURAL HISTORY & POPULAR SCIENCE	8
...OGRAPHICAL WORKS	3	PERIODICAL PUBLICATIONS	20
...EMISTRY, MEDICINE, SURGERY, and the ALLIED SCIENCES	9	POETRY and THE DRAMA	17
		RELIGIOUS and MORAL WORKS	13
...ITICISM, PHILOSOPHY, POLITY, &c.	4	RURAL SPORTS, &c.	18
...E ARTS and ILLUSTRATED EDITIONS	11	TRAVELS, VOYAGES, &c.	15
STORY, POLITICS, and HISTORICAL MEMOIRS	1	WORKS of FICTION	16
		WORKS of UTILITY and GENERAL	
...DEX	21—24	INFORMATION	19
...OWLEDGE for the YOUNG	20		

History, Politics, Historical Memoirs, &c.

The History of England from the Fall of Wolsey to the Defeat of the Spanish Armada. By JAMES ANTHONY FROUDE, M.A.
CABINET EDITION, 12 vols. cr. 8vo. £3 12*s*.
LIBRARY EDITION, 12 vols. 8vo. £8 18*s*.

The History of England from the Accession of James II. By Lord MACAULAY.
STUDENT'S EDITION, 2 vols. crown 8vo. 12*s*.
PEOPLE'S EDITION, 4 vols. crown 8vo. 16*s*.
CABINET EDITION, 8 vols. post 8vo. 48*s*.
LIBRARY EDITION, 5 vols. 8vo. £4.

Lord Macaulay's Works. Complete and uniform Library Edition. Edited by his Sister, Lady TREVELYAN. 8 vols. 8vo. with Portrait, price £5 5*s*. cloth, or £8 8*s*. bound in tree-calf by Rivière.

Varieties of Vice-Regal Life. By Major-General Sir WILLIAM DENISON, K.C.B. late Governor-General of the Australian Colonies, and Governor of Madras. With Two Maps. 2 vols. 8vo. 28*s*.

On Parliamentary Government in England: its Origin, Development, and Practical Operation. By ALPHEUS TODD, Librarian of the Legislative Assembly of Canada. 2 vols. 8vo. price £1 17*s*.

The Constitutional History of England since the Accession of George III. 1760—1860. By Sir THOMAS ERSKINE MAY, K.C.B. Cabinet Edition (the Third), thoroughly revised. 3 vols. crown 8vo. price 18*s*.

A Historical Account of the Neutrality of Great Britain during the American Civil War. By MOUNTAGUE BERNARD, M.A. Royal 8vo. price 16*s*.

The History of England, from the Earliest Times to the Year 1865. By C. D. YONGE, Regius Professor of Modern History in Queen's College, Belfast. New Edition. Crown 8vo. 7*s*. 6*d*.

Lectures on the History of England, from the Earliest Times to the Death of King Edward II. By WILLIAM LONGMAN. With Maps and Illustrations. 8vo. 15*s*.

The History of the Life and Times of Edward the Third. By WILLIAM LONGMAN. With 9 Maps, 8 Plates, and 16 Woodcuts. 2 vols. 8vo. 28*s*.

History of Civilization in England and France, Spain and Scotland. By HENRY THOMAS BUCKLE. New Edition of the entire work, with a complete INDEX. 3 vols. crown 8vo. 24*s*.

A

Realities of Irish Life. By W. STEUART TRENCH, Land Agent in Ireland to the Marquess of Lansdowne, the Marquess of Bath, and Lord Digby. Fifth Edition. Crown 8vo. 6s.

The Student's Manual of the History of Ireland. By M. F. CUSACK, Authoress of 'The Illustrated History of Ireland.' Crown 8vo. price 6s.

A Student's Manual of the History of India, from the Earliest Period to the Present. By Colonel MEADOWS TAYLOR, M.R.A.S. M.R.I.A. Crown 8vo. with Maps, 7s. 6d.

The History of India, from the Earliest Period to the close of Lord Dalhousie's Administration. By JOHN CLARK MARSHMAN. 3 vols. crown 8vo. 22s. 6d.

Indian Polity: a View of the System of Administration in India. By Lieut.-Col. GEORGE CHESNEY. Second Edition, revised, with Map. 8vo. 21s.

Home Politics: being a Consideration of the Causes of the Growth of Trade in relation to Labour, Pauperism, and Emigration. By DANIEL GRANT. 8vo. 7s.

Democracy in America. By ALEXIS DE TOCQUEVILLE. Translated by HENRY REEVE. 2 vols. 8vo. 21s.

Waterloo Lectures: a Study of the Campaign of 1815. By Colonel CHARLES C. CHESNEY, R.E. late Professor of Military Art and History in the Staff College. Second Edition. 8vo. with Map, 10s. 6d.

The Military Resources of Prussia and France, and Recent Changes in the Art of War. By Lieut.-Col. CHESNEY, R.E. and HENRY REEVE, D.C.L. Crown 8vo. 7s. 6d.

The Overthrow of the Germanic Confederation by Prussia in 1866. By Sir A. MALET, Bart. K.B.C. late H.B.M. Envoy and Minister at Frankfort. With 5 Maps. 8vo. 18s.

The Oxford Reformers—John Colet, Erasmus, and Thomas More; being a History of their Fellow-Work. By FREDERIC SEEBOHM. Second Edition. 8vo. 14s.

History of the Reformation in Europe in the Time of Calvin. By J. H. MERLE D'AUBIGNÉ, D.D. VOLS. I. and II. 8vo. 28s. VOL. III. 12s. VOL. IV. price 16s. and VOL. V. price 16s.

Chapters from French History St. Louis, Joan of Arc, Henri IV. wit Sketches of the Intermediate Periods. B J. H. GURNEY, M.A. New Edition. Fc 8vo. 6s. 6d.

The History of Greece. By C. THIR WALL, D.D. Lord Bishop of St. David 8 vols. fcp. 28s.

The Tale of the Great Persia War, from the Histories of Herodotus. F GEORGE W. COX, M.A. late Scholar Trin. Coll. Oxon. Fcp. 3s. 6d.

Greek History from Themistocle to Alexander, in a Series of Lives fro Plutarch. Revised and arranged by A.] CLOUGH. Fcp. with 44 Woodcuts, 6s.

Critical History of the Lan guage and Literature of Ancient Greec By WILLIAM MURE, of Caldwell. 5 vo 8vo. £3 9s.

History of the Literature of Ancient Greece. By Professor K. O. MÜLLE Translated by LEWIS and DONALDSO 3 vols. 8vo. 21s.

The History of Rome. By WILHEI IHNE. English Edition, translated ai revised by the Author. VOLS. I. and] 8vo. 30s.

History of the City of Rome fro1 its Foundation to the Sixteenth Century the Christian Era. By THOMAS H. DYE LL.D. 8vo. with 2 Maps, 15s.

History of the Romans unde the Empire. By Very Rev. CHARL MERIVALE, D.C.L. Dean of Ely. 8 vols. pc 8vo. price 48s.

The Fall of the Roman R, public; a Short History of the Last Ce tury of the Commonwealth. By the san Author. 12mo. 7s. 6d.

Historical and Chronologic: Encyclopædia; comprising Chronologic Notices of all the Great Events of Univers History, including Treaties, Alliance Wars, Battles, &c.; Incidents in the Liv of Eminent Men, Scientific and Geogr phical Discoveries, Mechanical Inventio and Social, Domestic, and Economical Ii provements. By the late B. B. WOODWAR B.A. and W. L. R. CATES. 1 vol. 8vo. [*In the press.*

An Historical View of Literatur: and Art in Great Britain from the Acce sion of the House of Hanover to the Rei, of Queen Victoria. By J. MURRAY GRAHA M.A. 8vo. price 14s.

History of European Morals from Augustus to Charlemagne. By W. E. H. LECKY, M.A. 2 vols. 8vo. price 28s.

History of the Rise and Influence of the Spirit of Rationalism in Europe. By the same Author. Cabinet Edition (the Fourth). 2 vols. crown 8vo. price 16s.

God in History; or, the Progress of Man's Faith in the Moral Order of the World. By the late Baron BUNSEN. Translated from the German by SUSANNA WINKWORTH; with a Preface by Dean STANLEY 3 vols. 8vo. 42s.

Socrates and the Socratic Schools. Translated from the German of Dr. E. ZELLER, with the Author's approval, by the Rev. OSWALD J. REICHEL, B.C.L. and M.A. Crown 8vo. 8s. 6d.

The Stoics, Epicureans, and Sceptics. Translated from the German of Dr. E. ZELLER, with the Author's approval, by OSWALD J. REICHEL, B.C.L. and M.A. Crown 8vo. 14s.

Saint-Simon and Saint-Simonism; a Chapter in the History of Socialism in France. By ARTHUR J. BOOTH, M.A. Crown 8vo. price 7s. 6d.

The History of Philosophy, from Thales to Comte. By GEORGE HENRY LEWES. Fourth Edition, corrected, and partly rewritten. 2 vols. 8vo. 32s.

The Mythology of the Aryan Nations. By GEORGE W. COX, M.A. late Scholar of Trinity College, Oxford. 2 vols. 8vo. price 28s.

The English Reformation. By F. C. MASSINGBERD, M.A. Chancellor of Lincoln. 4th Edition, revised. Fcp. 7s. 6d.

Maunder's Historical Treasury; comprising a General Introductory Outline of Universal History, and a Series of Separate Histories. Fcp. 6s.

Critical and Historical Essays contributed to the *Edinburgh Review* by the Right Hon. Lord MACAULAY:—
STUDENT'S EDITION, crown 8vo. 6s.
PEOPLE'S EDITION, 2 vols. crown 8vo. 8s.
CABINET EDITION, 4 vols. 24s.
LIBRARY EDITION, 3 vols. 8vo. 36s.

History of the Early Church, from the First Preaching of the Gospel to the Council of Nicæa, A.D. 325. By the Author of 'Amy Herbert.' New Edition. Fcp. 4s. 6d.

Sketch of the History of the Church of England to the Revolution of 1688. By the Right Rev. T. V. SHORT, D.D. Lord Bishop of St. Asaph. Eighth Edition. Crown 8vo. 7s. 6d.

History of the Christian Church, from the Ascension of Christ to the Conversion of Constantine. By E. BURTON, D.D. late Regius Prof. of Divinity in the University of Oxford. Fcp. 3s. 6d.

Biographical Works.

A Memoir of Daniel Maclise, R.A. By W. JUSTIN O'DRISCOLL, M.R.I.A. Barrister-at-Law. With Portrait and Woodcuts. Post 8vo. price 7s. 6d.

Memoirs of the Marquis of Pombal; with Extracts from his Writings and from Despatches in the State Papers Office. By the CONDE DA CARNOTA. New Edition. 8vo. price 7s.

Reminiscences of Fifty Years. By MARK BOYD. Post 8vo. price 10s. 6d.

The Life of Isambard Kingdom Brunel, Civil Engineer. By ISAMBARD BRUNEL, B.C.L. of Lincoln's Inn, Chancellor of the Diocese of Ely. With Portrait, Plates, and Woodcuts. 8vo. 21s.

The Life and Letters of the Rev. Sydney Smith. Edited by his Daughter, Lady HOLLAND, and Mrs. AUSTIN. New Edition, complete in One Volume. Crown 8vo. price 6s.

Some Memorials of R. D. Hampden, Bishop of Hereford. Edited by his Daughter, HENRIETTA HAMPDEN. 8vo. with Portrait, price 12s.

The Life and Travels of George Whitefield, M.A. By JAMES PATERSON GLEDSTONE. 8vo. price 14s.

'This pleasantly-written and genial biography of the man that extraordinary preacher that England ever produced endeavours, and we think with considerable success, to furnish the answer to a question which at first appears to be almost incapable of any satisfactory solution —What was the secret of his extraordinary power.'
ATHENÆUM.

Memoir of Pope Sixtus the Fifth. By Baron HÜBNER. Translated from the Original in French, with the Author's sanction, by HUBERT E. H. JERNINGHAM. 2 vols. 8vo. [*In the press.*

The Life and Letters of Faraday. By Dr. BENCE JONES, Secretary of the Royal Institution. Second Edition, with Portrait and Woodcuts. 2 vols. 8vo. 28s.

Faraday as a Discoverer. BY JOHN TYNDALL, LL.D. F.R.S. New and Cheaper Edition, with Two Portraits. Fcp. 8vo. price 3s. 6d.

Lives of the Lord Chancellors and Keepers of the Great Seal of Ireland, from the Earliest Times to the Reign of Queen Victoria. By J. R. O'FLANAGAN, M.R.I.A. Barrister. 2 vols. 8vo. 36s.

Dictionary of General Biography; containing Concise Memoirs and Notices of the most Eminent Persons of all Countries, from the Earliest Ages to the Present Time. Edited by WILLIAM L. R. CATES. 8vo. price 21s.

Life of the Duke of Wellington. By the Rev. G. R. GLEIG, M.A. Popular Edition, carefully revised; with copious Additions. Crown 8vo. with Portrait, 5s.

Father Mathew; a Biography. By JOHN FRANCIS MAGUIRE, M.P. Popular Edition, with Portrait. Crown 8vo. 3s. 6d.

History of my Religious Opinions. By J. H. NEWMAN, D.D. Being the Substance of Apologia pro Vitâ Suâ. Post 8vo. price 6s.

Letters and Life of Francis Bacon, including all his Occasional Works. Collected and edited, with a Commentary, by J. SPEDDING. VOLS. I. & II. 8vo. 24s. VOLS. III. & IV. 24s. VOL. V. 12s.

Felix Mendelssohn's Letters from *Italy and Switzerland,* and *Letters* from 1833 to 1847, translated by Lady WALLACE. With Portrait. 2 vols. crown 8vo. 5s. each.

Memoirs of Sir Henry Havelock, K.C.B. By JOHN CLARK MARSHMAN. People's Edition, with Portrait. Crown 8vo. price 3s. 6d.

Essays in Ecclesiastical Biography. By the Right Hon. Sir J. STEPHEN, LL.D. Cabinet Edition. Crown 8vo. 7s. 6d.

Vicissitudes of Families. By Sir J. BERNARD BURKE, C.B. Ulster King of Arms. New Edition, remodelled and enlarged. 2 vols. crown 8vo. 21s.

Lives of the Queens of England. By AGNES STRICKLAND. Library Edition; newly revised; with Portraits of every Queen, Autographs, and Vignettes. 8 vols post 8vo. 7s. 6d. each.

Maunder's Biographical Treasury. Thirteenth Edition, reconstructed and partly re-written, with above 1,000 additional Memoirs, by W. L. R. CATES. Fcp. 6s.

Criticism, Philosophy, Polity, &c.

On Representative Government. By JOHN STUART MILL. Third Edition. 8vo. 9s. crown 8vo. 2s.

On Liberty. By the same Author. Fourth Edition. Post 8vo. 7s. 6d. Crown 8vo. 1s. 4d.

Principles of Political Economy. By the same. Eighth Edition. 2 vols. 8vo. 30s. or in 1 vol. crown 8vo. 5s.

Utilitarianism. By the same. 4th Edit. 8vo. 5s.

Dissertations and Discussions. By the same Author. Second Edition. 3 vols. 8vo. price 36s.

Examination of Sir W. Hamilton's Philosophy, and of the principal Philosophical Questions discussed in his Writings. By the same. Third Edition. 8vo. 16s.

The Subjection of Women. By JOHN STUART MILL. New Edition. Post 8vo 5s.

Inaugural Address delivered to the University of St. Andrews. By JOHN STUART MILL. 8vo. 5s. Crown 8vo. 1s.

Analysis of the Phenomena o: the Human Mind. By JAMES MILL. A New Edition, with Notes, Illustrative and Critical, by ALEXANDER BAIN, ANDREW FINDLATER, and GEORGE GROTE. Edited with additional Notes, by JOHN STUART MILL. 2 vols. 8vo. price 28s.

The Elements of Political Economy. By HENRY DUNNING MACLEOD M.A. Barrister-at-Law. 8vo. 16s.

A Dictionary of Political Economy Biographical, Bibliographical, Historical and Practical. By the same Author. VOL I. royal 8vo. 30s.

Lord Bacon's Works, collected and edited by R. L. ELLIS, M.A. J. SPEDDING, M.A. and D. D. HEATH. New and Cheaper Edition. 7 vols. 8vo. price £3 13s. 6d.

A System of Logic, Ratiocinative and Inductive. By JOHN STUART MILL. Seventh Edition. 2 vols. 8vo. 25s.

Analysis of Mr. Mill's System of Logic. By W. STEBBING, M.A. New Edition. 12mo. 3s. 6d.

The Institutes of Justinian; with English Introduction, Translation, and Notes. By T. C. SANDARS, M.A. Barrister-at-Law. New Edition. 8vo. 15s.

The Ethics of Aristotle; with Essays and Notes. By Sir A. GRANT, Bart. M.A. LL.D. Second Edition, revised and completed. 2 vols. 8vo. price 28s.

The Nicomachean Ethics of Aristotle. Newly translated into English. By R. WILLIAMS, B.A. Fellow and late Lecturer Merton College, Oxford. 8vo. 12s.

Bacon's Essays, with Annotations. By R. WHATELY, D.D. late Archbishop of Dublin. Sixth Edition. 8vo. 10s. 6d.

Elements of Logic. By R. WHATELY, D.D. late Archbishop of Dublin. New Edition. 8vo. 10s. 6d. crown 8vo. 4s. 6d.

Elements of Rhetoric. By the same Author. New Edition. 8vo. 10s. 6d. Crown 8vo. 4s. 6d.

English Synonymes. By E. JANE WHATELY. Edited by Archbishop WHATELY. 5th Edition. Fcp. 3s.

An Outline of the Necessary Laws of Thought: a Treatise on Pure and Applied Logic. By the Most Rev. W. THOMSON, D.D. Archbishop of York. Ninth Thousand. Crown 8vo. 5s. 6d.

The Election of Representatives, Parliamentary and Municipal; a Treatise. By THOMAS HARE, Barrister-at-Law. Third Edition, with Additions. Crown 8vo. 6s.

Speeches of the Right Hon. Lord MACAULAY, corrected by Himself. People's Edition, crown 8vo. 3s. 6d.

Lord Macaulay's Speeches on Parliamentary Reform in 1831 and 1832. 16mo. price ONE SHILLING.

Walker's Pronouncing Dictionary of the English Language. Thoroughly revised Editions, by B. H. SMART. 8vo. 12s. 16mo. 6s.

A Dictionary of the English Language. By R. G. LATHAM, M.A. M.D. F.R.S. Founded on the Dictionary of Dr. S. JOHNSON, as edited by the Rev. H. J. TODD, with numerous Emendations and Additions. 4 vols. 4to. price £7.

Thesaurus of English Words and Phrases, classified and arranged so as to facilitate the expression of Ideas, and assist in Literary Composition. By P. M. ROGET, M.D. New Edition. Crown 8vo. 10s. 6d.

The Debater; a Series of Complete Debates, Outlines of Debates, and Questions for Discussion. By F. ROWTON. Fcp. 6s.

Lectures on the Science of Language. By F. MAX MÜLLER, M.A. &c. Foreign Member of the French Institute. Sixth Edition. 2 vols. crown 8vo price 16s.

Chapters on Language. By F. W. FARRAR, M.A. F.R.S. Head Master of Marlborough College. Crown 8vo. 8s. 6d.

Southey's Doctor, complete in One Volume, edited by the Rev. J. W. WARTER, B.D. Square crown 8vo. 12s. 6d.

Historical and Critical Commentary on the Old Testament; with a New Translation. By M. M. KALISCH, Ph.D. Vol. I. *Genesis*, 8vo. 18s. or adapted for the General Reader, 12s. Vol. II. *Exodus*, 15s. or adapted for the General Reader, 12s. Vol III. *Leviticus*, Part I. 15s. or adapted for the General Reader, 8s.

A Hebrew Grammar, with Exercises. By the same. Part I. *Outlines with Exercises*, 8vo. 12s. 6d. KEY, 5s. Part II. *Exceptional Forms and Constructions*, 12s. 6d.

Manual of English Literature, Historical and Critical: with a Chapter on English Metres. By THOMAS ARNOLD, M.A. Second Edition. Crown 8vo. 7s. 6d.

A Latin-English Dictionary. By JOHN T. WHITE, D.D. Oxon. and J. E. RIDDLE, M.A. Oxon. Third Edition, revised. 2 vols. 4to. pp. 2,128, price 42s.

White's College Latin-English Dictionary (Intermediate Size), abridged from the Parent Work for the use of University Students. Medium 8vo. pp. 1,048, price 18s

White's Junior Student's Complete Latin-English and English-Latin Dictionary. Revised Edition. Square 12mo. pp. 1,058, price 12s.

Separately { ENGLISH-LATIN, 5s. 6d.
{ LATIN-ENGLISH, 7s. 6d.

An English-Greek Lexicon, containing all the Greek Words used by Writers of good authority. By C. D. YONGE, B.A. New Edition. 4to. 21s.

Mr. Yonge's New Lexicon, English and Greek, abridged from his larger work (as above). Square 12mo. 8s. 6d.

The Mastery of Languages; or, the Art of Speaking Foreign Tongues Idiomatically. By THOMAS PRENDERGAST, late of the Civil Service at Madras. Second Edition. 8vo. 6s.

A Greek-English Lexicon. Compiled by H. G. LIDDELL, D.D. Dean of Christ Church, and R. SCOTT, D.D. Dean of Rochester. Sixth Edition. Crown 4to. price 36s.

A Lexicon, Greek and English, abridged for Schools from LIDDELL and SCOTT's *Greek-English Lexicon*. Twelfth Edition. Square 12mo. 7s. 6d.

A Practical Dictionary of the French and English Languages. By Professor LÉON CONTANSEAU, many years French Examiner for Military and Civil Appointments, &c. New Edition, carefully revised. Post 8vo. 10s. 6d.

Contanseau's Pocket Dictionary, French and English, abridged from the Practical Dictionary, by the Author. New Edition. 18mo. price 3s. 6d.

A Sanskrit-English Dictionary. The Sanskrit words printed both in the original Devanagari and in Roman letters; with References to the Best Editions of Sanskrit Authors, and with Etymologies and comparisons of Cognate Words chiefly in Greek, Latin, Gothic, and Anglo-Saxon. Compiled by T. BENFEY. 8vo. 52s. 6d.

New Practical Dictionary of the German Language; German-English, and English-German. By the Rev. W. L. BLACKLEY, M.A. and Dr. CARL MARTIN FRIEDLÄNDER. Post 8vo. 7s. 6d.

Miscellaneous Works and *Popular Metaphysics*.

The Essays and Contributions of A. K. H. B. Uniform Editions:—

Recreations of a Country Parson. FIRST and SECOND SERIES, 3s. 6d. each.

The Commonplace Philosopher in Town and Country. Crown 8vo. 3s. 6d.

Leisure Hours in Town; Essays Consolatory, Æsthetical, Moral, Social, and Domestic. Crown 8vo. 3s. 6d.

The Autumn Holidays of a Country Parson. Crown 8vo. 3s. 6d.

The Graver Thoughts of a Country Parson. FIRST and SECOND SERIES, crown 8vo. 3s. 6d. each.

Critical Essays of a Country Parson, selected from Essays contributed to *Fraser's Magazine*. Crown 8vo. 3s. 6d.

Sunday Afternoons at the Parish Church of a Scottish University City. Crown 8vo. 3s. 6d.

Lessons of Middle Age, with some Account of various Cities and Men. Crown 8vo. 3s. 6d.

Counsel and Comfort Spoken from a City Pulpit. Crown 8vo. 3s. 6d.

Changed Aspects of Unchanged Truths; Memorials of St. Andrews Sundays. Crown 8vo. 3s. 6d.

Present-Day Thoughts; Memorials of St. Andrews Sundays. Crown 8vo. 3s. 6d.

Short Studies on Great Subjects. By JAMES ANTHONY FROUDE, M.A. late Fellow of Exeter College, Oxford. Third Edition. 8vo. 12s. SECOND SERIES, 8vo. 12s.

Lord Macaulay's Miscellaneous Writings:—
LIBRARY EDITION, 2 vols. 8vo. Portrait, 21s.
PEOPLE'S EDITION, 1 vol. crown 8vo. 4s. 6d.

Lord Macaulay's Miscellaneous Writings and Speeches. Student's Edition, in One Volume, crown 8vo. price 6s.

The Rev. Sydney Smith's Miscellaneous Works, including Peter Plymley's Letters, Articles contributed to the *Edinburgh Review*, Letters to Archdeacon Singleton, and other Miscellaneous Writings. 1 vol. crown 8vo. 6s.

The Wit and Wisdom of the Rev. SYDNEY SMITH; a Selection of the most memorable Passages in his Writings and Conversation. Crown 8vo. 3s. 6d.

The Eclipse of Faith; or, a Visit to a Religious Sceptic. By HENRY ROGERS. Twelfth Edition. Fcp. 8vo. 5s.

Defence of the Eclipse of Faith, by its Author. Third Edition. Fcp. 8vo. 3s. 6d.

Selections from the Correspondence of R. E. H. Greyson. By the same Author. Third Edition. Crown 8vo. 7s. 6d.

Families of Speech, Four Lectures delivered at the Royal Institution of Great Britain. By the Rev. F. W. FARRAR, M.A. F.R.S. Post 8vo. with 2 Maps, 5s. 6d.

Chips from a German Workshop; being Essays on the Science of Religion, and on Mythology, Traditions, and Customs. By F. MAX MÜLLER, M.A. &c. Foreign Member of the French Institute. 3 vols. 8vo. £2.

An Introduction to Mental Philosophy, on the Inductive Method. By J. D. MORELL, M.A. LL.D. 8vo. 12s.

Elements of Psychology, containing the Analysis of the Intellectual Powers. By the same Author. Post 8vo. 7s. 6d.

The Secret of Hegel: being the Hegelian System in Origin, Principle, Form, and Matter. By JAMES HUTCHISON STIRLING. 2 vols. 8vo. 28s.

Sir William Hamilton; being the Philosophy of Perception: an Analysis. By the same Author. 8vo. 5s.

The Senses and the Intellect. By ALEXANDER BAIN, LL.D. Prof. of Logic in the Univ. of Aberdeen. Third Edition. 8vo. 15s.

Mental and Moral Science: a Compendium of Psychology and Ethics. By ALEXANDER BAIN, LL.D. Second Edition. Crown 8vo. 10s. 6d.

Ueberweg's System of Logic, and History of Logical Doctrines. Translated, with Notes and Appendices, by T. M. LINDSAY, M.A. F.R.S.E. 8vo. price 16s.

The Philosophy of Necessity; or, Natural Law as applicable to Mental, Moral, and Social Science. By CHARLES BRAY. Second Edition. 8vo. 9s.

The Education of the Feelings and Affections. By the same Author. Third Edition. 8vo. 3s. 6d.

On Force, its Mental and Moral Correlates. By the same Author. 8vo. 5s.

Time and Space; a Metaphysical Essay. By SHADWORTH H. HODGSON. 8vo. price 16s.

The Theory of Practice; an Ethical Inquiry. By SHADWORTH H. HODGSON. 2 vols. 8vo. price 24s.

A Treatise on Human Nature; being an Attempt to Introduce the Experimental Method of Reasoning into Moral Subjects. By DAVID HUME. Edited, with Notes, &c. by T. H. GREEN, Fellow, and T. H. GROSE, late Scholar, of Balliol College, Oxford. [*In the press.*

Essays Moral, Political, and Literary. By DAVID HUME. By the same Editors. [*In the press.*

*** The above will form a new edition of DAVID HUME's *Philosophical Works*, complete in Four Volumes, but to be had in Two separate Sections as announced.

Astronomy, Meteorology, Popular Geography, &c.

Outlines of Astronomy. By Sir J. F. W. HERSCHEL, Bart. M.A. Eleventh Edition, with Plates and Woodcuts. Square crown 8vo. 12s.

Other Worlds than Ours; the Plurality of Worlds Studied under the Light of Recent Scientific Researches. By R. A. PROCTOR, B.A. F.R.A.S. Second Edition, revised and enlarged; with 14 Illustrations. Crown 8vo. 10s. 6d.

The Sun; Ruler, Light, Fire, and Life of the Planetary System. By RICHARD A. PROCTOR, B.A. F.R.A.S. With 10 Plates (7 coloured) and 107 Woodcuts. Crown 8vo. price 14s.

Saturn and its System. By the same Author. 8vo. with 14 Plates, 14s.

Celestial Objects for Common Telescopes. By T. W. WEBB, M.A. F.R.A.S. Second Edition, revised and enlarged, with Map of the Moon and Woodcuts. 16mo. price 7s. 6d.

Navigation and Nautical Astronomy (Practical, Theoretical, Scientific) for the use of Students and Practical Men. By J. MERRIFIELD, F.R.A.S. and H. EVERS. 8vo. 14s.

The Canadian Dominion. By CHARLES MARSHALL. With 6 Illustrations on Wood. 8vo. price 12s. 6d.

A General Dictionary of Geography, Descriptive, Physical, Statistical, and Historical; forming a complete Gazetteer of the World. By A. KEITH JOHNSTON, F.R.S.E. New Edition. 8vo. price 31s. 6d.

NEW WORKS PUBLISHED BY LONGMANS AND CO.

A Manual of Geography, Physical, Industrial, and Political. By W. HUGHES, F.R.G.S. Prof. of Geog. in King's Coll. and in Queen's Coll. Lond. With 6 Maps. Fcp. 7s. 6d.

Maunder's Treasury of Geography, Physical, Historical, Descriptive, and Political. Edited by W. HUGHES, F.R.G.S. With 7 Maps and 16 Plates. Fcp. 6s.

The Public Schools Atlas of Modern Geography. In Thirty-one Maps, exhibiting clearly the more important Physical Features of the Countries delineated, and Noting all the Chief Places of Historical, Commercial, and Social Interest. Edited, with an Introduction, by the Rev. G. BUTLER, M.A. Imperial quarto, price 3s. 6d. sewed; 5s. cloth. [*Nearly ready.*

Natural History and *Popular Science.*

Ganot's Elementary Treatise on Physics, Experimental and Applied, for the use of Colleges and Schools. Translated and Edited with the Author's sanction by E. ATKINSON, Ph.D. F.C.S. New Edition, revised and enlarged; with a Coloured Plate and 620 Woodcuts. Post 8vo. 15s.

The Elements of Physics or Natural Philosophy. By NEIL ARNOTT, M.D. F.R.S. Physician-Extraordinary to the Queen. Sixth Edition, re-written and completed. 2 Parts, 8vo. 21s.

Dove's Law of Storms, considered in connexion with the ordinary Movements of the Atmosphere. Translated by R. H. SCOTT, M.A. T.C.D. 8vo. 10s. 6d.

Sound: a Course of Eight Lectures delivered at the Royal Institution of Great Britain. By Professor JOHN TYNDALL, LL.D. F.R.S. New Edition, with Portrait and Woodcuts. Crown 8vo. 9s.

Heat a Mode of Motion. By Professor JOHN TYNDALL, LL.D. F.R.S. Fourth Edition. Crown 8vo. with Woodcuts, price 10s. 6d.

Researches on Diamagnetism and Magne-Crystallic Action; including the Question of Diamagnetic Polarity. By Professor TYNDALL. With 6 Plates and many Woodcuts. 8vo. 14s.

Notes of a Course of Nine Lectures on Light, delivered at the Royal Institution, A.D. 1869. By Professor TYNDALL. Crown 8vo. 1s. sewed, or 1s. 6d. cloth.

Notes of a Course of Seven Lectures on Electrical Phenomena and Theories, delivered at the Royal Institution, A.D. 1870. By Professor TYNDALL. Crown 8vo. 1s. sewed, or 1s. 6d. cloth.

A Treatise on Electricity, in Theory and Practice. By A. DE LA RIVE, Prof. in the Academy of Geneva. Translated by C. V. WALKER, F.R.S. 3 vols. 8vo. with Woodcuts, £3 13s.

Fragments of Science for Unscientific People; a Series of detached Essays, Lectures, and Reviews. By JOHN TYNDALL, LL.D. F.R.S. Second Edition. 8vo. price 14s.

Light Science for Leisure Hours; a Series of Familiar Essays on Scientific Subjects, Natural Phenomena, &c. By R. A. PROCTOR, B.A. F.R.A.S. Crown 8vo. price 7s. 6d.

Light: its Influence on Life and Health. By FORBES WINSLOW, M.D. D.C.L. Oxon. (Hon.) Fcp. 8vo. 6s.

The Correlation of Physical Forces. By W. R. GROVE, Q.C. V.P.R.S. Fifth Edition, revised, and Augmented by a Discourse on Continuity. 8vo. 10s. 6d. The *Discourse,* separately, price 2s. 6d.

The Beginning: its When and its How. By MUNGO PONTON, F.R.S.E. Post 8vo. with very numerous Illustrations, 18s.

Manual of Geology. By S. HAUGHTON, M.D. F.R.S. Fellow of Trin. Coll. and Prof. of Geol. in the Univ. of Dublin. Second Edition, with 66 Woodcuts. Fcp. 7s. 6d.

Van Der Hoeven's Handbook of ZOOLOGY. Translated from the Second Dutch Edition by the Rev. W. CLARK, M.D. F.R.S. 2 vols. 8vo. with 24 Plates of Figures, 60s.

Professor Owen's Lectures on the Comparative Anatomy and Physiology of the Invertebrate Animals. Second Edition, with 235 Woodcuts. 8vo. 21s.

The Comparative Anatomy and Physiology of the Vertebrate Animals. By RICHARD OWEN, F.R.S. D.C.L. With 1,472 Woodcuts. 3 vols. 8vo. £3 13s. 6d.

Insects at Home. By the Rev. J. G. WOOD, M.A., F.L.S. With a Frontispiece in Colours, 21 full-page Illustrations and about 700 smaller Illustrations from original designs engraved on Wood by G. PEARSON. 8vo. price 21s.

Homes without Hands: a Description of the Habitations of Animals, classed according to their Principle of Construction. By Rev. J. G. WOOD, M.A. F.L.S. With about 140 Vignettes on Wood. 8vo. 21s.

Strange Dwellings; being a Description of the Habitations of Animals, abridged from 'Homes without Hands.' By J. G. WOOD, M.A. F.L.S. With a New Frontispiece and about 60 other Woodcut Illustrations. Crown 8vo. price 7s. 6d.

The Harmonies of Nature and Unity of Creation. By Dr. G. HARTWIG. 8vo. with numerous Illustrations, 18s.

The Sea and its Living Wonders. By the same Author. Third Edition, enlarged. 8vo. with many Illustrations, 21s.

The Tropical World. By the same Author. With 8 Chromoxylographs and 172 Woodcuts. 8vo. 21s.

The Subterranean World. By the same Author. With 3 Maps and about 80 Woodcut Illustrations, including 8 full size of page. 8vo. price 21s.

The Polar World: a Popular Description of Man and Nature in the Arctic and Antarctic Regions of the Globe. By the same Author. With 8 Chromoxylographs, 3 Maps, and 85 Woodcuts. 8vo. 21s.

The Origin of Civilisation and the Primitive Condition of Man; Mental and Social Condition of Savages. By Sir JOHN LUBBOCK, Bart. M.P. F.R.S. Second Edition, revised, with 25 Woodcuts. 8vo. price 16s.

The Primitive Inhabitants of Scandinavia. Containing a Description of the Implements, Dwellings, Tombs, and Mode of Living of the Savages in the North of Europe during the Stone Age. By SVEN NILSSON. 8vo. Plates and Woodcuts, 18s.

Bible Animals; being a Description of Every Living Creature mentioned in the Scriptures, from the Ape to the Coral. By the Rev. J. G. WOOD, M.A. F.L.S. With about 100 Vignettes on Wood. 8vo. 21s.

A Familiar History of Birds. By E. STANLEY, D.D. late Lord Bishop of Norwich. Fcp. with Woodcuts, 3s. 6d.

Kirby and Spence's Introduction to Entomology, or Elements of the Natural History of Insects. Crown 8vo. 5s.

Maunder's Treasury of Natural History, or Popular Dictionary of Zoology. Revised and corrected by T. S. COBBOLD, M.D. Fcp. with 900 Woodcuts, 6s.

The Elements of Botany for Families and Schools. Tenth Edition, revised by THOMAS MOORE, F.L.S. Fcp with 154 Woodcuts, 2s. 6d.

The Treasury of Botany, or Popular Dictionary of the Vegetable Kingdom; with which is incorporated a Glossary of Botanical Terms. Edited by J. LINDLEY, F.R.S. and T. MOORE, F.L.S. Pp. 1,274, with 274 Woodcuts and 20 Steel Plates. TWO PARTS, fcp. 8vo. 12s.

The Rose Amateur's Guide. By THOMAS RIVERS. New Edition. Fcp. 4s.

Loudon's Encyclopædia of Plants; comprising the Specific Character, Description, Culture, History, &c. of all the Plants found in Great Britain. With upwards of 12,000 Woodcuts. 8vo. 42s.

Maunder's Scientific and Literary Treasury; a Popular Encyclopædia of Science, Literature, and Art. New Edition, in part rewritten, with above 1,000 new articles, by J. Y. JOHNSON. Fcp. 6s.

A Dictionary of Science, Literature, and Art. Fourth Edition, re-edited by the late W. T. BRANDE (the Author) and GEORGE W. COX, M.A. 3 vols. medium 8vo. price 63s. cloth.

Chemistry, Medicine, Surgery, and the Allied Sciences.

A Dictionary of Chemistry and the Allied Branches of other Sciences. By HENRY WATTS, F.C.S. assisted by eminent Scientific and Practical Chemists. 5 vols. medium 8vo. price £7 3s.

Elements of Chemistry, Theoretical and Practical. By WILLIAM A. MILLER, M.D. LL.D. Professor of Chemistry, King's College, London. Fourth Edition. 3 vols. 8vo. £3.
PART I. CHEMICAL PHYSICS, 15s.
PART II. INORGANIC CHEMISTRY, 21s.
PART III. ORGANIC CHEMISTRY, 24s.

A Manual of Chemistry, Descriptive and Theoretical. By WILLIAM ODLING, M.B. F.R.S. PART I. 8vo. 9s. PART II. nearly ready.

A Course of Practical Chemistry, for the use of Medical Students. By W. ODLING, M.B. F.R.S. New Edition, with 70 new Woodcuts. Crown 8vo. 7s. 6d.

Select Methods in Chemical Analysis, chiefly Inorganic. By WILLIAM CROOKES, F.R.S. With 22 Woodcuts. Crown 8vo. price 12s. 6d.

A 3

Outlines of Chemistry; or, Brief Notes of Chemical Facts. By the same Author. Crown 8vo. 7s. 6d.

Lectures on Animal Chemistry Delivered at the Royal College of Physicians in 1865. By the same Author. Crown 8vo. 4s. 6d.

Lectures on the Chemical Changes of Carbon, delivered at the Royal Institution of Great Britain. By the same Author. Crown 8vo. 4s. 6d.

Chemical Notes for the Lecture Room. By THOMAS WOOD, F.C.S. 2 vols. crown 8vo. I. on Heat, &c. price 3s. 6d. II. on the Metals, price 5s.

A Treatise on Medical Electricity, Theoretical and Practical; and its Use in the Treatment of Paralysis, Neuralgia, and other Diseases. By JULIUS ALTHAUS, M.D. &c. Second Edition, with Plate and 62 Woodcuts. Post 8vo. price 15s.

The Diagnosis, Pathology, and Treatment of Diseases of Women; including the Diagnosis of Pregnancy. By GRAILY HEWITT, M.D. &c. President of the Obstetrical Society of London. Second Edition, enlarged; with 116 Woodcuts. 8vo. 24s.

Lectures on the Diseases of Infancy and Childhood. By CHARLES WEST, M.D. &c. Fifth Edition. 8vo. 16s.

On Some Disorders of the Nervous System in Childhood. Being the Lumleian Lectures delivered before the Royal College of Physicians in March 1871. By CHARLES WEST, M.D. Crown 8vo. 5s.

On the Surgical Treatment of Children's Diseases. By T. HOLMES, M.A. &c. late Surgeon to the Hospital for Sick Children. Second Edition, with 9 Plates and 112 Woodcuts. 8vo. 21s.

A System of Surgery, Theoretical and Practical, in Treatises by Various Authors. Edited by T. HOLMES, M.A. &c. Surgeon and Lecturer on Surgery at St. George's Hospital, and Surgeon-in-Chief to the Metropolitan Police. Second Edition, thoroughly revised, with numerous Illustrations. 5 vols. 8vo. £5 5s.

Lectures on the Principles and Practice of Physic. By Sir THOMAS WATSON, Bart. M.D. Physician-in-Ordinary to the Queen. Fifth Edition, thoroughly revised. 2 vols. 8vo. price 36s.

Lectures on Surgical Pathology. By Sir JAMES PAGET, Bart. F.R.S. Third Edition, revised and re-edited by the Author and Professor W. TURNER, M.B. 8vo. with 131 Woodcuts, 21s.

Cooper's Dictionary of Practical Surgery and Encyclopædia of Surgical Science. New Edition, brought down to the present time. By S. A. LANE, Surgeon to St. Mary's Hospital, &c. assisted by various Eminent Surgeons. VOL. II. 8vo. completing the work. [*In the press.*

On Chronic Bronchitis, especially as connected with Gout, Emphysema, and Diseases of the Heart. By E. HEADLAM GREENHOW, M.D. F.R.C.P. &c. 8vo. 7s. 6d

The Climate of the South of France as Suited to Invalids; with Notices of Mediterranean and other Winter Stations. By C. T. WILLIAMS, M.A. M.D. Oxon. Physician to the Hospital for Consumption at Brompton. Second Edition Crown 8vo. 6s.

Pulmonary Consumption; its Nature, Varieties, and Treatment: with an Analysis of One Thousand Cases to exemplify its Duration. By C. J. B. WILLIAMS M.D. F.R.S. and C. T. WILLIAMS, M.A. M.D. Oxon. Physicians to the Hospital for Consumption at Brompton. Post 8vo price 10s. 6d.

Clinical Lectures on Diseases of the Liver, Jaundice, and Abdominal Dropsy. By C. MURCHISON, M.D. Physician and Lecturer on the Practice of Medicine Middlesex Hospital. Post 8vo. with 2 Woodcuts, 10s. 6d.

Anatomy, Descriptive and Surgical. By HENRY GRAY, F.R.S. With about 410 Woodcuts from Dissections. Fifth Edition, by T. HOLMES, M.A. Cantab. With a New Introduction by the Editor. Royal 8vo. 28s.

Clinical Notes on Diseases of the Larynx, investigated and treated with the assistance of the Laryngoscope. By W. MARCET, M.D. F.R.S. Crown 8vo with 5 Lithographs, 6s.

The House I Live in; or, Popular Illustrations of the Structure and Function of the Human Body. Edited by T. G. GIRTIN New Edition, with 25 Woodcuts. 16mo price 2s. 6d.

Physiological Anatomy and Physiology of Man. By the late R. B. TODD M.D. F.R.S. and W. BOWMAN, F.R.S. King's College. With numerous Illustrations. VOL. II. 8vo. 25s.

VOL. I. New Edition by Dr. LIONEL BEALE, F.R.S. in course of publication with numerous Illustrations. PARTS I. and II. price 7s. 6d. each.

NEW WORKS PUBLISHED BY LONGMANS AND CO.

Outlines of Physiology, Human and Comparative. By JOHN MARSHALL, F.R.C.S. Professor of Surgery in University College, London, and Surgeon to the University College Hospital. 2 vols. crown 8vo. with 122 Woodcuts, 32s.

Copland's Dictionary of Practical Medicine, abridged from the larger work, and throughout brought down to the present state of Medical Science. 8vo. 36s.

A Manual of Materia Medica and Therapeutics, abridged from Dr. PEREIRA's *Elements* by F. J. FARRE, M.D. assisted by R. BENTLEY, M.R.C.S. and by R. WARINGTON, F.R.S. 1 vol. 8vo. with 90 Woodcuts, 21s.

Thomson's Conspectus of the British Pharmacopœia. Twenty-fifth Edition, corrected by E. LLOYD BIRKETT, M.D. 18mo. 6s.

The Fine Arts, and *Illustrated Editions.*

In Fairyland; Pictures from the Elf-World. By RICHARD DOYLE. With a Poem by W. ALLINGHAM. With Sixteen Plates, containing Thirty-six Designs printed in Colours. Folio, 31s. 6d.

Life of John Gibson, R.A. Sculptor. Edited by Lady EASTLAKE. 8vo. 10s. 6d.

Materials for a History of Oil Painting. By Sir CHARLES LOCKE EASTLAKE, sometime President of the Royal Academy. 2 vols. 8vo. 30s.

Albert Durer, his Life and Works; including Autobiographical Papers and Complete Catalogues. By WILLIAM B. SCOTT. With Six Etchings by the Author and other Illustrations. 8vo. 16s.

Half-Hour Lectures on the History and Practice of the Fine and Ornamental Arts. By. W. B. SCOTT. Second Edition. Crown 8vo. with 50 Woodcut Illustrations, 8s. 6d.

Italian Sculptors: being a History of Sculpture in Northern, Southern, and Eastern Italy. By C. C. PERKINS. With 30 Etchings and 13 Wood Engravings. Imperial 8vo. 42s.

Tuscan Sculptors, their Lives, Works, and Times. By the same Author. With 45 Etchings and 28 Wood Engravings. 2 vols. imperial 8vo. 63s.

The Chorale Book for England: the Hymns Translated by Miss C. WINKWORTH; the Tunes arranged by Prof. W. S. BENNETT and OTTO GOLDSCHMIDT. Fcp. 4to. 12s. 6d.

Six Lectures on Harmony. Delivered at the Royal Institution of Great Britain. By G. A. MACFARREN. 8vo. 10s. 6d.

The New Testament, illustrated with Wood Engravings after the Early Masters chiefly of the Italian School. Crown 4to. 63s. cloth, gilt top; or £5 5s. morocco.

The Life of Man Symbolised by the Months of the Year in their Seasons and Phases. Text selected by RICHARD PIGOT. 25 Illustrations on Wood from Original Designs by JOHN LEIGHTON, F.S.A. Quarto, 42s.

Cats' and Farlie's Moral Emblems; with Aphorisms, Adages, and Proverbs of all Nations: comprising 121 Illustrations on Wood by J. LEIGHTON, F.S.A. with an appropriate Text by R. PIGOT. Imperial 8vo. 31s. 6d.

Sacred and Legendary Art. By Mrs. JAMESON. 6 vols. square crown 8vo. price £5 15s. 6d. as follows:—

Legends of the Saints and Martyrs. Fifth Edition, with 19 Etchings and 187 Woodcuts. 2 vols. price 31s. 6d.

Legends of the Monastic Orders. Third Edition, with 11 Etchings and 88 Woodcuts. 1 vol. price 21s.

Legends of the Madonna. Third Edition, with 27 Etchings and 165 Woodcuts. 1 vol. price 21s.

The History of Our Lord, with that of His Types and Precursors. Completed by Lady EASTLAKE. Revised Edition, with 13 Etchings and 281 Woodcuts. 2 vols. price 42s.

Lyra Germanica, the Christian Year. Translated by CATHERINE WINKWORTH; with 125 Illustrations on Wood drawn by J. LEIGHTON, F.S.A. Quarto, 21s.

Lyra Germanica, the Christian Life. Translated by CATHERINE WINKWORTH; with about 200 Woodcut Illustrations by J. LEIGHTON, F.S.A. and other Artists. Quarto, 21s.

The Useful Arts, Manufactures, &c.

Gwilt's Encyclopædia of Architecture, with above 1,600 Woodcuts. Fifth Edition, with Alterations and considerable Additions, by WYATT PAPWORTH. 8vo. price 52s. 6d.

A Manual of Architecture : being a Concise History and Explanation of the principal Styles of European Architecture, Ancient, Mediæval, and Renaissance; with their Chief Variations and a Glossary of Technical Terms. By THOMAS MITCHELL. With 150 Woodcuts. Crown 8vo. 10s. 6d.

History of the Gothic Revival; an Attempt to shew how far the taste for Mediæval Architecture was retained in England during the last two centuries, and has been re-developed in the present. By CHARLES L. EASTLAKE, Architect. With many Illustrations. Imperial 8vo. price 31s. 6d.

Hints on Household Taste in Furniture, Upholstery, and other Details. By CHARLES L. EASTLAKE, Architect. Second Edition, with about 90 Illustrations. Square crown 8vo. 18s.

The Engineer's Handbook; explaining the principles which should guide the young Engineer in the Construction of Machinery. By C. S. LOWNDES. Post 8vo. 5s.

Lathes and Turning, Simple, Mechanical, and Ornamental. By W. HENRY NORTHCOTT. With about 240 Illustrations on Steel and Wood. 8vo. 18s.

Principles of Mechanism, designed for the use of Students in the Universities, and for Engineering Students generally. By R. WILLIS, M.A. F.R.S. &c. Jacksonian Professor in the Univ. of Cambridge. Second Edition; with 374 Woodcuts. 8vo. 18s.

Handbook of Practical Telegraphy. By R. S. CULLEY, Memb. Inst. C.E. Engineer-in-Chief of Telegraphs to the Post-Office. Fifth Edition, revised and enlarged; with 118 Woodcuts and 9 Plates. 8vo. price 14s.

Ure's Dictionary of Arts, Manufactures, and Mines. Sixth Edition, re-written and greatly enlarged by ROBERT HUNT, F.R.S. assisted by numerous Contributors. With 2,000 Woodcuts. 3 vols. medium 8vo. £4 14s. 6d.

Treatise on Mills and Millwork. By Sir W. FAIRBAIRN, Bart. F.R.S. New Edition, with 18 Plates and 322 Woodcuts. 2 vols. 8vo. 32s.

Useful Information for Engineers. By the same Author. FIRST, SECOND, and THIRD SERIES, with many Plates and Woodcuts. 3 vols. crown 8vo. 10s. 6d. each.

The Application of Cast and Wrought Iron to Building Purposes. By the same Author. Fourth Edition, with 6 Plates and 118 Woodcuts. 8vo. 16s.

Iron Ship Building, its History and Progress, as comprised in a Series of Experimental Researches. By Sir W. FAIRBAIRN, Bart. F.R.S. With 4 Plates and 130 Woodcuts, 8vo. 18s.

Encyclopædia of Civil Engineering, Historical, Theoretical, and Practical. By E. CRESY, C.E. With above 3,000 Woodcuts. 8vo. 42s.

A Treatise on the Steam Engine, in its various Applications to Mines, Mills, Steam Navigation, Railways, and Agriculture. By J. BOURNE, C.E. New Edition; with Portrait, 37 Plates, and 546 Woodcuts. 4to. 42s.

Catechism of the Steam Engine, in its various Applications to Mines, Mills, Steam Navigation, Railways, and Agriculture. By JOHN BOURNE, C.E. New Edition, with 89 Woodcuts. Fcp. 6s.

Recent Improvements in the Steam-Engine. By JOHN BOURNE, C.E. New Edition, including many New Examples, with 124 Woodcuts. Fcp. 8vo. 6s.

Bourne's Examples of Modern Steam, Air, and Gas Engines of the most Approved Types, as employed for Pumping, for Driving Machinery, for Locomotion, and for Agriculture, minutely and practically described. In course of publication, to be completed in Twenty-four Parts, price 2s. 6d. each, forming One Volume, with about 50 Plates and 400 Woodcuts.

A Treatise on the Screw Propeller, Screw Vessels, and Screw Engines, as adapted for purposes of Peace and War. By JOHN BOURNE, C.E. Third Edition, with 54 Plates and 287 Woodcuts. [Quarto, price 63s.

Handbook of the Steam Engine. By JOHN BOURNE, C.E. forming a KEY to the Author's Catechism of the Steam Engine. With 67 Woodcuts. Fcp. 9s.

A History of the Machine-Wrought Hosiery and Lace Manufactures. By WILLIAM FELKIN, F.L.S. F.S.S. With several Illustrations. Royal 8vo. 21s.

Mitchell's Manual of Practical Assaying. Third Edition for the most part re-written, with all the recent Discoveries incorporated. By W. CROOKES, F.R.S. With 188 Woodcuts. 8vo. 28s.

Reimann's Handbook of Aniline and its Derivatives; a Treatise on the Manufacture of Aniline and Aniline Colours. Revised and edited by WILLIAM CROOKES, F.R.S. 8vo. with 5 Woodcuts, 10s. 6d.

On the Manufacture of Beet-Root Sugar in England and Ireland. By WILLIAM CROOKES, F.R.S. With 11 Woodcuts. 8vo. 8s. 6d.

Practical Treatise on Metallurgy, adapted from the last German Edition of Professor KERL's *Metallurgy* by W. CROOKES, F.R.S. &c. and E. RÖHRIG, Ph.D. M.E. 3 vols. 8vo. with 625 Woodcuts, price £4 19s.

The Art of Perfumery; the History and Theory of Odours, and the Methods of Extracting the Aromas of Plants. By Dr. PIESSE, F.C.S. Third Edition, with 53 Woodcuts. Crown 8vo. 10s. 6d.

Chemical, Natural, and Physical Magic, for Juveniles during the Holidays. By the same Author. With 38 Woodcuts. Fcp. 6s.

Loudon's Encyclopædia of Agriculture: comprising the Laying-out, Improvement, and Management of Landed Property, and the Cultivation and Economy of the Productions of Agriculture. With 1,100 Woodcuts. 8vo. 21s.

Loudon's Encyclopædia of Gardening: comprising the Theory and Practice of Horticulture, Floriculture, Arboriculture, and Landscape Gardening. With 1,000 Woodcuts. 8vo. 21s.

Bayldon's Art of Valuing Rents and Tillages, and Claims of Tenants upon Quitting Farms, both at Michaelmas and Lady-Day. Eighth Edition, revised by J. C. MORTON. 8vo. 10s. 6d.

Religious and *Moral Works.*

Old Testament Synonyms, their Bearing on Christian Faith and Practice. By the Rev. R. B. GIRDLESTONE, M.A. 8vo. [*Nearly ready.*

Fundamentals; or, Bases of Belief concerning Man and God: a Handbook of Mental, Moral, and Religious Philosophy. By the Rev. T. GRIFFITH, M.A. 8vo. price 10s. 6d.

An Introduction to the Theology of the Church of England, in an Exposition of the Thirty-nine Articles. By the Rev. T. P. BOULTBEE, M.A. Fcp. 8vo. price 6s.

The Student's Compendium of the Book of Common Prayer; being Notes Historical and Explanatory of the Liturgy of the Church of England. By the Rev. H. ALLDEN NASH. Fcp. 8vo. price 2s. 6d.

Prayers Selected from the Collection of the late Baron Bunsen, and Translated by CATHERINE WINKWORTH. PART I. For the Family. PART II. Prayers and Meditations for Private Use. Fcp. 8vo. price 3s. 6d.

Churches and their Creeds. By the Rev. Sir PHILIP PERRING, Bart. late Scholar of Trin. Coll. Cambridge, and University Medallist. Crown 8vo. 10s. 6d.

The Bible and Popular Theology; a Re-statement of Truths and Principles, with special reference to recent works of Dr. Liddon, Lord Hatherley, and the Right Hon. W. E. Gladstone. By G. VANCE SMITH, B.A. Ph.D. 8vo. 7s. 6d.

The Truth of the Bible; Evidence from the Mosaic and other Records of Creation; the Origin and Antiquity of Man; the Science of Scripture; and from the Archæology of Different Nations of the Earth. By the Rev. B. W. SAVILE, M.A. Crown 8vo. 7s. 6d.

Considerations on the Revision of the English New Testament. By C. J. ELLICOTT, D.D. Lord Bishop of Gloucester and Bristol. Post 8vo. price 7s. 6d.

An Exposition of the 39 Articles, Historical and Doctrinal. By E. HAROLD BROWNE, D.D. Lord Bishop of Ely. Ninth Edition. 8vo. 16s.

Examination-Questions on Bishop Browne's Exposition of the Articles. By the Rev. J. GORLE, M.A. Fcp. 3s. 6d.

The Voyage and Shipwreck of St. Paul; with Dissertations on the Ships and Navigation of the Ancients. By JAMES SMITH, F.R.S. Crown 8vo. Charts, 10s. 6d.

The Life and Epistles of St. Paul. By the Rev. W. J. CONYBEARE, M.A. and the Very Rev. J. S. HOWSON, D.D. Dean of Chester. Three Editions:—

LIBRARY EDITION, with all the Original Illustrations, Maps, Landscapes on Steel, Woodcuts, &c. 2 vols. 4to. 48s.

INTERMEDIATE EDITION, with a Selection of Maps, Plates, and Woodcuts. 2 vols. square crown 8vo. 31s. 6d.

STUDENT'S EDITION, revised and condensed, with 46 Illustrations and Maps. 1 vol. crown 8vo. 9s.

Evidence of the Truth of the Christian Religion derived from the Literal Fulfilment of Prophecy. By ALEXANDER KEITH, D.D. 37th Edition, with numerous Plates, in square 8vo. 12s. 6d.; also the 39th Edition, in post 8vo. with 5 Plates, 6s.

The History and Destiny of the World and of the Church, according to Scripture. By the same Author. Square 8vo. with 40 Illustrations, 10s.

The History and Literature of the Israelites, according to the Old Testament and the Apocrypha. By C. DE ROTHSCHILD and A. DE ROTHSCHILD. Second Edition. 2 vols. crown 8vo. 12s. 6d.

VOL. I. *The Historical Books,* 7s. 6d.
VOL. II. *The Prophetic and Poetical Writings,* price 5s.

Ewald's History of Israel to the Death of Moses. Translated from the German. Edited, with a Preface and an Appendix, by RUSSELL MARTINEAU, M.A. Second Edition. 2 vols. 8vo. 24s.

The See of Rome in the Middle Ages. By the Rev. OSWALD J. REICHEL, B.C.L. and M.A. 8vo. 18s.

The Pontificate of Pius the Ninth; being the Third Edition, enlarged and continued, of 'Rome and its Ruler.' By J. F. MAGUIRE, M.P. Post 8vo. Portrait, price 12s. 6d.

Ignatius Loyola and the Early Jesuits. By STEWART ROSE. New Edition, revised. 8vo. with Portrait, 16s.

An Introduction to the Study of the New Testament, Critical, Exegetical, and Theological. By the Rev. S. DAVIDSON, D.D. LL.D. 2 vols. 8vo. 30s.

A Critical and Grammatical Commentary on St. Paul's Epistles. By C. J. ELLICOTT, D.D. Lord Bishop of Gloucester and Bristol. 8vo.

Galatians, Fourth Edition, 8s. 6d.
Ephesians, Fourth Edition, 8s. 6d.
Pastoral Epistles, Fourth Edition, 10s. 6d.
Philippians, Colossians, and Philemon, Third Edition, 10s. 6d.
Thessalonians, Third Edition, 7s. 6d.

Historical Lectures on the Life of Our Lord Jesus Christ: being the Hulsean Lectures for 1859. By C. J. ELLICOTT, D.D. Lord Bishop of Gloucester and Bristol. Fifth Edition. 8vo. 12s.

The Greek Testament; with Notes, Grammatical and Exegetical. By the Rev. W. WEBSTER, M.A. and the Rev. W. F. WILKINSON, M.A. 2 vols. 8vo. £2 4s.

Horne's Introduction to the Critical Study and Knowledge of the Holy Scriptures. Twelfth Edition; with 4 Maps and 22 Woodcuts. 4 vols. 8vo. 42s.

Compendious Introduction to the Study of the Bible. Edited by the Rev. JOHN AYRE, M.A. With Maps, &c. Post 8vo. 6s.

The Treasury of Bible Knowledge; being a Dictionary of the Books, Persons, Places, Events, and other Matters of which mention is made in Holy Scripture. By Rev. J. AYRE, M.A. With Maps, 15 Plates, and numerous Woodcuts. Fcp. 8vo. 6s.

Every-day Scripture Difficulties explained and illustrated. By J. E. PRESCOTT, M.A. I. *Matthew* and *Mark*; II. *Luke* and *John.* 2 vols. 8vo. price 9s. each.

The Pentateuch and Book of Joshua Critically Examined. By the Right Rev. J. W. COLENSO, D.D. Lord Bishop of Natal. Crown 8vo. price 6s.

The Four Cardinal Virtues; Six Sermons for the Day, in relation to the Public and Private Life of Catholics. By the Rev. ORBY SHIPLEY, M.A. Crown 8vo. with Frontispiece, 7s. 6d.

The Formation of Christendom. By T. W. ALLIES. PARTS I. and II. 8vo. price 12s. each.

Four Discourses of Chrysostom, chiefly on the parable of the Rich Man and Lazarus. Translated by F. ALLEN, B.A. Crown 8vo. 3s. 6d.

Christendom's Divisions; a Philosophical Sketch of the Divisions of the Christian Family in East and West. By EDMUND S. FFOULKES. Post 8vo. 7s. 6d. PART II. *Greeks and Latins*, price 15s.

Thoughts for the Age. By ELIZABETH M. SEWELL, Author of 'Amy Herbert.' New Edition. Fcp. 8vo. price 5s.

Passing Thoughts on Religion. By the same Author. Fcp. 5s.

Self-examination before Confirmation. By the same Author. 32mo. 1s. 6d.

Thoughts for the Holy Week, for Young Persons. By the same Author. New Edition. Fcp. 8vo. 2s.

Readings for a Month Preparatory to Confirmation from Writers of the Early and English Church. By the same. Fcp. 4s.

Readings for Every Day in Lent, compiled from the Writings of Bishop JEREMY TAYLOR. By the same Author. Fcp. 5s.

Preparation for the Holy Communion; the Devotions chiefly from the works of JEREMY TAYLOR. By the same. 32mo. 3s.

Principles of Education drawn from Nature and Revelation, and Applied to Female Education in the Upper Classes. By the same Author. 2 vols. fcp. 12s. 6d.

Bishop Jeremy Taylor's Entire Works; with Life by BISHOP HEBER. Revised and corrected by the Rev. C. P. EDEN. 10 vols. £5 5s.

England and Christendom. By ARCHBISHOP MANNING, D.D. Post 8vo. price 10s. 6d.

Singers and Songs of the Church: being Biographical Sketches of the Hymn-Writers in all the principal Collections; with Notes on their Psalms and Hymns. By JOSIAH MILLER, M.A. Post 8vo. 10s. 6d.

'Spiritual Songs' for the Sundays and Holidays throughout the Year. By J. S. B. MONSELL, LL.D. Vicar of Egham and Rural Dean. Fourth Edition, Sixth Thousand. Fcp. price 4s. 6d.

The Beatitudes. By the same Author. Third Edition, revised. Fcp. 3s. 6d.

His Presence not his Memory, 1855. By the same Author, in memory of his SON. Sixth Edition. 16mo. 1s.

Lyra Germanica, translated from the German by Miss C. WINKWORTH. FIRST SERIES, the *Christian Year*, Hymns for the Sundays and Chief Festivals of the Church; SECOND SERIES, the *Christian Life*. Fcp. 8vo. price 3s. 6d. each SERIES.

Lyra Eucharistica ; Hymns and Verses on the Holy Communion, Ancient and Modern: with other Poems. Edited by the Rev. ORBY SHIPLEY, M.A. Second Edition. Fcp. 5s.

Shipley's Lyra Messianica. Fcp. 5s.

Shipley's Lyra Mystica. Fcp. 5s.

Endeavours after the Christian Life: Discourses. By JAMES MARTINEAU. Fourth Edition. Post 8vo. price 7s. 6d.

Invocation of Saints and Angels; for the use of Members of the English Church. Edited by the Rev. ORBY SHIPLEY, M.A. 24mo. 3s. 6d.

Travels, Voyages, &c.

How to See Norway. By Captain J. R. CAMPBELL. With Map and 5 Woodcuts. Fcp. 8vo. price 5s.

Pau and the Pyrenees. By Count HENRY RUSSELL, Member of the Alpine Club. With 2 Maps. Fcp. 8vo. price 5s.

Scenes in the Sunny South; Including the Atlas Mountains and the Oases of the Sahara in Algeria. By Lieut.-Col. the Hon. C. S. VEREKER, M.A. Commandant of the Limerick Artillery Militia. 2 vols. post 8vo. price 21s.

Hours of Exercise in the Alps. By JOHN TYNDALL, LL.D., F.R.S. Second Edition, with Seven Woodcuts by E. Whymper. Crown 8vo. price 12s. 6d.

The Playground of Europe. By LESLIE STEPHEN, late President of the Alpine Club. With 4 Illustrations on Wood by E. Whymper. Crown 8vo. 10s. 6d.

Westward by Rail: the New Route to the East. By W. F. RAE. Second Edition, enlarged. Post 8vo. with Map, price 10s. 6d.

Travels in the Central Caucasus and Bashan, including Visits to Ararat and Tabreez and Ascents of Kazbek and Elbruz. By DOUGLAS W. FRESHFIELD. Square crown 8vo. with Maps, &c., 18s.

Cadore or Titian's Country. By JOSIAH GILBERT, one of the Authors of the 'Dolomite Mountains.' With Map, Facsimile, and 40 Illustrations. Imp. 8vo. 31s. 6d.

Zigzagging amongst Dolomites; with more than 300 Illustrations by the Author. By the Author of 'How we Spent the Summer.' Oblong 4to. price 15s.

The Dolomite Mountains. Excursions through Tyrol, Carinthia, Carniola, and Friuli. By J. GILBERT and G. C. CHURCHILL, F.R.G.S. With numerous Illustrations. Square crown 8vo. 21s.

How we Spent the Summer; or, a Voyage en Zigzag in Switzerland and Tyrol with some Members of the ALPINE CLUB. Third Edition, re-drawn. In oblong 4to. with about 300 Illustrations, 15s.

Pictures in Tyrol and Elsewhere. From a Family Sketch-Book. By the same Author. Second Edition. 4to. with many Illustrations, 21s.

Beaten Tracks; or, Pen and Pencil Sketches in Italy. By the same Author. With 42 Plates of Sketches. 8vo. 16s.

The Alpine Club Map of the Chain of Mont Blanc, from an actual Survey in 1863—1864. By A. ADAMS-REILLY, F.R.G.S. M.A.C. In Chromolithography on extra stout drawing paper 28in. × 17in. price 10s. or mounted on canvas in a folding case, 12s. 6d.

History of Discovery in our Australasian Colonies, Australia, Tasmania, and New Zealand, from the Earliest Date to the Present Day. By WILLIAM HOWITT. 2 vols. 8vo. with 3 Maps, 20s.

The Capital of the Tycoon; a Narrative of a 3 Years' Residence in Japan. By Sir RUTHERFORD ALCOCK, K.C.B. 2 vols. 8vo. with numerous Illustrations, 42s.

Pilgrimages in the Pyrenees and Landes. By DENYS SHYNE LAWLOR. Crown 8vo. with Frontispiece and Vignette, price 15s.

Guide to the Pyrenees, for the use of Mountaineers. By CHARLES PACKE. Second Edition, with Maps, &c. and Appendix. Crown 8vo. 7s. 6d.

The Alpine Guide. By JOHN BALL, M.R.I.A. late President of the Alpine Club. Post 8vo. with Maps and other Illustrations.

Guide to the Eastern Alps, price 10s. 6d.

Guide to the Western Alps, including Mont Blanc, Monte Rosa, Zermatt, &c. price 6s. 6d

Guide to the Central Alps, including all the Oberland District, price 7s. 6d.

Introduction on Alpine Travelling in general, and on the Geology of the Alps, price 1s. Either of the Three Volumes or Parts of the *Alpine Guide* may be had with this INTRODUCTION prefixed, price 1s. extra.

The Northern Heights of London; or, Historical Associations of Hampstead, Highgate, Muswell Hill, Hornsey, and Islington. By WILLIAM HOWITT. With about 40 Woodcuts. Square crown 8vo. 21s.

The Rural Life of England. By the same Author. With Woodcuts by Bewick and Williams. Medium 8vo. 12s. 6d.

Visits to Remarkable Places: Old Halls, Battle-Fields, and Scenes illustrative of striking Passages in English History and Poetry. By the same Author. 2 vols. square crown 8vo. with Wood Engravings, 25s.

Works of Fiction.

Novels and Tales. By the Right Hon. B. DISRAELI. Cabinet Editions, complete in Ten Volumes, crown 8vo. price 6s. each, as follows :—

LOTHAIR, 6s.	VENETIA, 6s.
CONINGSBY, 6s.	ALROY, IXION, &c. 6s.
SYBIL, 6s.	YOUNG DUKE, &c. 6s.
TANCRED, 6s.	VIVIAN GREY, 6s.
CONTARINI FLEMING, &c. 6s.	
HENRIETTA TEMPLE, 6s.	

A Visit to my Discontented Cousin. Reprinted, with some Additions, from *Fraser's Magazine*. Crown 8vo. price 7s. 6d.

Stories and Tales. By E. M. SEWELL. Comprising *Amy Herbert*; *Gertrude*; the *Earl's Daughter*; the *Experience of Life*; *Cleve Hall*; *Ivors*; *Katharine Ashton*; *Margaret Percival*; *Laneton Parsonage*; and *Ursula*. The Ten Works complete in Eight Volumes, crown 8vo. bound in leather and contained in a Box, price Two GUINEAS.

Our Children's Story. By One of their Gossips. By the Author of 'Voyage en Zigzag,' &c. Small 4to. with Sixty Illustrations by the Author, price 10s. 6d.

NEW WORKS PUBLISHED BY LONGMANS AND CO.   17

Cabinet Edition, in crown 8vo. of Stories and Tales by Miss SEWELL:—
AMY HERBERT, 2s. 6d.
GERTRUDE, 2s. 6d.
EARL'S DAUGHTER, 2s. 6d.
EXPERIENCE OF LIFE, 2s. 6d.
CLEVE HALL, 3s. 6d.
IVORS, 3s. 6d.
KATHARINE ASHTON, 3s. 6d.
MARGARET PERCIVAL, 5s.
LANETON PARSONAGE, 4s. 6d.
URSULA, 4s. 6d.

A Glimpse of the World. Fcp. 7s. 6d.

Journal of a Home Life. Post 8vo. 9s. 6d.

After Life; a Sequel to the 'Journal of a Home Life.' Post 8vo. 10s. 6d.

The Modern Novelist's Library. Each Work, in crown 8vo. complete in a Single Volume:—
MELVILLE'S GLADIATORS, 2s. boards; 2s. 6d. cloth.
——— GOOD FOR NOTHING, 2s. boards; 2s. 6d. cloth.
——— HOLMBY HOUSE, 2s. boards; 2s. 6d. cloth.
——— INTERPRETER, 2s. boards; 2s. 6d. cloth.
——— KATE COVENTRY, 2s. boards; 2s. 6d. cloth.
——— QUEEN'S MARIES, 2s. boards; 2s. 6d. cloth.
TROLLOPE'S WARDEN, 1s. 6d. boards; 2s. cloth.
——— BARCHESTER TOWERS, 2s. boards; 2s. 6d. cloth.
BRAMLEY-MOORE'S SIX SISTERS OF THE VALLEYS, 2s. boards; 2s. 6d. cloth.

Ierne; a Tale. By W. STEUART TRENCH, Author of 'Realities of Irish Life.' Second Edition. 2 vols. post 8vo. price 21s.

The Giant; a Witch's Story for English Boys. Edited by Miss SEWELL, Author of 'Amy Herbert,' &c. Fcp. 8vo. price 5s.

Uncle Peter's Fairy Tale for the XIXth Century. By the same Author and Editor. Fcp. 8vo. 7s. 6d.

The Home at Heatherbrae; a Tale. By the Author of 'Everley.' Fcp. 8vo. price 5s.

Becker's Gallus; or, Roman Scenes of the Time of Augustus. Post 8vo. 7s. 6d.

Becker's Charicles: Illustrative of Private Life of the Ancient Greeks. Post 8vo. 7s. 6d.

Tales of Ancient Greece. By GEORGE W. COX, M.A. late Scholar of Trin. Coll. Oxford. Crown 8vo. price 6s. 6d.

Cabinet Edition of Novels and Tales by G. J. WHYTE MELVILLE:—
THE GLADIATORS, 5s.
DIGBY GRAND, 5s.
KATE COVENTRY, 5s.
GENERAL BOUNCE, 5s.
HOLMBY HOUSE, 5s.
GOOD FOR NOTHING, 6s.
QUEEN'S MARIES, 6s.
THE INTERPRETER, 5s.

Wonderful Stories from Norway, Sweden, and Iceland. Adapted and arranged by JULIA GODDARD. With an Introductory Essay by the Rev. G. W. COX, M.A. and Six Illustrations. Square post 8vo. 6s.

Poetry and *The Drama.*

Thomas Moore's Poetical Works, the only Editions containing the Author's last Copyright Additions:—
Shamrock Edition, price 3s. 6d.
Ruby Edition, with Portrait, 6s.
Cabinet Edition, 10 vols. fcp. 8vo. 35s.
People's Edition, Portrait, &c. 10s. 6d.
Library Edition, Portrait & Vignette, 14s.

Moore's Lalla Rookh, Tenniel's Edition, with 68 Wood Engravings from Original Drawings and other Illustrations. Fcp. 4to. 21s.

Moore's Irish Melodies, Maclise's Edition, with 161 Steel Plates from Original Drawings. Super-royal 8vo. 31s. 6d.

Miniature Edition of Moore's Irish Melodies, with Maclise's Illustrations (as above), reduced in Lithography. Imp. 16mo. 10s. 6d.

Southey's Poetical Works, with the Author's last Corrections and copyright Additions. Library Edition. Medium 8vo. with Portrait and Vignette, 14s.

Lays of Ancient Rome; with *Ivry* and the *Armada*. By the Right Hon. LORD MACAULAY. 16mo. 4s. 6d.

Lord Macaulay's Lays of Ancient Rome. With 90 Illustrations on Wood, Original and from the Antique, from Drawings by G. SCHARF. Fcp. 4to. 21s.

Miniature Edition of Lord Macaulay's Lays of Ancient Rome, with Scharf's Illustrations (as above) reduced in Lithography. Imp. 16mo. 10s. 6d.

Goldsmith's Poetical Works, Illustrated with Wood Engravings from Designs by Members of the ETCHING CLUB. Imp. 16mo. 7s. 6d.

John Jerningham's Journal. Fcp. 8vo. price 3s. 6d.

The Mad War Planet, and other Poems. By WILLIAM HOWITT, Author of 'Visits to Remarkable Places,' &c. Fcp. 8vo. price 5s.

Eucharis; a Poem. By F. REGINALD STATHAM (Francis Reynolds), Author of 'Alice Rushton, and other Poems' and 'Glaphyra, and other Poems.' Fcp. 8vo. price 3s. 6d.

Poems of Bygone Years. Edited by the Author of 'Amy Herbert.' Fcp. 8vo. 5s.

Poems. By JEAN INGELOW. Fifteenth Edition. Fcp. 8vo. 5s.

Poems by Jean Ingelow. With nearly 100 Illustrations by Eminent Artists, engraved on Wood by DALZIEL Brothers. Fcp. 4to. 21s.

Mopsa the Fairy. By JEAN INGELOW. With Eight Illustrations engraved on Wood. Fcp. 8vo. 6s.

A Story of Doom, and other Poems. By JEAN INGELOW. Third Edition. Fcp. price 5s.

Bowdler's Family Shakspeare, cheaper Genuine Edition, complete in 1 vol. large type, with 36 Woodcut Illustrations, price 14s. or in 6 pocket vols. 3s. 6d. each.

Arundines Cami. Collegit atque edidit H. DRURY, M.A. Editio Sexta, curavit H. J. HODGSON, M.A. Crown 8vo. price 7s. 6d.

Horatii Opera, Pocket Edition, with carefully corrected Text, Marginal References, and Introduction. Edited by the Rev. J. E. YONGE, M.A. Square 18mo. 4s. 6d.

Horatii Opera, Library Edition, with Copious English Notes, Marginal References and Various Readings. Edited by the Rev. J. E. YONGE, M.A. 8vo. 21s.

The Æneid of Virgil Translated into English Verse. By JOHN CONINGTON, M.A. Corpus Professor of Latin in the University of Oxford. New Edition. Crown 8vo. 9s.

Hunting Songs and Miscellaneous Verses. By R. E. EGERTON WARBURTON. Second Edition. Fcp. 8vo. 5s.

Works by Edward Yardley:—
FANTASTIC STORIES, fcp. 3s. 6d.
MELUSINE and other POEMS, fcp. 5s.
HORACE'S ODES translated into ENGLISH VERSE, crown 8vo. 6s.
SUPPLEMENTARY STORIES and POEMS, fcp. 3s. 6d.

Rural Sports, &c.

Encyclopædia of Rural Sports; a Complete Account, Historical, Practical, and Descriptive, of Hunting, Shooting, Fishing, Racing, &c. By D. P. BLAINE. With above 600 Woodcuts (20 from Designs by JOHN LEECH). 8vo. 21s.

The Dead Shot, or Sportsman's Complete Guide; a Treatise on the Use of the Gun, Dog-breaking, Pigeon-shooting, &c. By MARKSMAN. Fcp. with Plates, 5s.

A Book on Angling: being a Complete Treatise on the Art of Angling in every branch, including full Illustrated Lists of Salmon Flies. By FRANCIS FRANCIS. Second Edition, with Portrait and 15 other Plates, plain and coloured. Post 8vo. 15s.

Wilcocks's Sea-Fisherman: comprising the Chief Methods of Hook and Line Fishing in the British and other Seas, a glance at Nets, and remarks on Boats and Boating. Second Edition, enlarged, with 80 Woodcuts. Post 8vo. 12s. 6d.

The Fly-Fisher's Entomology. By ALFRED RONALDS. With coloured Representations of the Natural and Artificial Insect. Sixth Edition, with 20 coloured Plates. 8vo. 14s.

The Book of the Roach. By GREVILLE FENNELL, of 'The Field.' Fcp. 8vo. price 2s. 6d.

Blaine's Veterinary Art: a Treatise on the Anatomy, Physiology, and Curative Treatment of the Diseases of the Horse, Neat Cattle, and Sheep. Seventh Edition, revised and enlarged by C. STEEL. 8vo. with Plates and Woodcuts, 18s.

Horses and Stables. By Colonel F. FITZWYGRAM, XV. the King's Hussars. With 24 Plates of Woodcut Illustrations, containing very numerous Figures. 8vo. 15s.

Youatt on the Horse. Revised and enlarged by W. WATSON, M.R.C.V.S. 8vo. with numerous Woodcuts, 12s. 6d.

Youatt on the Dog. (By the same Author.) 8vo. with numerous Woodcuts, 6s.

The Dog in Health and Disease By STONEHENGE. With 70 Wood Engravings. New Edition. Square crown 8vo. 10s. 6d.

The Greyhound. By the same Author. Revised Edition, with 24 Portraits of Greyhounds. Square crown 8vo. 10s. 6d.

Robbins's Cavalry Catechism; or, Instructions on Cavalry Exercise and Field Movements, Brigade Movements, Outpost Duty, Cavalry supporting Artillery, Artillery attached to Cavalry. 12mo. price 5s.

The Horse's Foot, and how to keep it Sound. By W. MILES, Esq. Ninth Edition, with Illustrations. Imp. 8vo. 12s. 6d.

A Plain Treatise on Horse-shoeing. By the same Author. Sixth Edition, post 8vo. with Illustrations, 2s. 6d.

Stables and Stable Fittings. By the same. Imp. 8vo. with 13 Plates, 15s.

Remarks on Horses' Teeth, addressed to Purchasers. By the same. Post 8vo. 1s. 6d

The Ox, his Diseases and their Treatment; with an Essay on Parturition in the Cow. By J. R. DOBSON, M.R.C.V.S. Crown 8vo. with Illustrations, 7s. 6d.

Works of Utility and *General Information.*

The Law of Nations Considered as Independent Political Communities. By Sir TRAVERS TWISS, D.C.L. 2 vols. 8vo. 30s. or separately, PART I. *Peace*, 12s. PART II. *War*, 18s.

The Theory and Practice of Banking. By HENRY DUNNING MACLEOD, M.A. Barrister-at-Law. Second Edition. entirely remodelled. 2 vols. 8vo. 30s.

M'Culloch's Dictionary, Practical, Theoretical, and Historical, of Commerce and Commercial Navigation. New Edition, revised throughout and corrected to the Present Time; with a Biographical Notice of the Author. Edited by H. G. REID, Secretary to Mr. M'Culloch for many years. 8vo. price 63s. cloth.

Modern Cookery for Private Families, reduced to a System of Easy Practice in a Series of carefully-tested Receipts. By ELIZA ACTON. Newly revised and enlarged; with 8 Plates, Figures, and 150 Woodcuts. Fcp. 6s.

A Practical Treatise on Brewing; with Formulæ for Public Brewers, and Instructions for Private Families. By W. BLACK. Fifth Edition. 8vo. 10s. 6d.

The Cabinet Lawyer; a Popular Digest of the Laws of England, Civil, Criminal, and Constitutional. Twenty-third Edition, corrected and brought up to the Present Date. Fcp. 8vo. price 7s. 6d.

Maunder's Treasury of Knowledge and Library of Reference: comprising an English Dictionary and Grammar, Universal Gazetteer, Classical Dictionary, Chronology, Law Dictionary, Synopsis of the Peerage, Useful Tables, &c. Fcp. 6s.

Chess Openings. By F. W. LONGMAN, Balliol College, Oxford. Fcp. 8vo. 2s. 6d.

Hints to Mothers on the Management of their Health during the Period of Pregnancy and in the Lying-in Room. By THOMAS BULL, M.D. Fcp. 5s.

The Maternal Management of Children in Health and Disease. By THOMAS BULL, M.D. Fcp. 5s.

How to Nurse Sick Children; containing Directions which may be found of service to all who have charge of the Young. By CHARLES WEST, M.D. Second Edition. Fcp. 8vo. 1s. 6d.

Notes on Lying-In Institutions; with a Proposal for Organising an Institution for Training Midwives and Midwifery Nurses. By FLORENCE NIGHTINGALE. With several Illustrations. 8vo. price 7s. 6d.

Notes on Hospitals. By FLORENCE NIGHTINGALE. Third Edition, enlarged; with 13 Plans. Post 4to. 18s.

Tidd Pratt's Law relating to Benefit Building Societies; with Practical Observations on the Act and all the Cases decided thereon, also a Form of Rules and Forms of Mortgages. Fcp. 3s. 6d.

Collieries and Colliers: a Handbook of the Law and Leading Cases relating thereto. By J. C. FOWLER, Barrister. Second Edition. Fcp. 8vo. 7s. 6d.

Coulthart's Decimal Interest Tables at Twenty-four Different Rates not exceeding Five per Cent. Calculated for the use of Bankers. To which are added Commission Tables at One-eighth and One-fourth per Cent. 8vo. 15s.

Willich's Popular Tables for Ascertaining the Value of Lifehold, Leasehold, and Church Property, Renewal Fines, &c.; the Public Funds; Annual Average Price and Interest on Consols from 1731 to 1867; Chemical, Geographical, Astronomical, Trigonometrical Tables, &c. Post 8vo. 10s.

Pewtner's Comprehensive Specifier; a Guide to the Practical Specification of every kind of Building-Artificer's Work: with Forms of Building Conditions and Agreements, an Appendix, Foot-Notes, and Index. Edited by W. YOUNG. Architect. Crown 8vo. 6s.

Periodical Publications.

The Edinburgh Review, or Critical Journal, published Quarterly in January, April, July, and October. 8vo. price 6s. each Number.

Notes on Books: An Analysis of the Works published during each Quarter by Messrs. LONGMANS & Co. The object is to enable Bookbuyers to obtain such information regarding the various works as is usually afforded by tables of contents and explanatory prefaces. 4to. Quarterly. *Gratis.*

Fraser's Magazine. Edited by JAMES ANTHONY FROUDE, M.A. New Serie published on the 1st of each Month. 8vo. price 2s. 6d. each Number.

The Alpine Journal; A Record of Mountain Adventure and Scientific Observation. By Members of the Alpine Club. Edited by LESLIE STEPHEN. Published Quarterly, May 31, Aug. 31, Nov. 30, Feb. 28. 8vo. price 1s. 6d. each Number.

Knowledge for the Young.

The Stepping Stone to Knowledge: Containing upwards of Seven Hundred Questions and Answers on Miscellaneous Subjects, adapted to the capacity of Infant Minds. By a MOTHER. New Edition, enlarged and improved. 18mo. price 1s.

The Stepping Stone to Geography: Containing several Hundred Questions and Answers on Geographical Subjects. 18mo. 1s.

The Stepping Stone to English History: Containing several Hundred Questions and Answers on the History of England. 1s.

The Stepping Stone to Bible Knowledge: Containing several Hundred Questions and Answers on the Old and New Testaments. 18mo. 1s.

The Stepping Stone to Biography: Containing several Hundred Questions and Answers on the Lives of Eminent Men and Women. 18mo. 1s.

Second Series of the Stepping Stone to Knowledge: containing upwards of Eight Hundred Questions and Answers on Miscellaneous Subjects not contained in the FIRST SERIES. 18mo. 1s.

The Stepping Stone to French Pronunciation and Conversation: Containing several Hundred Questions and Answers. By Mr. P. SADLER. 18mo. 1s.

The Stepping Stone to English Grammar: Containing several Hundred Questions and Answers on English Grammar. By Mr. P. SADLER. 18mo. 1s.

The Stepping Stone to Natural History: VERTEBRATE OR BACKBONED ANIMALS. PART I. *Mammalia*; PART II. *Birds, Reptiles, Fishes.* 18mo. 1s. each Part.

INDEX.

ACTON'S Modern Cookery	19
ALCOCK'S Residence in Japan	16
ALLIES on Formation of Christendom	14
ALLEN'S Discourses of Chrysostom	14
Alpine Guide (The)	16
——— Journal	20
ALTHAUS on Medical Electricity	10
ARNOLD'S Manual of English Literature	5
ARNOTT'S Elements of Physics	8
Arundines Cami	18
Autumn Holidays of a Country Parson	6
AYRE'S Treasury of Bible Knowledge	14
BACON'S Essays by WHATELY	5
——— Life and Letters, by SPEDDING	4
——— Works	5
BAIN'S Mental and Moral Science	7
——— on the Senses and Intellect	7
BALL'S Guide to the Central Alps	16
———Guide to the Western Alps	16
———Guide to the Eastern Alps	16
BAYLDON'S Rents and Tillages	13
Beaten Tracks	16
BECKER'S *Charicles* and *Gallus*	17
BENFEY'S Sanskrit-English Dictionary	6
BERNARD on British Neutrality	1
BLACK'S Treatise on Brewing	19
BLACKLEY'S German-English Dictionary	6
BLAINE'S Rural Sports	18
——— Veterinary Art	18
BOOTH'S Saint-Simon	3
BOULTBEE on 39 Articles	13
BOURNE on Screw Propeller	12
———'s Catechism of the Steam Engine	12
——— Examples of Modern Engines	12
——— Handbook of Steam Engine	12
——— Treatise on the Steam Engine	12
——— Improvements in the same	12
BOWDLER'S Family SHAKSPEARE	18
BOYD'S Reminiscences	3
BRAMLEY-MOORE'S Six Sisters of the Valley	17
BRANDE'S Dictionary of Science, Literature, and Art	9
BRAY'S (C.) Education of the Feelings	7
——— Philosophy of Necessity	7
——— On Force	7
BROWNE'S Exposition of the 39 Articles	13
BRUNEL'S Life of BRUNEL	3
BUCKLE'S History of Civilisation	1
BULL'S Hints to Mothers	19
——— Maternal Management of Children	19
BUNSEN'S God in History	3
——— Prayers	13
BURKE'S Vicissitudes of Families	4
BURTON'S Christian Church	3
Cabinet Lawyer	19
CAMPBELL'S Norway	15
CARNOTA'S Memoirs of Pombal	3
CATES'S Biographical Dictionary	4
CATS and FARLIE'S Moral Emblems	11
Changed Aspects of Unchanged Truths	6
CHESNEY'S Indian Polity	2
——— Waterloo Campaign	2
CHESNEY'S and REEVE'S Military Essays	2
Chorale Book for England	11
CLOUGH'S Lives from Plutarch	2
COLENSO (Bishop) on Pentateuch and Book of Joshua	14
Commonplace Philosopher in Town and Country	6
CONINGTON'S Translation of Virgil's Æneid	18
CONTANSEAU'S Two French Dictionaries	6
CONYBEARE and HOWSON'S Life and Epistles of St. Paul	14
COOPER'S Surgical Dictionary	10
COPLAND'S Dictionary of Practical Medicine	11
COULTHART'S Decimal Interest Tables	19
Counsel and Comfort from a City Pulpit	6
Cox's (G. W.) Aryan Mythology	3
——— Tale of the Great Persian War	2
——— Tales of Ancient Greece	17
CRESY'S Encyclopædia of Civil Engineering	12
Critical Essays of a Country Parson	6
CROOKES on Beet-Root Sugar	13
———'s Chemical Analysis	9
CULLEY'S Handbook of Telegraphy	12
CUSACK'S Student's History of Ireland	2
D'AUBIGNÉ'S History of the Reformation in the time of CALVIN	2
DAVIDSON'S Introduction to New Testament	14
Dead Shot (The), by MARKSMAN	18
DE LA RIVE'S Treatise on Electricity	8
DENISON'S Vice-Regal Life	1
DE TOCQUEVILLE'S Democracy in America	2
DISRAELI'S Lothair	16
——— Novels and Tales	16
DOBSON on the Ox	19
DOVE'S Law of Storms	8
DOYLE'S Fairyland	11
DYER'S City of Rome	2
EASTLAKE'S Gothic Revival	12
——— Hints on Household Taste	12
——— History of Oil Painting	11
——— Life of Gibson	11
Edinburgh Review	20
Elements of Botany	9

ELLICOTT on the Revision of the English
  New Testament 13
  ———'s Commentary on Ephesians 14
  ——————— Lectures on Life of Christ 14
  ——————— Commentary on Galatians 14
  ——————————————— Pastoral Epist. 14
  ——————————————— Philippians,&c. 14
  ——————————————— Thessalonians 14
EWALD'S History of Israel 14

FAIRBAIRN'S Application of Cast and
  Wrought Iron to Building 12
  ——————— Information for Engineers 12
  ——————— Treatise on Mills and Millwork 12
  ——————— Iron Shipbuilding 12
FARADAY'S Life and Letters 4
FARRAR'S Chapters on Language 5
  ——————— Families of Speech 7
FELKIN on Hosiery & Lace Manufactures.. 13
FENNEL'S Book of the Roach 18
FFOULKES'S Christendom's Divisions 15
FITZWYGRAM on Horses and Stables 18
FOWLER'S Collieries and Colliers 19
FRANCIS'S Fishing Book 18
FRASER'S Magazine....................... 20
FRESHFIELD'S Travels in the Caucasus 15
FROUDE'S History of England 1
  ——————— Short Studies 6

GANOT'S Elementary Physics 8
GIANT (The) 17
GILBERT'S Cadore 15
  ——— and CHURCHILL'S Dolomites 16
GIRDLESTONE'S Bible Synonyms 13
GIRTIN'S House I Live In 10
GLEDSTONE'S Life of WHITEFIELD 3
GODDARD'S Wonderful Stories 17
GOLDSMITH'S Poems, Illustrated 17
GRAHAM'S View of Literature and Art ... 2
GRANT'S Ethics of Aristotle............... 5
  ——————— Home Politics.................... 2
Graver Thoughts of a Country Parson...... 6
Gray's Anatomy........................... 10
GREENHOW on Bronchitis 10
GRIFFITH'S Fundamentals 13
GROVE on Correlation of Physical Forces .. 9
GURNEY'S Chapters of French History 2
GWILT'S Encyclopædia of Architecture 12

HAMPDEN'S (Bishop) Memorials 3
Hare on Election of Representatives 5
HARTWIG'S Harmonies of Nature.......... 9
  ——————— Polar World 9
  ——————— Sea and its Living Wonders.... 9
  ——————— Subterranean World 9
  ——————— Tropical World.............. 9
HAUGHTON'S Manual of Geology 8
HERSCHEL'S Outlines of Astronomy........ 7
HEWITT on the Diseases of Women 10
HODGSON'S Time and Space............... 7
  ——————— Theory of Practice 9
HOLMES'S Surgical Treatment of Children.. 10
  ——————— System of Surgery 10
Home (The) at Heatherbrae 17
HORNE'S Introduction to the Scriptures .. 14
  ——————— Compendium of the Scriptures .. 14
How we Spent the Summer................. 16

HOWITT'S Australian Discovery............ 16
  ——————— Mad War Planet................. 18
  ——————— Northern Heights of London.... 16
  ——————— Rural Life of England 16
  ——————— Visits to Remarkable Places 16
HÜBNER'S Pope Sixtus 4
HUGHES'S Manual of Geography 8
HUME'S Essays 7
  ——————— Treatise on Human Nature........ 7

IHNE'S History of Rome ....
INGELOW'S Poems 18
  ——————— Story of Doom 18
  ——————— Mopsa 18

JAMESON'S Legends of Saints and Martyrs.. 11
  ——————— Legends of the Madonna...... 11
  ——————— Legends of the Monastic Orders 11
  ——————— Legends of the Saviour........ 11
JOHN JERNINGHAM'S Journal 18
JOHNSTON'S Geographical Dictionary 7

KALISCH'S Commentary on the Bible...... 5
  ——————— Hebrew Grammar............... 5
KEITH on Destiny of the World............ 14
  ——————— Fulfilment of Prophecy.......... 14
KERL'S Metallurgy, by CROOKES and
  RÖHRIG 13
KIRBY and SPENCE'S Entomology.......... 9

LATHAM'S English Dictionary.............. 5
LAWLOR'S Pilgrimages in the Pyrenees 16
LECKY'S History of European Morals 3
  ——————— Rationalism.................... 3
Leisure Hours in Town.................... 6
Lessons of Middle Age 6
LEWES'S Biographical History of Philosophy 3
LIDDELL and SCOTT'S Greek-English Lexicon 6
  ——————————————— Abridged ditto 6
Life of Man Symbolised................... 11
LINDLEY and MOORE'S Treasury of Botany 9
LONGMAN'S Edward the Third 1
  ——————— Lectures on History of England 1
  ——————— Chess Openings................ 19
LOUDON'S Encyclopædia of Agriculture 13
  ——————————————— Gardening 13
  ——————————————— Plants 9
LOWNDES'S Engineer's Handbook.......... 12
LUBBOCK'S Origin of Civilisation 9
Lyra Eucharistica 15
  ——— Germanica 11, 15
  ——— Messianica 15
  ——— Mystica 15

MACAULAY'S (Lord) Essays 3
  ——————— History of England .. 1
  ——————— Lays of Ancient Rome 17
  ——————— Miscellaneous Writings 6
  ——————— Speeches 5
  ——————— Works 1
MACFARREN'S Lectures on Harmony 11
MACLEOD'S Elements of Political Economy 4
  ——————— Dictionary of Political Economy 4
  ——————— Theory and Practice of Banking 19
MCCULLOCH'S Dictionary of Commerce 19

NEW WORKS PUBLISHED BY LONGMANS AND CO. 23

MAGUIRE's Life of Father Mathew 4
——— PIUS IX.................... 14
MALET's Overthrow of the Germanic Confederation 2
MANNING's England and Christendom 15
MARCET on the Larynx 10
MARSHALL's Canadian Dominion........... 7
———— Physiology 11
MARSHMAN's History of India 2
————Life of Havelock 4
MARTINEAU's Endeavours after the Christian Life 15
MASSINGBERD's History of the Reformation 3
MAUNDER's Biographical Treasury 4
———— Geographical Treasury 8
———— Historical Treasury 3
———— Scientific and Literary Treasury 9
———— Treasury of Knowledge........ 19
———— Treasury of Natural History .. 9
MAY's Constitutional History of England.. 1
MELVILLE's Digby Grand.................. 17
———— General Bounce 17
———— Gladiators 17
———— Good for Nothing 17
———— Holmby House................ 17
———— Interpreter 17
———— Kate Coventry................ 17
———— Queen's Maries 17
MENDELSSOHN's Letters 4
MERIVALE's Fall of the Roman Republic .. 2
———— Romans under the Empire 2
MERRIFIELD and EVERS's Navigation ... 7
MILES on Horse's Foot and Horse Shoeing. 19
——— on Horses' Teeth and Stables 19
MILL (J.) on the Mind 4
MILL (J. S.) on Liberty 4
———— Subjection of Women 4
———— on Representative Government 4
———— on Utilitarianism 4
———'s Dissertations and Discussions...... 4
———— Political Economy 4
———— System of Logic.............. 5
———— Hamilton's Philosophy 4
———— Inaugural Address at St. Andrew's. 4
MILLER's Elements of Chemistry 9
———— Hymn Writers 15
MITCHELL's Manual of Architecture 12
———— Manual of Assaying 13
MONSELL's Beatitudes 15
———— His Presence not his Memory.. 15
———— 'Spiritual Songs' 15
MOORE's Irish Melodies.................. 17
———— Lalla Rookh 17
———— Poetical Works............. 17
MORELL's Elements of Psychology 7
MORELL's Mental Philosophy 7
MÜLLER's (MAX) Chips from a German Workshop 7
———— Lectures on the Science of Language 5
———— (K. O.) Literature of Ancient Greece 3
MURCHISON on Liver Complaints 10
MURE's Language and Literature of Greece 2

NASH's Compendium of the Prayer-Book .. 13
New Testament Illustrated with Wood Engravings from the Old Masters 11
NEWMAN's History of his Religious Opinions 4

NIGHTINGALE's Notes on Hospitals 19
———— Lying-In Institutions 19
NILSSON's Scandinavia 9
NORTHCOTT on Lathes and Turning 12
Notes on Books......................... 20

ODLING's Animal Chemistry 10
———— Course of Practical Chemistry .. 9
— ———— Manual of Chemistry........... 9
———— Lectures on Carbon 10
———— Outlines of Chemistry 10
O'DRISCOLL's Memoir of Macliso 3
O'FLANAGAN's Irish Chancellors 4
Our Children's Story 16
OWEN's Comparative Anatomy and Physiology of Vertebrate Animals 8
———— Lectures on the Invertebrata...... 8

PACKE's Guide to the Pyrenees 16
PAGET's Lectures on Surgical Pathology .. 10
PEREIRA's Manual of Materia Medica...... 11
PERKINS's Italian and Tuscan Sculptors .. 11
PERRING's Churches and Creeds 13
PEWTNER's Comprehensive Specifier 20
Pictures in Tyrol 16
PIESSE's Art of Perfumery 13
———— Chemical, Natural, and Physical Magic 13
PONTON's Beginning 8
PRATT's Law of Building Societies 19
PRENDERGAST's Mastery of Languages 6
PRESCOTT's Scripture Difficulties.......... 14
Present-Day Thoughts, by A. K. H. B. 6
PROCTOR's Plurality of Worlds 7
———— Saturn 7
———— Scientific Essays 8
———— Sun......................... 7
Public Schools Atlas 8

RAE's Westward by Rail 15
Recreations of a Country Parson 6
REICHEL's See of Rome.................... 14
REILLY's Map of Mont Blanc.............. 16
REIMANN on Aniline Dyes 13
RIVERS's Rose Amateur's Guide 9
ROBBINS's Cavalry Catechism............ 19
ROGERS's Correspondence of Greyson 6
———— Eclipse of Faith 6
———— Defence of Faith 6
ROGET's Thesaurus of English Words and Phrases 5
RONALDS's Fly-Fisher's Entomology 18
ROSE's Loyola 14
ROTHSCHILD's Israelites 14
ROWTON's Debater 5
RUSSELL's Pau and the Pyrenees......... 15

SANDARS's Justinian's Institutes 5
SAVILE on Truth of the Bible............. 13
SCOTT's Lectures on the Fine Arts 11
———— Albert Durer................. 11
SEEBOHM's Oxford Reformers of 1498 2
SEWELL's After Life 17
———— Glimpse of the World 17
———— History of the Early Church.... 3
———— Journal of a Home Life 17

SEWELL's Passing Thoughts on Religion .. 15
—— Poems of Bygone Years 18
—— Preparation for Communion 15
—— Principles of Education 15
—— Readings for Confirmation 15
—— Readings for Lent 15
—— Examination for Confirmation .. 15
—— Stories and Tales .... 16 & 17
—— Thoughts for the Age 15
—— Thoughts for the Holy Week 15
SHIPLEY's Four Cardinal Virtues......... 14
—— Invocation of Saints............ 15
SHORT's Church History 3
Smart's WALKER's English Dictionaries .. 5
SMITH'S (V.) Bible and Popular Theology.. 13
—— Paul's Voyage and Shipwreck 13
—— (SYDNEY) Life and Letters 3
—————— Miscellaneous Works .. 6
—————— Wit and Wisdom 6
SOUTHEY's Doctor 5
—— Poetical Works................ 17
STANLEY's History of British Birds........ 9
STATHAM's Eucharis.................... 18
STEBBING's Analysis of MILL's Logic...... 5
STEPHEN's Ecclesiastical Biography 4
—— Playground of Europe 15
Stepping-Stone to Knowledge, &c. 20
STIRLING's Secret of Hegel.............. 7
—— Sir WILLIAM HAMILTON 7
STONEHENGE on the Dog................ 19
—— on the Greyhound 19
STRICKLAND's Queens of England 4
Sunday Afternoons at the Parish Church of
a Scottish University City 6

TAYLOR's History of India 2
—— (Jeremy) Works, edited by EDEN 15
THIRLWALL's History of Greece 2
THOMSON's Conspectus 11
—— Laws of Thought 5
TODD (A.) on Parliamentary Government .. 1
—— and BOWMAN's Anatomy and Physiology of Man 10
TRENCH's Ierne 17
—— Realities of Irish Life 2
TROLLOPE's Barchester Towers............ 17
—— Warden 17
TWISS's Law of Nations 19
TYNDALL's Diamagnetism 8
—— Faraday as a Discoverer........ 4
—— Fragments of Science........ 8
—— Hours of Exercise in the Alps.. 15
—— Lectures on Electricity 8

TYNDALL's Lectures on Light ....
—— Lectures on Sound ....
—— Heat a Mode of Motion........

UEBERWEG's System of Logic ....
Uncle PETER's Fairy Tale 18
URE's Dictionary of Arts, Manufactures, and
Mines 12

VAN DER HOEVEN's Handbook of Zoology..
VEREKER's Sunny South................. 15
Visit to my Discontented Cousin 16

WARBURTON's Hunting Songs 18
WATSON's Principles and Practice of Physic 1
WATTS's Dictionary of Chemistry.........
WEBB's Objects for Common Telescopes....
WEBSTER & WILKINSON's Greek Testament 14
WELLINGTON's Life, by GLEIG 4
WEST on Children's Diseases 10
—— on Children's Nervous Disorders 10
—— on Nursing Sick Children 19
WHATELY's English Synonymes 5
—— Logic 5
—— Rhetoric 5
WHITE and RIDDLE's Latin Dictionaries .. 5
WILCOCKS's Sea Fisherman............... 18
WILLIAMs Aristotle's Ethics 5
WILLIAMS on Climate of South of France.. 10
—— Consumption............... 10
WILLICH's Popular Tables 20
WILLIS's Principles of Mechanism 12
WINSLOW on Light..................... 8
WOOD's (J. G.) Bible Animals............. 9
—— Homes without Hands 9
—— Insects at Home 8
—— Strange Dwellings 8
—— (T.) Chemical Notes 10
WOODWARD and CATES's Encyclopædia .. 2

YARDLEY's Poetical Works................ 18
YONGE's History of England 1
—— English-Greek Lexicons ....
—— Two Editions of Horace 18
YOUATT on the Dog 18
—— on the Horse................

ZELLER's Socrates ....
—— Stoics, Epicureans, and Sceptics..
Zigzagging amongst Dolomites ....

www.ingramcontent.com/pod-product-compliance
Lightning Source LLC
Chambersburg PA
CBHW030548300426
44111CB00009B/905